A Dictionary of
Shakespeare

STANLEY WELLS

with the assistance of JAMES SHAW

OXFORD
UNIVERSITY PRESS

OXFORD

UNIVERSITY PRESS

Great Clarendon Street, Oxford OX2 6DP

Oxford University Press is a department of the University of Oxford.
It furthers the University's objective of excellence in research, scholarship,
and education by publishing worldwide in

Oxford New York
Auckland Cape Town Dar es Salaam Hong Kong Karachi
Kuala Lumpur Madrid Melbourne Mexico City Nairobi
New Delhi Shanghai Taipei Toronto

With offices in
Argentina Austria Brazil Chile Czech Republic France Greece
Guatemala Hungary Italy Japan Poland Portugal Singapore
South Korea Switzerland Thailand Turkey Ukraine Vietnam

Oxford is a registered trade mark of Oxford University Press
in the UK and in certain other countries

Published in the United States
by Oxford University Press Inc., New York

British Library Cataloguing in Publication Data
Data available

Library of Congress Cataloging in Publication Data
Data available

Typeset by SNP Best-set Typesetter Ltd, Hong Kong
Printed in Great Britain by
Clays Ltd, St Ives plc

ISBN 0-19-280638-6   978-0-19-280638-3

1

Preface

This volume is intended as a companion and guide to reading Shakespeare's plays and to experiencing them where they belong, in the theatre. The previous version of this work, published as *Shakespeare: An Illustrated Dictionary* (1978, 2nd edn. 1986), has undergone a thorough revision, and there are many new entries resulting from advances in Shakespeare scholarship and from the constantly changing treatment of the plays in the theatre. Each play has a separate entry giving the basic information about its date, sources, and first publication, followed by a selective account of the history of its theatrical presentation. Other entries are concerned with Shakespeare's life, his contemporaries, his interpreters, creative artists who have come under his influence, and other topics likely to interest those who enjoy Shakespeare's works, and who want to know more about him and them. Selectivity has been essential. It would have been possible, for example, to fill the volume with entries for Shakespeare's theatrical interpreters alone. We have tried to choose the great figures of the past along with those who are most active as Shakespeare performers at present. The section on Further Reading at the end of the book points to additional sources of information. An asterisk indicates that there is a separate entry in the dictionary for the topic so marked. The volume also includes a finding list of the characters in Shakespeare's plays, a conjectural chronology, and a statistical appendix providing interesting facts about Shakespeare's work.

Normally, quotations from early printed books and documents are given in modern form. Quotations from Shakespeare are from the Oxford *Complete Works*, General Editors Stanley Wells and Gary Taylor (1986, etc.). In compiling the many facts for this book, the library staffs of the Shakespeare Institute and Shakespeare Centre, Stratford-upon-Avon, have been a constant help, and we would like to thank Christine Buckley for her scrupulous copy-editing.

S.W.W.

J.S.

Acknowledgements

The authors and publishers would like to thank the following for permission to reproduce photographs on the pages listed:

The Bodleian Library, University of Oxford: 114 (Malone 389), 148 (Arch Gd. 41), 191 (Arch Ge. 31)

The photographs on pages 13 (C57b42), 64 (C34k1), 126 (ADD MS70438) by permission of the British Library

The College of Arms: 7

The Guildhall Library: 79

Holy Trinity Church, Stratford-upon-Avon: 14, 49.

The photograph on page 101 is reproduced by permission of the Marquess of Bath, Longleat House, Warminster, Great Britain

The photograph on page 27 by courtesy of the National Portrait Gallery, London

The Public Record Office: 167

The Royal Shakespeare Company Collection with permission of the Governors of the Royal Shakespeare Theatre: 54

The Shakespeare Birthplace Trust: 28, 44, 45, 55, 92, 121, 146, 169

Contents

A

act-and-scene divisions None of the *quarto editions of Shakespeare's plays issued before the First *Folio appeared, in 1623, is divided into scenes, and only one, *Othello*, printed in 1622, is divided into acts.

In the Folio, six plays are undivided; *Hamlet* is only partially divided; eleven plays are divided into acts only; the remaining eighteen are divided into acts and scenes. Some of the divided plays are ones which had been printed without divisions in quarto.

For most of its career, Shakespeare's company seems not to have observed act-breaks, though they may have been introduced after the acquisition of the *Blackfriars Theatre. Evidence such as the placing of the *Choruses in *Henry V* and *Pericles* shows that Shakespeare was conscious of the conventional five-act structure.

The divisions marked in modern editions are basically those established by the early eighteenth-century editors, Nicholas *Rowe and Alexander *Pope.

ACTER (A Center for Theater, Education and Research) Founded in 1967 by Homer Swander, producing small-scale productions, often featuring *Royal Shakespeare Company actors, touring throughout the USA.

actresses No professional actresses appeared on the English stage until after the Restoration, in 1660. Female roles in Shakespeare's plays were written for male actors, usually, if not invariably, boys. (*See* BOY ACTORS.)

Admiral's Men A theatre company, known first as Lord Howard's Men, under the patronage from 1576/7 to 1603 of Charles, Lord Howard, first Earl of Nottingham, who became Lord High Admiral in 1585. On *James I's accession, they became Prince Henry's Men (1603–12), and after that the Elector Palatine's, or Palsgrave's, Men (1613–25).

They were the main rivals to Shakespeare's company, the *Lord Chamberlain's (later King's) Men. From about 1589, perhaps earlier, to 1597, and 1600 to 1605, their leading actor was Edward *Alleyn, Richard *Burbage's chief rival. Their principal financier was Philip

*Henslowe, who owned the Rose Theatre, built in 1587, where the company mainly played from 1594 till they moved to his *Fortune Theatre in 1600. This burned down in 1621. The company, greatly harmed, survived only till 1625.

advice to the Players, Hamlet's Hamlet's speeches to the actors, III. ii. 1–45.

Age of Kings, An A BBC television serial based on Shakespeare's English history plays (*see* HISTORIES), directed by Peter Dews, and transmitted in 1961.

Aldridge, Ira (*c.*1807–67) The USA's first prominent black actor: he achieved international success, being acclaimed as the 'African Roscius'. He excelled as Othello, Aaron, Richard III, King Lear, and Macbeth.

Alexander, Bill (1948–) British director, whose productions with the *Royal Shakespeare Company include *Henry IV, Parts 1 and 2 (1980), *Richard III (1984), The *Merry Wives of Windsor (1985), A *Midsummer Night's Dream (1986), *Twelfth Night, The *Merchant of Venice, *Cymbeline (1987), *Much Ado About Nothing (1990), The *Taming of the Shrew (1992), *Titus Andronicus (2003) and King Lear (2004). After a short period of working in the USA, he became artistic director of the Birmingham Repertory Theatre in 1992, where he directed *Othello (1993), The *Tempest (1994), *Macbeth (1995), and The *Merchant of Venice (1997).

Alexander, Peter (1894–1969) British scholar whose edition of Shakespeare appeared in 1951.

Alleyn, Edward (1566–1626) Leading actor of the *Admiral's Men and founder of Dulwich College. He was famous particularly as *Marlowe's Faustus, Tamburlaine, and Barabas. He retired from 1597 to 1600, then returned to the stage till 1605, after which he continued as theatre manager. He was married first to Philip *Henslowe's stepdaughter, Joan, then (in 1623) to John Donne's daughter, Constance.

All for Love *See* DRYDEN, JOHN; ANTONY AND CLEOPATRA.

All is True (Henry VIII) This play was first published in the First *Folio (1623). It is generally, though not unanimously, believed that Shakespeare collaborated in its composition with John *Fletcher. There is no external evidence about this. The *Globe Theatre burned down during one of the early performances of the play, on 29 June 1613. The event was described in a letter by Sir Henry *Wotton, who refers to the play as *All is True*. His account, along with those of the other contemporary writers, names the play *All is True*. The title *Henry VIII* probably derives from the editors of the First Folio. The main source is *Holinshed's *Chronicles*, supplemented by *Halle's *Union of the Two Noble and Illustre Families of Lancaster and York*.

The second recorded performance was given at the second Globe Theatre on 29 July 1628, at the request of the then Duke of Buckingham, who left after the Buckingham of the play went to his execution.

After the Restoration, Thomas *Betterton played the King, giving the role up only in 1709, the year before he died. The play was frequently revived during the eighteenth century. A *Drury Lane production of 1727 celebrated George II's coronation with an elaborate procession which was repeated for many years afterwards. John Philip *Kemble revived the play at *Drury Lane in 1788 with Sarah *Siddons as Queen Katherine, a role in which she excelled and continued to appear till 1816. Kemble frequently played Wolsey, as, later, did W. C. *Macready, Samuel *Phelps, and, in 1855, Charles *Kean in his own spectacular production at the Princess's, with a real barge and an elaborate panoramic view of London. Henry *Irving also played Wolsey, with Ellen *Terry as Katherine, in 1892.

Nineteenth-century productions generally cut the play heavily, especially in the last two acts. Beerbohm *Tree acted Wolsey in 1910. Since then, less emphasis has been placed on this character. Sybil *Thorndike excelled as Katherine at the Empire in 1925. Tyrone *Guthrie directed the play at *Sadler's Wells in 1933, with Charles Laughton as Henry, in 1949 at Stratford-upon-Avon, with Anthony *Quayle as Henry, and in 1951 at the *Old Vic, in honour of the coronation of Elizabeth II. Michael *Benthall's Old Vic production in 1958 had John *Gielgud as Wolsey and Edith *Evans as Katherine. The Stratford-upon-Avon productions of 1969, directed by Trevor *Nunn (with Donald *Sinden as Henry and Peggy *Ashcroft as Katherine), and 1983, directed by Howard Davies, were both influenced by Brechtian staging methods. There was a lavish restaging by Ian Judge (Chichester, 1991), and a strong revival by Greg Doran at the *Swan, Stratford-upon-Avon (1996).

All is True is not one of Shakespeare's most popular plays, but its fine acting roles and opportunities for spectacle have kept it alive in the theatre.

All's Well that Ends Well Shakespeare's comedy was first printed in the First *Folio (1623). Though it was not directly mentioned by Francis *Meres in 1598, it has sometimes been identified with his *Love's Labour's Won, but resemblances to *Measure for Measure cause it most often to be dated 1602–3. It is based on a story from *Boccaccio's Decameron, probably in *Painter's translation.

It has never been a favourite with audiences. Its first recorded performance is in 1741. Subsequent performances tended to emphasize the role of Parolles (or Paroles). J. P. *Kemble tried, with little success, to restore the balance of the play at *Drury Lane in 1794. A musical version was played at *Covent Garden in 1832, and Samuel *Phelps presented the original at *Sadler's Wells in 1852. Barry *Jackson produced a modern-dress version at Birmingham Repertory Theatre in 1927, with the young Laurence *Olivier as Parolles. Tyrone *Guthrie directed a brilliant, if eccentric, production at *Stratford, Ontario, in 1957; this was repeated in 1959 at Stratford-upon-Avon, where in 1981 Trevor *Nunn directed a highly successful version in an Edwardian setting. In 1992, Peter Hall directed the play in the Swan Theatre, where also in 2003 Gregory Doran directed it with Judi Dench as a superb Countess. Elijah Moshinsky's production for the *BBC television series was also much admired.

All's Well that Ends Well has perhaps suffered by being labelled, since about 1900, a *problem play. It has excellent acting roles, good comedy, and fine, if rarefied, poetry.

Animated Shakespeare Thirty-minute adaptations by Leon Garfield preserving Shakespeare's lines in abbreviated form, and using a variety of animation techniques. The project was run by S4C and the Russian State Animation Studio and was first screened in 1992. It has been much used in schools.

Anne Hathaway's Cottage See HATHAWAY, ANNE. The house was bought by the *Shakespeare Birthplace Trust in 1892, and is maintained as a showplace.

Antony and Cleopatra Shakespeare's Roman tragedy was first printed in the First *Folio (1623). It had been entered in the *Stationers' Register in 1608, and is usually dated 1606–7. The main source is *Plutarch's Lives of the Noble Grecians and Romans. Shakespeare's wording is often close to *North's translation. No early performance is recorded.

*Dryden treated the subject in his *All for Love* (1678), with some debt to Shakespeare, and this probably had the effect of keeping Shakespeare's play off the stage. David *Garrick revived it in a version prepared by Edward *Capell, in 1759, without success. J. P. *Kemble's acting version of 1813 incorporated passages from *All for Love*. It too failed, as did W. C. *Macready's performances in 1833. The play had little success generally on the nineteenth-century stage.

Beerbohm *Tree presented a spectacular revival in 1906. Robert *Atkins's *Old Vic production of 1922 successfully abandoned realistic settings in favour of a bare stage. The play has continued to prove intractable, though Stratford-upon-Avon productions by Glen Byam *Shaw (1953) with Michael *Redgrave and Peggy *Ashcroft, by Trevor *Nunn (1972) with Richard Johnson and Janet *Suzman, and the St James's, London, production (1951) with Laurence *Olivier and Vivien Leigh, have enjoyed some success, as did a New York production of 1947 with Godfrey Tearle and Katharine Cornell. Helen *Mirren was a fine Cleopatra in Adrian *Noble's production at The *Other Place in 1982. Peter *Hall directed Judi *Dench and Anthony Hopkins at the *National Theatre in 1987 and Richard Johnson took the lead again in 1992 in John *Caird's production at Stratford-upon-Avon.

The fact that the play lags behind the 'great' tragedies in theatrical popularity may be attributed to its structural peculiarities, to the difficulty experienced by directors in finding a workable style for its presentation, and to challenges posed by the role of Cleopatra. Critically, it has aroused much interest, and it contains some of Shakespeare's greatest dramatic poetry, along with some of his most fascinating touches of characterization.

Apocryphal works A number of works attributed to Shakespeare in his own time and later are now not generally accepted as his. These include six plays added to the second issue (1664) of the Third *Folio: *The *London Prodigal*, *Thomas, *Lord Cromwell, Sir John *Oldcastle, The *Puritan, A *Yorkshire Tragedy*, and *Locrine. Other plays attributed to Shakespeare in the seventeenth and eighteenth centuries include *The Birth of Merlin*, *The Merry Devil of Edmonton*, *Mucedorus, *The Second Maiden's Tragedy, Fair Em*, and *Arden of Faversham*. More recently, claims have been made for the lyric *'Shall I die?', the manuscript play *Edmund Ironside*, and 'A *Funeral Elegy.' It has been long believed that passages in the manuscript play *Sir Thomas More are by Shakespeare and certain scenes in *Edward III* have often been attributed to him; more recently the whole of the latter play has been claimed as his. It is printed in the New *Riverside edition (1997) and is to appear in the *New Cambridge series and in the revised Oxford Complete Works.

Performances of the apocryphal plays are rare, but *Arden of Faversham* has been successfully staged, notably in Terry *Hands's production of 1982, and is the subject of an opera (*Arden Muss Sterben—Arden Must Die*, 1967) by Alexander Goehr.

Apollonius of Tyre The hero of a romantic tale, well-known in the Middle Ages and Renaissance, and often retold. Shakespeare uses it in the framework of The *Comedy of Errors* and as the main tale of *Pericles*.

Arcadia, The A lengthy prose romance by Sir Philip *Sidney, based on Greek romances. It exists in two forms: the 'old' *Arcadia*, and an incompleted revision, the 'New' *Arcadia*. Shakespeare drew on it for the Gloucester sub-plot of *King Lear*.

Arden edition A multi-volume edition of Shakespeare which first appeared under the General Editorship of W. J. Craig, from 1891 to 1906, then of R. H. Case, from 1906 to 1924. A plan to revise the original volumes was soon scrapped in favour of entirely new editions which began to appear in 1951 under the General Editorship of Una Ellis-Fermor, succeeded in 1958 by Harold F. Brooks and Harold Jenkins, later joined by Brian Morris and Richard Proudfoot. This series, unofficially known as the New Arden, included some distinguished and highly influential volumes such as *Macbeth* and *King Lear* edited by Kenneth *Muir, *Hamlet* edited by Jenkins, and *Coriolanus* edited by Philip Brockbank. A new series, known as Arden 3, began to appear in 1995 under the General Editorship of Proudfoot, Ann Thompson, and David Scott Kastan. Each volume of all the series has full scholarly apparatus, including an extended introduction, collations, detailed annotations, and reprints of source material.

Arden, Mary (d. 1608) Youngest daughter of Robert Arden of Wilmcote near Stratford-upon-Avon; married Shakespeare's father, *John, about 1557. *See* MARY ARDEN'S HOUSE.

Armin, Robert (*c*.1568–1615) An actor and writer who seems to have joined Shakespeare's company, the *Lord Chamberlain's Men, by 1599. The author of a book called *Foole upon Foole* (1600), he specialized in comic roles, and may have succeeded Will *Kemp. No

John Shakespeare's coat of arms, from the document assigning it to him (1596)

Shakespearian roles can certainly be assigned to him, but it seems likely that he played Dogberry, Touchstone, Feste, and Lear's Fool.

arms, Shakespeare's Shakespeare's father approached the Heralds' Office about a coat of arms shortly after becoming bailiff of Stratford-upon-Avon in 1568, but did not proceed far. He (or perhaps his son on his behalf) renewed the application in 1596. Sir William Dethick, Garter King-of-Arms, granted the request. Two rough drafts survive.

The shield was to be 'gold on a bend sables, a spear of the first steeled argent, and for his crest or cognizance a falcon, his wings displayed argent, standing on a wreath of his colours, supporting a spear gold, steeled as aforesaid, set upon a helmet with mantles and tassels as hath been accustomed and doth more plainly appear depicted on this margin'.

A rough sketch of the shield and crest appears on both drafts. The motto, which Shakespeare is not known to have used, is 'Non Sans Droit'—'Not Without Right'. The grant of arms gave to John *Shakespeare and his family the status of gentlefolk.

In 1599, John Shakespeare applied for the right to impale his arms with those of his wife's family, the Ardens, but this seems not to have been allowed. His right to arms was challenged in 1602, but the official reply was that he was 'a magistrate in Stratford-upon-Avon. A Justice of Peace, he married a daughter and heir of Arden, and was of good substance and habilité.'

Arne, Thomas (1710–78) Composer of delightful settings of songs from several of Shakespeare's plays, and of the music for *Garrick's Ode for the Jubilee of 1769.

arras A curtain or wall-hanging which appears to have been used on the Elizabethan stage, as for the eavesdropping Polonius (*Hamlet*, III. i), and the snoring Falstaff (I *Henry IV*, II. iv).

Ashcroft, Dame Peggy (1907–91) British actress who had a strong influence on company approach to theatre, notably with the *Royal Shakespeare Company which she joined at its inception in 1960. Her many roles included Margaret of Anjou in the 1963 *Wars of the Roses*, which involved ageing sixty years and earned a major revaluation of the role. Other roles included Desdemona (Savoy, 1930, with Paul Robeson), Imogen (*Old Vic, 1932, Stratford-upon-Avon, 1957), Juliet (Old Vic, 1932, New Theatre, with Laurence *Olivier and John *Gielgud, changing roles in mid-run, as Romeo and Mercutio), Portia (Queen's, 1935, Stratford-upon-Avon, 1953), Viola (Phoenix, 1938 and Old Vic, 1950), Ophelia (*Haymarket, with Gielgud, 1944), and (all at Stratford-upon-Avon) Beatrice (1950, etc.), Cordelia (1950), Cleopatra (with Michael *Redgrave, 1953), Rosalind (1957), Katherina (1960), Paulina (1960), Queen Katherine (1969); and the Countess in *All's Well that Ends Well* (1981).

Ashland, Oregon *See* OREGON SHAKESPEARE FESTIVAL.

As You Like It Shakespeare's pastoral comedy, first printed in the First *Folio (1623), is first heard of in the *Stationer's Register in 1600, and was probably written not long before. It is based directly on Thomas *Lodge's prose romance *Rosalynde*, first printed in 1590. Shakespeare adapted the story and added the characters of Jaques, Touchstone, Audrey, William, and Sir Oliver Martext.

No early performances are certainly recorded. In 1723 parts of the play were used in an odd compilation by Charles Johnson, *Love in a Forest*, which also draws on A *Midsummer Night's Dream* and other plays. Shakespeare's play was revived in 1740 by Charles *Macklin, with songs by Thomas *Arne. Since then it has been regularly performed, usually in picturesque settings, and often during the past hundred years in the open air. Many leading actresses, including Dorothea *Jordan, Ada *Rehan, Mary Anderson, Edith *Evans, Peggy *Ashcroft, Margaret Leighton, Vanessa *Redgrave, and Juliet *Stevenson have excelled in the demanding role of Rosalind. In 1967 Clifford Williams directed an all-male version with the *National Theatre company at the Old Vic, a concept repeated with great success by *Cheek by Jowl (1991, 1994). The play was filmed in 1992 by Christine Edzard, who chose an inner-city wasteland to represent the forest.

As You Like It is a play in which ideas are never far below the surface. It portrays contrasting attitudes to life, using an original technique of tolerant juxtaposition rather than presentation by intrigue or argument. The style of both its verse and its prose is exceptionally limpid and unforced, and though Rosalind is the dominating character, other roles, especially Jaques, Touchstone, Audrey, Corin, and William, offer opportunities for creative acting.

Atkins, Robert (1886–1972) English actor and director much associated with Shakespeare's plays at the *Old Vic, Stratford-upon-Avon, the *Regent's Park Open-Air Theatre, and elsewhere.

Aubrey, John (1626–97) His posthumously published *Brief Lives* include gossip about Shakespeare, some of it from William Beeston, son of Christopher, a member of Shakespeare's company. He describes Shakespeare as 'a handsome, well-shaped man: very good company, and of a very ready and pleasant smooth wit', and says that he was 'the more to be admired [because] he was not a company keeper . . . wouldn't be debauched, and if invited to, writ he was in pain.' From him comes the statement that Shakespeare 'had been in his younger years a schoolmaster in the country', as well as the suggestion that William *Davenant was Shakespeare's natural son.

authorship The first suggestion that Shakespeare did not write the plays attributed to him appears to have been made by the Revd James Wilmot, who ascribed them to Francis Bacon around 1785. He did not publish his conclusion. The next appearance of the idea is in a book called *The Romance of Yachting*, published in 1848 by an eccentric New

York lawyer, Colonel Joseph C. Hart. He was influenced by a denigratory life of Shakespeare in Dionysius Lardner's *Cabinet Cyclopaedia*, which found that the plays 'absolutely teem with the grossest impurities,—more gross by far than can be found in any contemporary dramatist.' Hart fantasized that Shakespeare 'purchased or obtained surreptitiously' other men's plays which he then 'spiced with obscenity, blackguardism and impurities'. He did not identify the original author.

The first extended attempt to prove Bacon's authorship was in an article by Delia Bacon, also an American, published in 1856. Later that year she spent a night in *Holy Trinity Church with the intention of opening Shakespeare's grave, but abandoned the plan. Her theory was elaborated in her book *The Philosophy of the Plays of Shakespeare Unfolded* (1857).

The 'anti-Stratfordian' movement, as it has come to be called, developed. An English Bacon Society, producing a periodical, was founded in 1885, and an American Society followed in 1892. Much intellectual effort and learning have been expended in the attempt to find cryptograms and other clues to authorship in the texts and other places, such as the *Droeshout engraving. The movement has had some distinguished adherents, including Mark Twain and Sigmund *Freud.

In more recent years splinter groups have attempted to replace Shakespeare with many different names, including those of the Earl of Derby, the Earl of *Essex, Queen *Elizabeth, Christopher *Marlowe, the Earl of *Oxford, and the Earl of *Rutland. An excellent account of the whole topic is given in Part Six of S. *Schoenbaum's *Shakespeare's Lives* (1970, revised 1991).

All alternative claims depend on conspiracy theory: that, for example, Marlowe's death—one of the best authenticated episodes in literary history—was a cover-up, and that he lived on writing plays for another twenty years, otherwise leaving no trace of his previously colourful personality, and generously giving credit for his work to Shakespeare (whose supposedly early works have to be redated), and that Shakespeare co-operated in the conspiracy by pretending to be the author of works he had not written, and by somehow concealing their authorship from all his theatrical and literary colleagues, and from those who published them.

Evidence that the plays were written by someone called William Shakespeare (occasionally in collaboration with, for example, John

*Fletcher) abounds, occurring in title-pages, in printed tributes and allusions, in manuscripts not intended for publication, and elsewhere. Evidence that the Shakespeare who wrote the works was the Shakespeare of Stratford-upon-Avon includes the references in his will to *Heminges and *Condell, who were closely involved with the publication of the First *Folio; the inscriptions on Shakespeare of Stratford's *monument, one in Latin comparing him to great figures of antiquity, the other in English specifically praising him as a writer; Ben *Jonson's verses in the First Folio calling him 'sweet Swan of Avon'; and the lines in the same volume by Leonard *Digges referring to his 'Stratford monument'.

Evidence for authorship may be both external or internal. External evidence is not completely reliable. Both A *Yorkshire Tragedy and The *London Prodigal were clearly attibuted to Shakespeare on the title-pages of their first publication and on their reprinting in 1619, but this evidence is generally discredited, helped by the fact that they were not included in the First Folio. Internal evidence based on stylistic analysis, aided in recent times by computerization, has had limited success. There is fairly general agreement about the passages in The *Two Noble Kinsmen and *All is True (Henry VIII) for which Shakespeare and Fletcher respectively were primarily responsible, but elaborate stylistic tests on *Edward III and 'A *Funeral Elegy' have not won general assent.

Attempts to discredit Shakespeare's authorship seem to be based mainly on snobbery—the idea that a man of relatively humble origins without a university education could have written works of genius; or on the desire for notoriety; or on mere folly.

B

Bacon, Delia *See* AUTHORSHIP.

Bacon, Francis *See* AUTHORSHIP.

bad quarto A technical term devised by the bibliographer A. W. Pollard to refer to certain early texts of Shakespeare's plays which he believed were not printed from an authoritative manuscript. These include the first *quartos of *Romeo and Juliet* (1597), *Henry V* (1600), The *Merry Wives of Windsor* (1602), and *Hamlet* (1603). The theory, forwarded by Pollard, that all these texts were reconstructed from memory by some of the actors is now under attack. Alternative theories are that some or all of them are early versions by Shakespeare, or abbreviations made either for Shakespeare's company or for other companies. There are two new editions including reprints of the early quartos, New Cambridge Shakespeare: the Early Quartos (Cambridge University Press, 1994–), and Shakespearean Originals: First Editions (Harvester Wheatsheaf, 1992–). Though they have no textual authority they may assist in the effort to establish a true text, especially in their *stage directions which sometimes give us our only evidence as to pieces of stage business.

Balakirev, Mily Alexeievich (1837–1910) The Russian composer wrote an overture (1859) *King Lear* and published an extended suite of incidental music for the play in 1904.

baptism, Shakespeare's The baptism of 'Gulielmus filius Johannes Shakspere' is recorded in the Stratford-upon-Avon Parish Register on 26 April 1564. The register, a transcript dated 1600, is now in the custody of the *Shakespeare Birthplace Trust.

Barker, Harley Granville *See* GRANVILLE-BARKER, HARLEY.

Barry, Elizabeth (*c.*1658–1713) English actress, mistress of the Earl of Rochester; she acted with Thomas *Betterton, and played Cordelia in Nahum *Tate's version of *King Lear*, Mrs Ford in The *Merry Wives of Windsor*, Queen Katherine in *Henry VIII*, and Lady Macbeth.

Ham. To be, or not to bè, I there's the point,
To Die, to sleepe, is that all? I all:
No, to sleepe, to dreame, I mary there it goes,
For in that dreame of death, when wee awake,
And borne before an euerlasting Iudge,
From whence no passenger euer retur'nd,
The vndiscouered country, at whose sight
The happy smile, and the accursed damn'd.
But for this, the ioyfull hope of this,
Whol'd beare the scornes and flattery of the world,
Scorned by the right rich, the rich cursſed of the poore?

The

" *Prince of Denmarke*

The widow being oppresſed, the orphan wrong'd,
The taste of hunger, or a tirants raigne,
And thousand more calamities besides,
To grunt and sweate vnder this weary life,
When that he may his full *Quietus* make,
With a bare bodkin, who would this indure,
But for a hope of something after death?
Which pusles the braine, and doth confound the sence,
Which makes vs rather beare those euilles we haue,
Than flie to others that we know not of.
I that, O this conscience makes cowardes of vs all,
Lady in thy orizons, be all my sinnes remembred.

Hamlet's 'To be or not to be . . .' as it appeared in the 'bad quarto' of 1603

Barry, Spranger (1717?–77) Irish actor, chief rival of David *Garrick, with whom he acted in his later years; most successful as Romeo, Hamlet, Othello, Macbeth, Lear, and Richard III. A female admirer, comparing him with Garrick as Romeo, said, 'Had I been Juliet to Garrick's Romeo—so ardent and impassioned was he, I should have expected he would have *come up* to me in the balcony; but had I been Juliet to Barry's Romeo—so tender, so eloquent, and so seductive was he, I should certainly have *gone down* to him!' In Lear, however, Barry was said to be 'every inch a King', but Garrick 'every inch King Lear!'

The entry of Shakespeare's birth in the Stratford-upon-Avon Parish Register

Bartlett, John (1820–1905) American compiler of a *Complete Concordance to Shakespeare's Dramatic Works and Poems*, published in 1894, standard until the publication of *Spevack's more truly 'complete' work.

Barton, John Associate director of the *Royal Shakespeare Company 1964–91, and advisory director 1991– , whose work includes distinguished productions of The *Taming of the Shrew (1960), *Love's Labour's Lost (1965 and 1978), *All's Well that Ends Well (1967), *Coriolanus (1967), *Troilus and Cressida (1968, 1976), *Twelfth Night (1969), *Measure for Measure (1970), *Othello (1971) and *Much Ado About Nothing (1976), and The *Merchant of Venice (1978 and 1981). He adapted the texts of the early history plays to make The *Wars of the Roses (1963 etc.), which he directed with Peter *Hall, and also adapted *King John (1974). In 1992 he directed *Measure for Measure and *As You Like It at National Theatret, Oslo. His television series *Playing Shakespeare*, and book of the same name, appeared in 1984.

Basse, William (1583?–1653?) English poet, author of a manuscript sonnet-epitaph on Shakespeare written before 1623, beginning:

> Renowned Spenser, lie a thought more nigh
> To learnèd Chaucer, and rare Beaumont, lie
> A little nearer Spenser to make room
> For Shakespeare in your three-fold, four-fold tomb.

Baylis, Lilian (1874–1937) *See* OLD VIC.

BBC Television Shakespeare In 1978 the BBC, which had sporadically televised a number of Shakespeare's plays, embarked on a plan to produce all of them at the rate of about six a year. Cedric Messina was originally in charge of the project; Jonathan *Miller took over after two years, to be succeeded by Shaun Sutton. Directors include Miller himself, Elijah Moshinsky, Jane Howell, David Jones, etc. Some cuts are made (*The *Taming of the Shrew* loses the Christopher Sly scenes), though the early histories, for example, are given in exceptionally full texts. The costumes are mostly of Shakespeare's time or of the historical period represented, and settings are generally representational. They include distinguished performances by e.g. John *Gielgud, Celia Johnson, Claire Bloom, Derek *Jacobi, Richard *Pasco, Helen *Mirren, Michael Hordern, and others, sometimes repeating roles they have played on stage. Production styles have been criticized as unadventurous; some of the less popular plays (e.g. *All's Well that Ends Well*, *Henry VIII*) have succeeded best. The series was completed in 1985 with *Titus Andronicus* and has had an international distribution. An account of the venture is provided by *The BBC Shakespeare Plays: Making the Televised Canon* (1991) by Susan Willis. Plays have subsequently been commissioned and filmed by the BBC, e.g. *Measure for Measure* (1994), *Henry IV* (1995), and the Bard on the Box season of programmes in 1995 included documentaries, workshops, and performances.

bear One of the more surprising stage directions in Shakespeare occurs in *The *Winter's Tale*, III. iii. 59, when Antigonus is required to 'Exit, pursued by a bear', which devours him.

Beaumont, Francis (*c.*1584–1616) English dramatist, collaborator with John *Fletcher and author of independent plays. *The Woman Hater* (*c.*1606) quotes a phrase from *Hamlet* in a comic context, and in *The Knight of the Burning Pestle* (*c.*1607) are lines which appear to be an early allusion to *Macbeth*. They are spoken by Jasper 'with his face mealed', and evidently refer to the appearance of Banquo's ghost, and to record a piece of stage business—the dropping of the cup—used by many later actors. They are:

> When thou art at thy table with thy friends,
> Merry in heart, and filled with swelling wine,
> I'll come in midst of all thy pride and mirth,
> Invisible to all men but thyself,
> And whisper such a sad tale in thine ear

> Shall make thee let the cup fall from thy hand,
> And stand as mute and pale as death itself. (v. i. 26–32)

bed-trick The deceptive substitution of one woman in a man's bed for another, a common motif of romance literature, used by Shakespeare in both *All's Well that Ends Well* and *Measure for Measure*.

Beerbohm, Max (1872–1956) English satirical writer and artist who reviewed many productions of Shakespeare's plays (see Stanley Wells, 'Shakespeare in Max Beerbohm's Theatre Criticism', *Shakespeare Survey 29*, 1976), and drew several cartoons featuring Shakespeare, including one alluding to the *authorship controversy.

Beethoven, Ludwig van (1770–1827) Beethoven's overture *Coriolan* (1807) was written for a play 'after Shakespeare' by a Viennese playwright, H. Collin, but he may have had Shakespeare's play in mind. The slow movement of his first string quartet, Opus 18 No. 1, is said to have been inspired by the last scene of *Romeo and Juliet*, and when asked the meaning of the first movement of his piano sonata in D minor, Opus 31 No. 2, he replied 'Read Shakespeare's *The Tempest*.'

Bell, John (1745–1831) A London publisher who brought out an edition of Shakespeare's plays (printed 1773–5) based on the prompt-books of the Theatres Royal, edited and introduced by Francis *Gentleman, which is invaluable to the theatre historian. The plays not in the theatres' repertoires are also printed, in complete texts with Gentleman's suggestions for omissions. The edition is accompanied with two plates for each play, one illustrating an actor as one of the characters, the other portraying a scene from the play. The plates were published separately, and are not necessarily included in sets of the plays. Bell also published a conventional edition, based on the text of Samuel *Johnson and George *Steevens, in 1788.

Belleforest, François de (1530–83) French writer; his continuation of Pierre Boaistuau's translation of Matteo Bandello's *Novelle*, as *Histoires Tragiques* (1559–82), includes a version of a legend from *Saxo Grammaticus which influenced *Hamlet (perhaps indirectly), and a story which may have influenced *Much Ado About Nothing*.

Belott, Stephen *See* MOUNTJOY, CHRISTOPHER.

Benson, Sir Francis (Frank) Robert (1858–1939) Actor–manager whose first appearance was at the *Lyceum, in 1882, under Henry

*Irving. From 1883 to 1919 he managed a company which presented most of Shakespeare's plays, mainly in the English provinces, including Stratford-upon-Avon. He produced the plays singly, with few cuts. He gave a full text of *Hamlet at the Lyceum in 1900. In 1906 his company gave the English history plays (omitting 1 *Henry IV) at Stratford-upon-Avon, where from 1888 to 1919 he managed the Festival. His own best roles included Hamlet, Richard II (finely reviewed by C. E. Montague), Richard III, Petruchio, and Caliban.

Benthall, Michael (1919–74) English director who worked at Stratford-upon-Avon (1947–51) and directed the *Old Vic Theatre from 1953 to 1958, during which time all Shakespeare's plays were put on, many of them under the direction of Benthall.

Benson, John (d. 1667) A London publisher who brought out an edition of Shakespeare's *Poems* in 1640. It omits *Venus and Adonis* and The *Rape of Lucrece* and includes many non-Shakespearian poems along with inauthentic versions of most of the *Sonnets.

Bergman, Ingmar (1918–) Swedish director who mounted a series of impressive productions at the Royal Dramatic Theatre, Stockholm, including *King Lear* (1984), *Twelfth Night, *Hamlet* (1986), and The *Winter's Tale* (1992).

Berlioz, Hector (1803–69) French composer greatly influenced by Shakespeare, especially in his fantasia for chorus and orchestra on The Tempest (1830, incorporated into Lélio, 1832); his concert overture King Lear (1831); his dramatic symphony Romeo and Juliet (1839); his choral and orchestral pieces The Death of Ophelia (originally for voice and piano) and 'Funeral March for Hamlet' (1848); his comic opera Beatrice and Benedict (1862), and, less directly but no less profoundly, his opera The Trojans (1858).

Bernard, Sir John (1605–74) Second husband of Shakespeare's granddaughter, Elizabeth *Hall.

Bernhardt, Sarah (1834–1923) French actress who made an early success as Cordelia in a translation of *King Lear*, and later played Hamlet. She was 54 at the time. Max *Beerbohm, reviewing the performance, wrote, 'Her friends ought to have restrained her. The native critics ought not to have encouraged her. The custom-house officials at Charing Cross ought to have confiscated her sable doublet and hose . . . the

HECTOR BERLIOZ *(1803–69) on the impact of Shakespeare; from his*
Memoirs *(1870), translated by David Cairns*

Shakespeare, coming upon me unawares, struck me like a
thunderbolt. The lightning flash of that discovery revealed to me
at a stroke the whole heaven of art, illuminating it to its remotest
corners. I recognized the meaning of grandeur, beauty, dramatic
truth, and I could measure the utter absurdity of the French view
of Shakespeare which derives from Voltaire:

> That ape of genius, sent
> By Satan among men to do his work

and the pitiful narrowness of our own worn-out academic,
cloistered traditions of poetry. I saw, I undertood, I felt . . . that I
was alive and that I must arise and walk. . . .

As I came out of *Hamlet*, shaken to the depths by the
experience, I vowed not to expose myself a second time to the
flame of Shakespeare's genius.

Next day the playbills announced *Romeo and Juliet*. I had my
pass to the pit. But to make doubly sure of getting in, just in case
the doorkeeper at the Odéon might have had orders to suspend
the free list, I rushed round to the box office the moment I saw the
posters and bought a stall. My fate was doubly sealed.

only compliment one can conscientiously pay her is that her Hamlet
was, from first to last, *très grande dame*.'

Bestrafte Brudermord, Der *See* FRATRICIDE PUNISHED.

Betterton, Thomas (1635–1710) The leading actor of the Restoration
period, also involved with theatre management. After a short period
with Thomas *Killigrew and the King's Men, he joined William
*Davenant and the Duke's Men, and in 1661 played Hamlet with them
'beyond imagination', according to *Pepys. He went on playing Hamlet until he was over seventy, and his other Shakespeare roles included Brutus, Macbeth, Mercutio, Sir Toby Belch, Lear, Henry VIII,
Othello, and *Falstaff.

Betty, Master William (1791–1874) A child prodigy, known as the
'Young Roscius', he had a period of sensational popularity from 1803

to 1808, playing Romeo, Hamlet, Richard III, and Macbeth, among other roles. His fame was such that the Prime Minister, William Pitt, adjourned the House of Commons in order to see Betty's performance as Hamlet.

Bevington edition A one-volume edition of the Complete Works, with annotations and other editorial material, prepared under the supervision of the American scholar David Bevington. Originally published in 1973 as a revision of an edition by Hardin *Craig, it has itself undergone radical revisions in 1980 and 1997.

Bible Shakespeare's plays show a familiar acquaintance with both the Geneva Bible (1560) and the Bishops' Bible (1568). The most complete study is Naseem Shaheen's multi-volume study of biblical references in Shakespeare's plays, 1987– .

Birmingham Shakespeare Library *See* SHAKESPEARE MEMORIAL LIBRARY, BIRMINGHAM.

birthday, Shakespeare's Shakespeare was baptized on 26 April 1564, probably only a few days after his birth, traditionally celebrated on St George's Day, 23 April, the date of his death. The annual celebrations at Stratford-upon-Avon include a flag-unfurling ceremony, a procession including diplomatic representatives of many nations, a luncheon at which the Immortal Memory of William Shakespeare is toasted by a distinguished speaker, a performance of one of the plays, a church service with a special sermon, and a lecture.

birthplace, Shakespeare's When Shakespeare was born, in 1564, his father owned two adjacent houses in Henley Street, Stratford-upon-Avon, and another in Greenhill Street. Legal records show that he was living in Henley Street in 1552 and as late as 1597. There is no reason to suppose that he lived elsewhere during this period, so the Henley Street property is likely to be that in which Shakespeare was born.

When Shakespeare died, his sister, Joan Hart, was living in the western part of the property, and he left her a life-tenancy in it for an annual rent of one shilling. His granddaughter left both houses to Joan's descendants, who lived in the western one and rented the other. They sold the property in 1806, when the western wing became a butcher's shop. The property was bought as a public trust (*see* SHAKESPEARE BIRTHPLACE TRUST) in 1847.

Bishop, Sir Henry Rowley (1786–1855) English composer who worked with Frederick *Reynolds on musical versions of several of Shakespeare's plays at *Covent Garden, and also wrote incidental music. His best-known setting of Shakespeare is 'Lo, here the gentle lark', words from *Venus and Adonis* introduced into The *Comedy of Errors* (1819).

Blackfriars Gatehouse In March 1613 Shakespeare bought a house in the Blackfriars, in the eastern part of the City of London, close to the theatre, for £140. He appears not to have lived in it, and to have bought it as an investment.

Blackfriars Theatre A disused monastery in the Blackfriars area of London, used sporadically as a theatre by children's companies between 1576 and 1608, when it was acquired for the King's (formerly *Lord Chamberlain's) Men, who used it as a winter house from autumn 1609 to 1642. It was a *'private' theatre, roofed, with higher admission charges than the 'public' theatres, and holding only about 700 spectators, and the staging possibilities may have been influential in the inclusion of *masque elements in the *late plays. It was demolished in 1655. A reconstruction opened in Staunton, Virginia, in 2001.

Blake, William (1757–1827) The English poet and artist produced more than twenty highly imaginative pictorial treatments of Shakespearian themes.

blank verse Unrhymed verse, with five iambic feet to a line, a measure introduced into England by the Earl of Surrey (c.1517–47), the poet, which became the basic verse form of Elizabethan drama.

Bloch, Ernest (1880–1959) The Swiss composer of an opera (1910), *Macbeth*, based on Shakespeare's play.

blocking entry An entry in the *Stationers' Register which seems designed to establish a claim to the right of printing a work rather than as an immediate preliminary to printing it. Several of Shakespeare's plays were entered in this way.

Boccaccio, Giovanni (1313–75) Italian writer best known for his *Decameron* (1353), a collection of 100 tales. Among those translated by William Painter in his *Palace of Pleasure* (1567) was that of Giletta of Narbonne, used by Shakespeare for *All's Well that Ends Well*.

Bogdanov, Michael (1938–) British director who directed for the *Royal Shakespeare Company and the *National Theatre before forming the *English Shakespeare Company in 1985 with actor Michael *Pennington. Director of politically-charged productions with contemporary social references. In his *Romeo and Juliet* (Stratford-upon-Avon, 1986) Tybalt entered the stage in an Alfa Romeo sports car and Romeo killed himself using a hypodermic needle. Other productions include for the Royal Shakespeare Company, The *Taming of the Shrew* (1978), and for the English Shakespeare Company, *Wars of the Roses* (1986–9) history cycle, *Coriolanus and The *Winter's Tale* (1990), and *Macbeth, The *Tempest* (1992).

Bohemia, sea-coast of Shakespeare's attribution in The *Winter's Tale* of a sea-coast to Bohemia has often been held against him. It troubled Sir Thomas *Hanmer so much that he supposed it to be a mistake for Bithynia, a reading which Charles *Kean adopted in his acting version.

Bond, Edward (1934–) British dramatist whose plays include the Shakespeare-related *Lear* (Royal Court, 1971), and *Bingo* (Northcott Theatre, Exeter, 1973). The latter is based on Shakespeare's final days, and presents an embittered playwright who chooses suicide.

Booth, Edwin (1833–93) American actor and manager, son of Junius Brutus *Booth, successful also in London. He excelled as Hamlet, Iago, Brutus, and Lear.

Booth, Junius Brutus (1796–1852) English tragedian, at first an imitator of Edmund *Kean; he worked in America from 1821, and toured regularly. His Shakespeare roles included Richard III, Shylock, Iago, Hamlet, Macbeth, Lear, Othello, and Cassius. He was the father of three actors: Junius, Edwin, and John Wilkes, who assassinated Abraham Lincoln.

Bouncing Knight, The *See* HENRY IV, PART ONE.

Bowdler, Miss Henrietta Maria (1754–1830) Sister of Dr Thomas *Bowdler, and the editor of the first anonymous edition of the *Family Shakespeare*, in which twenty of Shakespeare's plays were published, expurgated, in 1807. She also published best-selling sermons and religious poems and essays.

Bowdler, Dr Thomas (1754–1825) Notorious as the editor of an expurgated ('bowdlerized') edition of Shakespeare. Twenty of the plays appeared in the *Family Shakespeare* in 1807. This was issued anonymously, and was the work of Bowdler's sister, *Henrietta. Thomas Bowdler expurgated the remaining plays for the second edition, of 1818. His principle was that 'If any word or expression is of such a nature that the first impression it excites is an impression of obscenity, that word ought not to be spoken nor written or printed; and, if printed, it ought to be erased.' His edition was often reprinted. The title-page reads 'The Family Shakespeare, in ten volumes; in which nothing is added to the original text; but those words and expressions are omitted which cannot with propriety be read aloud in a family'. He also published (posthumously) Edward Gibbon's *History of the Decline and Fall of the Roman Empire, for the use of Families and Young Persons, reprinted from the original text with the careful omissions of all passages of an irreligious or immoral tendency* (1826).

boy actors No professional actresses appeared on the English stage before 1660. All the female roles in Shakespeare's plays were originally played by male actors. This is no doubt one explanation of the popularity of plots in which girls dress up as boys.

Boy actors underwent a rigorous training as apprentices to senior members of the acting companies, and there is no reason to suppose that they lacked expertise. In Shakespeare's time there were also companies composed exclusively of boys, which at times constituted serious rivals to the adult companies. A passage in *Hamlet* (II. ii. 339–61) alludes to their success.

Boydell's Shakespeare Gallery Alderman John Boydell (1719–1804) commissioned paintings of scenes from Shakespeare by the leading British artists of the day, including Henry *Fuseli, William *Hogarth, Sir Joshua Reynolds, George Romney, Robert Smirke, Richard Westall, and Francis Wheatley. A gallery for their exhibition was opened in Pall Mall, London, in 1789. About 170 paintings were completed, and many of them engraved, but Boydell had money troubles, and the collection was sold by auction in 1805. There is an account of the venture in W. M. Merchant's *Shakespeare and the Artist* (1959), and a more recent study is *The Boydell Shakespeare Gallery*, edited by Walter Pape and Frederick Burwick (1996).

Boys from Syracuse, The A musical, loosely related to *The *Comedy of Errors*, by Richard Rodgers and Lorenz Hart, staged 1938, filmed 1940.

Bradley, Andrew Cecil (1851–1935) Professor of Poetry at Oxford, 1901–6, author of *Shakespearean Tragedy* (1904), essays on *Antony and Cleopatra* and 'The Rejection of Falstaff' published in *Oxford Lectures on Poetry* (1909), and a British Academy lecture on *Coriolanus*. He has been criticized for treating Shakespeare's characters too much as if they were real people, but his writings are classics of criticism.

Branagh, Kenneth (1960–) British actor and director. Played Henry V for the *Royal Shakespeare Company in 1984 at the age of 24 and Hamlet in a full-text production for the same company in 1992. In 1986 he formed the Renaissance Theatre Company for which he has played Romeo (1986), Hamlet, Benedick, Touchstone (1988), Quince, Edgar (1990), and Coriolanus (1992). He directed and played the leading male roles in films of *Henry V* (1989), *Much Ado About Nothing* (1993), *Hamlet* (1996), and *Love's Labour's Lost* (1999), and he also played Iago in *Othello* (1995) directed by Oliver Parker.

Brecht, Bertolt (1898–1956) German playwright, director, and theoretician of 'epic theatre'. His adaptations of *Measure for Measure* and *Coriolanus* gave the plays marked contemporary relevance.

Bremer Shakespeare Company Formed in 1983 as an unsubsidized ensemble company with no recognized artistic director, dedicated to playing Shakespeare. Among their notable productions was an all-male *Merry Wives of Windsor*, which was shown live on German television. They were the first company to perform an entire Shakespeare play at the *International Shakespeare Globe Centre.

Bridges-Adams, William (1889–1965) English director of the festival seasons at the *Shakespeare Memorial Theatre, Stratford-upon-Avon, from 1919 to 1934.

Britten, Lord (Benjamin Britten; 1913–76) English composer whose settings for Shakespeare include the opera *A Midsummer Night's Dream* (1960).

Brook, Peter (1925–) English director whose British productions have mainly been given at Stratford-upon-Avon. These include *Romeo and Juliet* and *Love's Labour's Lost* (1946), *Measure for Measure* and The *Winter's Tale* (both with *Gielgud, 1951), *Titus Andronicus* (with *Olivier) and *Hamlet* (1955), *King Lear* (with *Scofield, 1962, filmed 1970), *A Midsummer Night's Dream* (1970), and *Antony and Cleopatra* (1978). In 1971 he founded International Center of Theater Research in Paris, where his Shakespeare work includes *Timon of Athens* (1974), *Measure for Measure* (1978), The *Tempest* (1990), and an adaptation of *Hamlet, Qui est là* (1995).

Brooke, Arthur (d. 1563) English author of the long poem, *The Tragical History of Romeus and Juliet* (1562), on which Shakespeare based *Romeo and Juliet*.

Burbage, James (*c*.1530–97) A joiner who became an actor with the Earl of Leicester's Men and, in 1576, built the *Theatre; father of Cuthbert (1566–1636, also a theatre owner) and *Richard.

Burbage, Richard (*c*.1567–1619) Son of James; leading actor in Shakespeare's company throughout his career; known to have played, probably at their first performances, Richard III, Hamlet, King Lear, and Othello. An elegy ascribed to 'Jo Fletcher' includes the lines:

> He's gone, and with him what a world are dead,
> Which he revived, to be revivèd so.
> No more young Hamlet, old Hieronimo,
> Kind Lear, the grievèd Moor, and more beside,
> That lived in him, have now forever died . . .

He was a painter (*see* RUTLAND, FRANCIS MANNERS); an anecdote about him and Shakespeare is told by John *Manningham.

Burton, Richard (1925–84) Celebrated film actor who played many Shakespeare roles early in his career, succeeding particularly as heroic characters. His roles include Hal, Henry V (1951, *Shakespeare Memorial Theatre), Hamlet, Bastard (*King John*), Toby Belch, Coriolanus, Caliban, Othello–Iago (alternated with John Neville), Henry V (1952–6, *Old Vic). Also played Hamlet in John *Gielgud's 1964 New York production, and Petruchio opposite Elizabeth Taylor in Franco *Zeffirelli's 1966 film of The *Taming of the Shrew.

Bury, John (1925–2000) British designer, head of design at the *Royal Shakespeare Company (1965–8) and *National Theatre (1973–85). His many Shakespeare productions include an influential metallic design for the 1963 *Wars of the Roses (Stratford-upon-Avon).

C

Caird, John (1948–) Canadian-born director who first worked with the *Royal Shakespeare Company in 1978. Known for irreverent interpretations which have seen Puck enter on stage reading the text of A *Midsummer Night's Dream* (1989), and an *As You Like It* (1989) in a set devised to resemble the Royal Shakespeare Theatre foyer. His other Shakespeare productions include *Romeo and Juliet, *Twelfth Night* (1983), The *Merchant of Venice* (1984), and *Antony and Cleopatra* (1992, all Royal Shakespeare Company), *Hamlet* (with Simon Russell Beale, National, 2000) and for BBC television *Henry IV*, adapted from Parts 1 and 2 (1995).

Cambridge Shakespeare An edition in nine volumes, prepared by W. G. Clark, J. Glover, and W. A. Wright, published from 1863 to 1866. It includes footnotes recording variant readings from all editions before 1700 and from selected later editions. It was reprinted in one volume as the Globe Shakespeare in 1864, without footnotes but with act, scene, and line numbering which became the standard form of reference. A second edition of the full-scale work, revised by Wright, appeared in 1891–3.

cancel A bibliographical term referring to a leaf which is substituted for one removed by the printers because of an error or other reason for change. The first *quarto of *Troilus and Cressida* has a title-page which exists in both cancelled and uncancelled states.

Capell, Edward (1713–81) English scholar whose ten-volume edition of Shakespeare appeared in 1768; it is based on a careful collation of early editions, and he is the first editor to have realized the full importance of the good *quartos.

Cardenio A lost play acted by the *King's Men in 1613 and entered in the *Stationers' Register in 1653 as 'The History of Cardenio, by Mr Fletcher and Shakespeare'. If it was printed, no copies are known. In 1727 Lewis *Theobald prepared for the stage a play, *The Double Falsehood*, which he claimed to be by Shakespeare and is based on the story of Cardenio and Lucinda in Cervantes's *Don Quixote*, which had appeared in English in 1612. Theobald stated that he had 'revised' the play and 'adapted [it] to the stage' from an old manuscript. He did not include it in his edition of Shakespeare. The story may be true.

Casson, Sir Lewis (1875–1969) English actor and producer, husband of Sybil *Thorndike, much associated with Shakespeare.

Castelnuovo-Tedesco, Mario (1895–1968) The Italian-born composer wrote operas based on *All's Well that Ends Well* (1958) and The *Merchant of Venice* (1961), overtures to seven of Shakespeare's plays, and settings to all of Shakespeare's songs.

cast-off copy To 'cast-off' printer's copy is to estimate in advance how many sheets will be required to print a given manuscript, and to estimate the amount of copy needed to fill a single sheet. The practice meant that work could be shared out among a number of men working simultaneously. It was adopted for the Shakespeare First *Folio. Mistakes could result in the spreading out of a small amount of material over a large space, or in the crowding, even omission, of lines. In *Titus Andronicus*, for instance, at the foot of a page, a single line of verse is printed as two lines (III. i. 95), whereas on the crowded last page of *Much Ado About Nothing*, verse is printed as prose, words are omitted, and abbreviated forms are used to save space.

Catherine and Petruchio An adaptation by David *Garrick of The *Taming of the Shrew*, which first appeared in 1754 and held the stage for over a hundred years.

censorship In Shakespeare's time, plays had to be licensed for performance and, from 1607, for printing by the *Master of the Revels. An ordinance of 1559 required the censoring of 'matters of religion or of the governance of the estate of the common weal'. The absence of the deposition scene from the first three *quartos of Shakespeare's *Richard II* is presumably the result of censorship. In 1606, an Act 'to restrain abuses of players', known as the Profanity Act, required that 'any person or persons' who 'in any stage play, interlude, show, may-game, or pageant, jestingly or profanely speak or use the holy name of God or of Christ Jesus, or of the Holy Ghost or of the Trinity' should 'forfeit for every such offence by him or them committed ten pounds'. This is reflected in a number of Shakespeare's plays. For example, in the *Folio text (1623) of The *Merry Wives of Windsor*, 'heaven' several times replaces 'God' in the quarto of 1602 and, after the Profanity Act, Shakespeare's plays were mainly set in pre-Christian times.

Chamberlain's Men *See* LORD CHAMBERLAIN'S MEN.

Chambers, Sir Edmund Kerchever (1866–1953) English scholar, author of *The Medieval Stage* (2 vols., 1903), *The Elizabethan Stage* (4 vols., 1923), *William Shakespeare: A Study of Facts and Problems* (2 vols., 1930), and other works. His *Shakespeare* is an authoritative compilation of reference material, partially superseded by S. *Schoenbaum's *William Shakespeare: A Documentary Life* (1975, compact edition, 1977).

Chandos portrait of Shakespeare An early seventeenth-century portrait believed to have belonged to William *Davenant, then to Thomas *Betterton; later in the possession of the Dukes of Chandos; given by the Earl of Ellesmere to the newly founded National Portrait Gallery in 1856. It may be an authentic portrait of Shakespeare. Many copies of it exist, including one made by Sir Godfrey Kneller for *Dryden. It was frequently engraved, and became the dominant source of eighteenth-century images of Shakespeare.

The Chandos portrait

Chapman, George (*c*.1560–1634) English poet, playwright, translator of Homer; sometimes conjecturally identified as the *rival poet of Shakespeare's *Sonnets.

Charlecote House *See* LUCY, SIR THOMAS.

Cheek by Jowl Co-founded in 1981 by Declan Donnellan (1953–) and Nick Ormerod (1951–). Their small-scale touring productions of classical theatre have received critical acclaim for fast-paced, inventive interpretations. Productions include *Othello* (1982), *Pericles* (1984), *A *Midsummer Night's Dream* (1985), *Twelfth Night* (1986), *Macbeth* (1987), *The *Tempest* (1988), *Hamlet* (1990), an all-male *As You Like It* (1991, 1994), *Measure for Measure* (1994), and *Much Ado About Nothing*.

Chesterfield portrait of Shakespeare An early variation on the *Chandos portrait, perhaps by the Dutch painter Pieter Borseler, who worked in England in the 1660s and 1670s. It now hangs in the *Shakespeare Centre, Stratford-upon-Avon.

Chettle, Henry (*c*.1560–*c*.1607) English printer and writer, author of *Kind-heart's Dream* (1592), in which he expresses regret that, in preparing *Greene's Groatsworth of Wit* for the press, he did not 'moderate the heat' of *Greene's reference to Shakespeare: 'I am as sorry as if the original fault had been my fault, because myself have seen his

The Chesterfield portrait

demeanour no less civil than he excellent in the quality he professes. Besides, divers of worship have reported his uprightness of dealing, which argues his honesty, and his facetious grace in writing, that approves his art.' It has been suggested, but not proven, that Chettle had in fact written the *Groatsworth* himself in order to stir up controversy.

children's companies *See* BOY ACTORS.

Chorus Shakespeare makes varied use of chorus figures. *Romeo and Juliet* has a prologue to Acts I and II; 2 *Henry IV* opens with a speech by Rumour, 'painted full of tongues'; each act of *Henry V* is introduced by a Chorus, who speaks some of the finest poetry in the play; in *Pericles*, too, Chorus has an extended role, in the figure of the poet, John *Gower; the gap of sixteen years in the action of The *Winter's Tale* is bridged by Time, as Chorus; and both *All is True* (*Henry VIII*) and *The *Two Noble Kinsmen* have introductory prologues.

The authenticity of the prologue to Act II of *Romeo and Juliet* is sometimes doubted, and the prologue to *The Two Noble Kinsmen* is usually attributed to *Fletcher. (*See also* EPILOGUE.)

chronicle play A play based closely on material from chronicle sources of English history. *See* HOLINSHED and HALLE.

chronology The precise dating, and the order of composition, of Shakespeare's plays have been a major concern of scholarship for many years, and are not likely ever to be finally determined. The two most important sources of evidence are the list of plays given by Francis *Meres in his book, *Palladis Tamia*, of 1598, and the entries of plays in the *Stationers' Register. Other clues are given by the dates of *sources, contemporary allusions within and outside the plays, and stylistic evidence. The subject is treated in the *Oxford *Textual Companion*. Particular doubt attaches to the relative order of the plays written before 1598, and we have no real evidence as to when Shakespeare began to write. See also the table on p. 244.

Cibber, Colley (1671–1757) English actor and playwright. His adaptation of *Richard III* had long-lasting influence. He also adapted *King John*, as *Papal Tyranny in the Reign of King John* (1737).

Cibber, Theophilus (1703–58) Son of Colley; *see* HENRY VI, PART THREE.

Cinthio, Giovanni Battista Giraldi (1504–73) Italian writer best known for *Hecatommithi* (1565), a collection of prose tales. *Othello* is fairly closely based on one of the tales. No translation is known to have existed, so Shakespeare may have read it in Italian. Another tale was used by *Whetstone for *Promos and Cassandra*, a source of *Measure for Measure*.

Clarke, Mary Cowden *See* GIRLHOOD OF SHAKESPEARE'S HEROINES, THE.

Clemen, Wolfgang H. (1909–90) German scholar and critic; Professor at the University of Munich, 1946–74; author of *The Development of Shakespeare's Imagery* (1951; original, German version, 1936), a seminal work of criticism; *A Commentary on Shakespeare's 'Richard III'* (tr. 1968); *Shakespeare's Dramatic Art* (1974), etc.

clown In Shakespeare's time this term could be used for a rustic fellow, not necessarily a conscious entertainer, but it is often equated with *'fool'. Modern criticism distinguishes between the naturally comic characters, or clowns, such as Lance, Bottom, Dogberry, etc., and the professional fools, or jesters, such as Touchstone, Feste, and Lear's Fool.

Cobbler of Preston, The *See* TAMING OF THE SHREW, THE.

Coghill, Nevill (1899–1980) Merton Professor of English at Oxford, 1952–66; author of *Shakespeare's Professional Skills* (1964); influential as director of Shakespeare's plays with the Oxford University Dramatic Society (*OUDS) between 1934 and 1966.

Coleridge, Samuel Taylor (1772–1834) English poet, and the most influential of the Romantic critics of Shakespeare. His most important extended essay is 'The specific symptoms of poetic power elucidated in a critical analysis of Shakespeare's *Venus and Adonis* and *The Rape of Lucrece*', published as Chapter XV of *Biographia Literaria* (1817). His main concern was to demonstrate the organic unity of Shakespeare's plays. Most of his criticism has to be assembled from letters, marginalia, lecture notes, reports of lectures, and so on. It is collected by T. M. Raysor (*Coleridge's Shakespearean Criticism*, 2 vols., 1930; revised edn., Everyman's Library, 1960), and by Terence Hawkes (*Coleridge's Writings on Shakespeare*, 1959, reprinted as *Coleridge on Shakespeare*, 1969).

collation The process of comparing different copies of the same edition of a work, in order to discover alterations made during printing, or of comparing copies of different editions in order to discover variations. For example, the collation of a *quarto of a Shakespeare play against the text in the *Folio invariably reveals many differences, for which various explanations may be offered.

The word also means a formula to describe the make-up of a printed book.

Collier, John Payne (1789–1883) English scholar who forged many documents, annotations, poems, etc., apparently relating to Shakespeare. Any manuscript or copy of a book which he is known to have handled must be viewed with suspicion.

Collins, Francis (d. 1617) Shakespeare left him twenty marks and asked him to oversee his *will. As an attorney, he drew up the will, which may be in his handwriting.

Colman, George (the Elder, 1732–94) English playwright and theatre manager who in 1763 revised *The Fairies*, *Garrick's adaptation of *A *Midsummer Night's Dream*, as *A Fairy Tale*, for *Drury Lane, and who revised Nahum *Tate's version of *King Lear* for *Covent Garden in 1768, restoring many of Shakespeare's lines.

Combe family Neighbours of Shakespeare in Stratford-upon-Avon. William (1551–1610) sold land to Shakespeare in 1602. His nephew John (c.1560–1614), a usurer, left Shakespeare £5 and had other business dealings with the family, as did his brother, Thomas (d. 1609). Shakespeare left his sword to Thomas's younger son, also called Thomas (1589–1657).

Comedies The *Folio distinguishes fourteen of Shakespeare's plays as comedies. To these may be added *Cymbeline*, called a tragedy in the Folio, and *Pericles*, not included in the Folio. The plays are sometimes grouped as *Early Comedies; *Romantic Comedies; Problem Comedies (or *Problem Plays), or Dark Comedies; and *Last Plays, or *Romances. Though Shakespeare was unquestionably aware of the traditional genres he refused to be bound by them, and the First Folio's rigid demarcation may be more misleading than helpful.

Comedy of Errors, The Shakespeare's comedy, his shortest play, was first printed in the First *Folio (1623), probably from the author's manuscript. Its date is uncertain, but it appears to have been performed at the Christmas revels of Gray's Inn (*see* GESTA GRAYORUM) in 1594. It is based on *The Menaechmi*, by *Plautus, with additional material from Plautus's *Amphitruo* and, for the framework story, from the traditional tale of *Apollonius of Tyre, which Shakespeare also used in *Pericles*. *The Comedy of Errors* and *The *Tempest* are his only two plays which conform to the principles of the unities of plot, time, and place advocated by neo-classical theoreticians.

It was played at Court at Christmas 1604. The first recorded revival was in adaptation, as a farce called *Every Body Mistaken* (*Lincoln's Inn Fields, 1716). Numerous subsequent adaptations have included *See If You Like It, or 'Tis All a Mistake* (*Covent Garden, 1734), *The Twins*, by Thomas Hull (1762), J. P. *Kemble's revision of this (1808), and Frederick *Reynolds's musical version (Covent Garden, 1819).

Samuel *Phelps revived the original play at *Sadler's Wells in 1855, but, perhaps because of its brevity and its relative lightness, it has continued to be padded out with extraneous material, as in Trevor *Nunn's musical version (Stratford, 1976), and to be treated as a vehicle for directorial inventiveness to emphasize the farcical elements as by Adrian *Noble and Ian Judge at Stratford in 1983 and 1990. More rounded Stratford productions were provided by Clifford Williams (1962, etc.) and Tim Supple (1996).

Although this is Shakespeare's only play with the word 'comedy' in its title, it is often labelled a farce as an excuse for evading the basis of real human emotion which Shakespeare is careful to provide for the comic complications of the action. It is a brilliantly constructed comedy which far transcends its sources and reveals Shakespeare's early mastery of theatrical and verbal techniques.

Comical Gallant, The *See* DENNIS, JOHN.

'commodity' speech The Bastard's speech, *King John*, II. i. 561–99, in which he comments ironically on the King of France's withdrawal of support from Prince Arthur under the temptation of 'commodity' (i.e. self-interest):

> That smooth-faced gentleman, tickling commodity,
> Commodity, the bias of the world . . .

Condell, Henry (d. 1627) An actor and shareholder in the same company as Shakespeare; with John *Heminges, he was responsible for the publication of the First *Folio. Shakespeare left him 26s. 8d. to buy a mourning ring.

Cons, Emma *See* OLD VIC THEATRE.

'Contention' plays The *bad quartos of the plays printed in the First *Folio as 2 and 3 *Henry VI, published as *The First Part of the Contention betwixt the Two Famous Houses of York and Lancaster* ... (1594) and *The True Tragedy of Richard, Duke of York, and the Death of Good King Henry the Sixth, with the Whole Contention between the Two Houses Lancaster and York* ... (1595, actually an *octavo). They were both reprinted in 1600 and 1619.

Cooke, George Frederick (1756–1811) English actor, famous as Richard III, *Falstaff, Shylock, Henry VIII, etc.

Copeau, Jacques (1879–1949) Influential French director who founded the Théâtre du Vieux-Colombier in Paris in 1913. In work similar to Harley *Granville-Barker's, Copeau broke proscenium conventions to concentrate on the text, actors, and bare stage. Productions include *Twelfth Night* (1914) and *The *Winter's Tale* (1920).

Corambis Name for Polonius in the *'bad' quarto (1603) of *Hamlet*.

Coriolanus Shakespeare's *Roman tragedy was first printed in the First *Folio (1623), and is usually dated 1607–8, mainly on stylistic evidence. It is based principally on *Plutarch's *Lives of the Noble Grecians and Romans* in Sir Thomas *North's translation. No early performances are recorded.

Nahum *Tate's adaptation, as *The Ingratitude of a Commonwealth, or the Fall of Caius Martius Coriolanus*, was played in 1681, with little success. John *Dennis's adaptation, *The Invader of his Country or The Fatal Resentment* (1719), was no better received. Shakespeare's play had a few revivals around the same time. In 1749 appeared James Thomson's *Coriolanus*, an independent play which Thomas Sheridan drew on in a spectacular adaptation of Shakespeare at *Covent Garden in 1754, in which year Shakespeare's play, abbreviated, was given at *Drury Lane. In 1789 J. P. *Kemble also amalgamated Shakespeare and Thomson, at Drury Lane. His sister, Sarah *Siddons, and he had lasting success as Volumnia and Coriolanus. Edmund *Kean's attempt to restore Shakespeare in 1820 failed, but W. C. *Macready had more success on various occasions from 1819 to 1839. Samuel *Phelps gave the play four times at *Sadler's Wells (1848, 1850, and March and September 1860). Edwin *Forrest gave successful performances in New York in the later nineteenth century.

*Benson's London revival of 1901 had Geneviève Ward as a powerful Volumnia, a role which she continued to play over about twenty years. *Irving's *Lyceum production, also of 1901, with Ellen *Terry as Volumnia, failed. The aged William *Poel offered a rewritten, Napoleonic version at the Chelsea Palace in 1931. In 1933–4 the play was given at the Comédie Française in an adaptation aimed at over-throwing democratic government; riots resulted. Laurence *Olivier played the hero with great success at the *Old Vic in 1938, with Sybil *Thorndike as his mother, and again at Stratford-upon-Avon in 1959, with Edith *Evans. In 1972 the play was directed at Stratford-upon-Avon by Trevor *Nunn as one of a cycle of *Roman plays with Ian Hogg as Coriolanus, succeeded by Nicol Williamson at the Aldwych in 1973. Alan Howard played the title-role in both Terry *Hands's Stratford-upon-Avon production (1977) and the *BBC television version (1984). Peter *Hall directed Ian McKellen as Coriolanus at the *National Theatre in 1984 and in Hands's 1989 Stratford production Charles Dance played the lead. Michael *Bogdanov directed an overtly political production for the *English Shakespeare Company (1990), and David Thacker directed a young Toby Stephens at Stratford-upon-Avon in 1994. In 1963, an unfinished adaptation by Bertolt *Brecht was given by the Berliner Ensemble. Gunter Grass's play *The Plebeians Rehearse the Uprising* (Aldwych, 1970) shows Brecht rehearsing his *Coriolan*, and John Osborne wrote a 're-working' of Shakespeare's play as *A Place Calling Itself Rome* (1973).

   Coriolanus has a reputation of being one of Shakespeare's less popular plays, partly because of its unsympathetic hero, It offers a serious but realistically powerful study of the relationship between individual personality and politics, and is a remarkable illustration of Shakespeare's capacity to understand and portray an alien culture.

Covent Garden Theatre The first theatre in Covent Garden, in central London, was opened in 1732. A *patent theatre, it was the chief rival to *Drury Lane. Rebuilt in 1787, it burned down in 1808. A new building also burned down, in 1856, having been used mainly for opera for some years. The present opera house was built in 1858.

Cowley, Richard (d. 1619) An actor in Shakespeare's company. His name is printed as a speech-prefix for Verges in *Much Ado About Nothing*, suggesting that Shakespeare had him in mind as he wrote.

crabtree, Shakespeare's An anonymous letter-writer in the *British Magazine*, 1762, tells the story that the landlord of the White Lion in Stratford-upon-Avon took him to Bidford-on-Avon, some miles away, and showed him 'in the hedge a crabtree called "Shakespeare's Canopy", because under it our poet slept one night; for he, as well as Ben Jonson, loved a glass for the pleasure of society; and he, having heard much of the men of that village as deep drinkers and merry fellows one day went over to Bidford to take a cup with them. He enquired of a shepherd for the Bidford drinkers, who replied they were absent, but the Bidford sippers were at home: "and, I suppose", continued the sheepkeeper, "they will be sufficient for you"; and so indeed they were. He was forced to take up his lodging under that tree for some hours.' *See also* Villages, the Shakespeare.

Craig, (Edward) Gordon (1872–1968) English actor and influential stage designer, son of Ellen *Terry, author of several books on the theatre.

Craig, Hardin (1875–1968) American scholar, author of *The Enchanted Glass* (1936), a book concerned with ideas in the Elizabethan period, and editor of a complete edition of Shakespeare (1951).

Crane, Ralph (1550(60?)–*c*.1632) A scribe who worked mainly for lawyers but also for theatre companies. Some of his scribal characteristics, particularly the 'massing' of entries (i.e. the listing at the head of a scene of all the characters who appear in it) are found in certain plays of the First *Folio, which he appears to have helped to prepare for the press.

Crowne, John (*c*.1640–1703) English playwright who made adaptations of the *Henry VI* plays.

Cushman, Charlotte (1816–76) American actress who became well known as Lady Macbeth, Volumnia, Gertrude, Emilia, and Queen Katherine. She also played male roles, such as Romeo (restoring Shakespeare's text in place of *Garrick's), Hamlet, and Cardinal Wolsey.

Cymbeline Shakespeare's romance was first printed in the First *Folio (1623), with the title '*The Tragedie of Cymbeline*'. The play is usually dated 1609–10, mainly on stylistic grounds. The historical part is based on *Holinshed's *Chronicles*. The wager plot derives from *Boccaccio's *Decameron*, perhaps indirectly through a pamphlet of 1560, *Frederick of Jennen*. The Belarius story may come from an anonymous play, printed in 1589, *The Rare Triumphs of Love and Fortune*. The

---

ALFRED, LORD TENNYSON *(1809–92) on Shakespeare's simplicities; from*
Life and Works, *ed. Hallam, Lord Tennyson, 1898*

There are three repartees in Shakespeare which always bring tears
to my eyes from their simplicity.

One is in *King Lear*, when Lear says to Cordelia, 'So young and
so untender,' and Cordelia lovingly answers, 'So young, my lord,
and true.' And in *The Winter's Tale*, when Florizel takes Perdita's
hand to lead her to the dance, and says, 'So turtles pair that never
mean to part,' and the little Perdita answers, giving her hand to
Florizel, 'I'll swear for 'em.' And in *Cymbeline*, when Imogen in
tender rebuke says to her husband:

> 'Why did you throw your wedded lady from you?
> Think that you are upon a rock; and now,
> Throw me again!'

and Posthumus does not ask forgiveness, but answers, kissing her:

> 'Hang there like fruit, my soul,
> Till the tree die.'

---

authenticity of the vision scene (v. iv) has often been questioned, but
is nowadays generally defended.

Simon *Forman, who died in 1611, recorded seeing a performance
without saying when, and the play was presented at Court in 1634. An
adaptation by Thomas D'Urfey, *The Injured Princess or The Fatal Wager*,
was written about 1673 and held the stage. Shakespeare's play was
revived in 1746. David *Garrick put on a revised version in 1761, and
frequently played Posthumus, a role later taken by John Philip
*Kemble, with Mrs *Siddons as a notable Imogen.

Imogen's name is in doubt. Holinshed and Forman call her
'Innogen', as does the *Oxford edition. The character was idealized by
nineteenth-century readers and audiences. Swinburne said that 'in
Imogen we find half-glorified already the immortal godhead of wom-
anhood', and Tennyson (who is said to have died with a copy of the
play open on his lap) shared his opinion. The most distinguished representatives of the role after Mrs Siddons were Helena *Faucit and
Ellen *Terry.

Twentieth-century productions have had limited success. Bernard *Shaw, who wrote fascinating letters to Ellen Terry about her preparation to play Imogen, also wrote his own version of the last act, which has occasionally been performed. Peggy *Ashcroft played Imogen at Stratford-upon-Avon in 1957, and Vanessa *Redgrave in 1962. A considerably shortened version at Stratford-upon-Avon in 1974 had Susan Fleetwood as an affecting Imogen. Bill *Alexander directed an emotionally strong production at The *Other Place (Stratford, 1987), and Peter *Hall staged the play in a season of *late plays (*National Theatre, 1988). Adrian *Noble's 1997 production at Stratford-upon-Avon gave the play an oriental setting. Dominic Cooke directed Emma Fielding in a fine production at the Swan (2003).

Cymbeline is a fantasy, highly elaborated in both style and action, experimental in its technique, which achieves some brilliant effects but is challenging both structurally and stylistically. The song 'Hark, hark, the lark' has become independently famous in *Schubert's setting, and the dirge ('Fear no more the heat o'th' sun') is also well known apart from the rest of the play.

D

Daly, Augustin (1838–99) American director whose London theatre (Daly's) opened in 1893 with a performance of The *Taming of the Shrew* given by his company led by Ada *Rehan, to whom much of his success was due. He took many liberties with the texts of Shakespeare, and *Shaw wrote caustic reviews of his spectacular productions, but admired Ada Rehan, especially as Kate, in The *Taming of the Shrew*, and as Rosalind, in *As You Like It*. Shaw described Theseus' panoramic passage from the forest to Athens as 'more absurd than anything that occurs in the tragedy of Pyramus and Thisbe'.

Daniel, Samuel (1562–1619) English poet and dramatist, author of a popular sonnet-cycle, *Delia* (1592), a closet drama, The Tragedy of *Cleopatra* (1593), The Civil Wars (first four books 1595, complete version, as The Civil Wars between the Houses of Lancaster and York 1609), etc. Shakespeare's *Richard II seems to have been influenced by The Civil Wars, and Shakespeare may have drawn on Daniel's *Cleopatra* in *Antony and Cleopatra.

Daniels, Ron British director with the *Royal Shakespeare Company 1978–89, later based in the United States. Productions for the RSC include *Pericles (1979), *Romeo and Juliet, *Timon of Athens (1980), A *Midsummer Night's Dream (1981), The *Tempest (1982), *Julius Caesar (1983), *Much Ado About Nothing (1986), *Hamlet (1988–9), *Richard II (1990), *Henry V (1997), and his work abroad includes Hamlet (American Repertory Theatre Company, 1991), *Titus Andronicus (Tokyo, 1992), 1 and 2 *Henry IV (American Repertory Theatre Company, 1993).

Dark Lady of the Sonnets The woman referred to, and addressed, in many of Shakespeare's *Sonnets 127–54, and possibly in others. Many attempts have been made to identify her with a real person, such as Mary *Fitton, one of Queen *Elizabeth's maids of honour. A. L. Rowse suggested Emilia *Lanier, put forward in his Shakespeare the Man (1973), and Jonathan Bate, in The Genius of Shakespeare (1997), argued for the wife of John *Florio. Neither of these claims can be supported by hard evidence.

Davenant, Sir William (1606–68) English poet, playwright, and theatre manager whose father was a vintner at the Crown Tavern, Oxford. He wrote many plays and masques, and was appointed Poet Laureate in 1638. A royalist, he took part in the Civil War.

At the Restoration, in 1660, he and Thomas *Killigrew both received patents enabling them to form an acting company and to manage a theatre. Davenant established the Duke's Men, performing first in the old Salisbury Court Theatre and, from 1661, at the *Lincoln's Inn Fields Theatre, under the patronage of the Duke of York. The right to perform Shakespeare's plays was divided between Davenant and Killigrew.

Davenant was largely responsible for carrying into the public theatres the staging techniques used at Court before the Restoration, greatly influencing the future development of the English theatre. He adapted some of Shakespeare's plays to the taste of his age: *Macbeth (1663), The *Two Noble Kinsmen (as The Rivals, 1664), The *Tempest (with *Dryden, as The Enchanted Isle, 1667), and *Measure for Measure, into which he interpolated scenes from *Much Ado About Nothing, to make The Law Against Lovers (1662). Macbeth and The Tempest were particularly influential.

According to John *Aubrey, Davenant boasted that he was Shakespeare's natural son.

Davies, John, of Hereford (c.1565–1618) English poet and writing-master. His Scourge of Folly (c.1610) includes a cryptic epigram 'To our English Terence, Mr Will Shakespeare':

> Some say, good Will, which I in sport do sing,
> Hadst thou not played some kingly parts in sport,
> Thou hadst been a companion for a king,
> And been a king among the meaner sort.
> Some others rail; but, rail as they think fit,
> Thou hast no railing, but a reigning wit;
> And honesty thou sow'st, which they do reap,
> So to increase their stock which they do keep.

Davies, Richard (d. 1708) An Oxford man who in 1688 inherited papers belonging to a Gloucestershire clergyman, William Fulman, including notes on Shakespeare. Davies added the first account of Shakespeare's deer-stealing from Sir Thomas *Lucy, and the statement that Shakespeare 'died a papist'.

death-mask *See* KESSELSTADT DEATH MASK.

death of Shakespeare *See* WARD, JOHN.

dedications The only works bearing dedications by Shakespeare are
Venus and Adonis (1593) and The *Rape of Lucrece* (1594), both addressed
to Henry *Wriothesley, 3rd Earl of Southampton. The *Sonnets bear
a publisher's dedication to Mr W. H. The First *Folio is dedicated by
*Heminges and *Condell to William and Philip *Herbert, Earls of
Pembroke and Montgomery.

'degree' speech Ulysses' speech in *Troilus and Cressida* (I. iii. 74–137),
which expounds the common notion of a hierarchical principle
binding the universe and preventing it from falling back into chaos.
The speech has frequently been taken as evidence of Shakespeare's
conservatism but the broader context of the play and characterization of Ulysses contradict such a simplistic suggestion.

Dench, Dame Judi (1934–   ) Actress whose versatility and commitment
to theatre have made her one of Britain's foremost classical per-
formers. Her roles have included Isabella and Titania (both 1962),
Hermione and Perdita (doubled), Viola (both 1969), Portia (1971), Beat-
rice and Lady Macbeth (both 1976, all *Royal Shakespeare Company),
Cleopatra (1987), Gertrude (1989, both *Royal National Theatre),
Volumnia (1992, Renaissance Theatre Company), and the Countess in
All's Well That Ends Well (Stratford, 2003). As director, *Much Ado About
Nothing* (1988, Renaissance Theatre Company), The *Boys from Syracuse*
(1991), *Romeo and Juliet* (1993, both *Regent's Park Open-Air Theatre).

Dennis, John (1657–1734) English dramatist and critic, who adapted
The *Merry Wives of Windsor* in 1702 as The Comical Gallant. His Epistle to
this is the source of the legend that the play was written at the command of Queen *Elizabeth, 'and by her direction, and she was so
eager to see it acted that she commanded it to be finished in fourteen
days'.

Two years later Dennis improved the story by saying that Elizabeth
commanded Shakespeare to write the play 'in ten days' time'.
Nicholas *Rowe elaborated further: 'She was so well pleased with that
admirable character of Falstaff, in the two Parts of *Henry the Fourth*,
that she commanded him to continue it for one play more, and to
show him in love.'

In 1710, Charles *Gildon conflated the anecdotes: 'the Queen ... who had obliged him to write a play of Sir John Falstaff in love and which I am very well assured he performed in a fortnight.'

Dennis also adapted *Coriolanus as The Invader of his Country (1719).

de Quincey, Thomas (1785–1859) English essayist who wrote the article on Shakespeare in the seventh edition (1838) of the Encyclopaedia Britannica, and a famous essay (1823) 'On the Knocking at the Gate in Macbeth'.

Dering manuscript A manuscript version of 1 and 2 *Henry IV written about 1613 and revised about 1623, by Sir Edward Dering (1598–1644), probably for private performance. It is (except for *Sir Thomas More) the earliest known manuscript of a Shakespeare play.

Devine, George (1910–66) English director who attempted to introduce European theatrical influences into British theatre. His early productions were traditional but an increasing desire to experiment culminated in the 1955 *King Lear (Stratford-upon-Avon), which used abstract settings designed by Noguchi. In 1956, he left classical theatre to set up the English Stage Company at the Royal Court. Other productions include The *Tempest (1940, *Old Vic), A *Midsummer Night's Dream (1948, Young Vic), The *Taming of the Shrew, *King Lear (1953), A *Midsummer Night's Dream (1954, all *Shakespeare Memorial Theatre), and King John (1953, Old Vic).

de Witt, Johannes (work flourished 1583–96) A Dutchman who visited the *Swan Theatre in 1596. His drawing of it, done from memory and surviving only in an early copy, is our only detailed picture of the interior of an Elizabethan theatre. He also described it, in Latin, saying that it held three thousand people.

Diana A Spanish prose romance by Jorge de Montemayor (c.1521–61), translated into French by Nicholas Colin (1578) and into English by Bartholomew Yonge (1592, not published till 1598). The *Two Gentlemen of Verona is based, perhaps indirectly, on a section of it.

Dibdin, Charles (1745–1814) English composer of music for the *Garrick Jubilee in 1769, including a cantata, 'Queen Mab, or the Fairies' Jubilee', and the songs 'The Warwickshire Lad' and 'Sweet Willy O'.

Dickens, Charles (1812–70) The great English novelist's works include many allusions to Shakespeare. He was deeply interested in the theatre, and himself performed Justice Shallow in The *Merry Wives of Windsor*. He sponsored an appeal to endow a curatorship of *Shakespeare's Birthplace, and to this end organized amateur theatrical performances with casts including distinguished literary figures, but the project was unsuccessful. A recent study of value is Valerie Gager's *Shakespeare and Dickens: the dynamics of influence* (1996).

Digges, Leonard (1588–1635) English poet and translator, stepson of Thomas *Russell; probably known to Shakespeare. He contributed a poem in Shakespeare's memory to the First *Folio, and another to the 1640 edition of Shakespeare's *Poems*, in which he praises Shakespeare above *Jonson for his theatrical success:

CHARLES DICKENS *(1812–70): Mr Wopsle plays Hamlet; from* Great Expectations *(1860–1)*

Whenever that undecided Prince had to ask a question or state a doubt, the public helped him out with it. As for example; on the question whether 'twas nobler in the mind to suffer, some roared yes, and some no, and some inclining to both opinions said 'toss up for it;' and quite a Debating Society arose. When he asked what should such fellows as he do crawling between earth and heaven, he was encouraged with loud cries of 'Hear, hear!' When he appeared with his stocking disordered (its disorder expressed, according to usage, by one very neat fold in the top, which I suppose to be always got up with a flat iron), a conversation took place in the gallery respecting the paleness of his leg, and whether it was occasioned by the turn the ghost had given him. On his taking the recorders—very like a little black flute that had just been played in the orchestra and handed out at the door—he was called upon unanimously for Rule Britannia. When he recommended the player not to saw the air thus, the sulky man said, 'And don't *you* do it, neither; you're a deal worse than *him!*' And I grieve to add that peals of laughter greeted Mr. Wopsle on every one of these occasions.

                           let but Falstaff come,
         Hal, Poins, the rest, you scarce shall have a room,
         All is so pestered. Let but Beatrice
         And Benedick be seen, lo, in a trice
         The Cockpit galleries, boxes, all are full
         To hear Malvolio, that cross-gartered gull.

Dorset Garden Theatre, London Known as the second Duke's House
because it was planned by William *Davenant for the Duke of York's
Men, this fine theatre, designed by Christopher Wren, opened in 1671
and was directed initially by Thomas *Betterton and Henry Harris. It
was used for many Shakespeare performances, but declined after the
*King's and the Duke's Men combined, in 1682, making *Drury Lane
their headquarters. It is last heard of in 1706.

Double Falsehood, The *See* CARDENIO.

Dowden, Edward (1843–1913) Professor of English at Trinity College,
Dublin, author of *Shakspere: A Critical Study of his Mind and Art* (1875), an
attempt to trace the growth of Shakespeare's 'intellect and character
from youth to full maturity'. His *Shakspere Primer* (1877) includes the
once well-known division of Shakespeare's career into periods
labelled 'In the Workshop', 'In the World', 'Out of the Depths', and
'On the Heights'.

Dowland, John (1563–1626) Lutenist, and one of the greatest of English
song composers. There is a complimentary allusion to him in a poem
by Richard Barnfield which was included in *The *Passionate Pilgrim*,
ascribed to Shakespeare.

Drayton, Michael (1563–1631) Warwickshire poet, author of the long
topographical poem *Polyolbion* (1612, 1622), probably a friend of
Shakespeare (*see* WARD, JOHN). He was treated by Dr John *Hall. In a
poem published in 1627 he wrote:

                           And be it said of thee,
         Shakespeare, thou hadst as smooth a comic vein,
         Fitting the sock, and in thy natural brain,
         As strong conception, and as clear a rage,
         As anyone that trafficked with the stage.

Droeshout, Martin (1601–c.1650) Engraver of the frontispiece
portrait of Shakespeare in the First *Folio. Droeshout was only 15

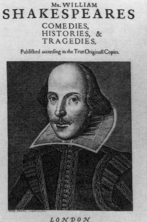

Mr. WILLIAM
SHAKESPEARES
COMEDIES,
HISTORIES, &
TRAGEDIES.
Published according to the True Originall Copies.

LONDON
Printed by Isaac Iaggard, and Ed. Blount. 1623.

Droeshout's engraving of Shakespeare, printed on the title-page of the First Folio (1623)

when Shakespeare died, and the engraving must be from an unknown drawing, but, except for the bust on the *monument, it is the only portrait with any convincing claim to authenticity (*see* PORTRAITS OF SHAKESPEARE). It exists in three states, with only slight variants.

drolls Brief adaptations of comic scenes from popular plays made during the closing of the theatres, 1642–60. In 1662 Francis Kirkman published a collection, including some based on Shakespeare, as *The Wits, or Sport upon Sport*. Its frontispiece, possibly depicting an improvised stage, shows characters from several different plays, including Falstaff who was known as the Bouncing Knight.

Drummond, William, of Hawthornden *See* JONSON, BEN.

Drury Lane Theatre A theatre between Bridge Street and Drury Lane, London, was opened by Thomas *Killigrew in 1663. It burned down in 1672, and was replaced by a new Theatre Royal probably designed by Christopher Wren, opened in 1674. David *Garrick managed it from 1747 to 1776. Rebuilt and enlarged in 1794, it burned down in 1809. The present theatre opened in 1812, and continued as a *patent theatre till 1843. It has seen many great Shakespeare performances.

Dryden, John (1631–1700) The great English poet, dramatist, and critic wrote the first important criticism of Shakespeare, mainly in the *Essay*

Frontispiece of Kirkman's The Wits *(1662)*

JOHN DRYDEN *(1631–1700) on Shakespeare; from his Preface to* All for Love; or The World Well Lost *(1678)*

He was the man who of all Modern, and perhaps Ancient Poets, had the largest and most comprehensive soul. All the Images of Nature were still present to him, and he drew them not laboriously, but luckily: when he describes any thing, you more than see it, you feel it too. Those who accuse him to have wanted learning, give him the greater commendation: he was naturally learn'd; he needed not the spectacles of Books to read Nature; he look'd inwards, and found her there. I cannot say he is every where alike; were he so, I should do him injury to compare him with the greatest of Mankind. He is many times flat, insipid; his Comick wit degenerating into clenches, his serious swelling into Bombast. But he is always great, when some great occasion is presented to him: no man can say he ever had a fit subject for his wit, and did not then raise himself as high above the rest of Poets.

of Dramatic Poesy (1688), the *Essay on the Dramatic Poetry of the Last Age* (1672), and the Preface to *Troilus and Cressida* (1679), an adaptation of Shakespeare's play. He collaborated with William *Davenant in an adaptation of *The *Tempest, The Enchanted Isle* (1667); and his tragedy *All for Love* (1677) derives partly from *Antony and Cleopatra*. He described his intentions in the preface to *Troilus and Cressida* as 'to remove that heap of Rubbish, under which many excellent thoughts lay wholly buried'.

Duffett, Thomas (fl. 1673–8) English playwright whose *Empress of Morocco* (c.1673) has an Epilogue burlesquing the production of the witch scenes in William *Davenant's adaptation of *Macbeth* as performed at *Dorset Garden Theatre, London, in 1673. His *The Mock-Tempest, or The Enchanted Castle* (1674) is a full-scale burlesque of the production, also at the Dorset Garden Theatre, of *Shadwell's operatic version of *The *Tempest*.

Dugdale, Sir William (1605–86) English antiquary. His *Antiquities of Warwickshire* (1656) includes the first representation of Shakespeare's *monument.

Duke's Men *See* Davenant, William.

Dvořák, Antonín (1841–1904) The Czech composer wrote a concert overture, 'Othello' (1891).

E

Early Comedies Shakespeare's earliest comedies are *The* **Two Gentlemen of Verona*, *The* *Comedy of Errors, *The* **Taming of the Shrew*, and **Love's Labour's Lost*. *A* **Midsummer Night's Dream* is also sometimes classed as an early comedy.

education, Shakespeare's *See* Grammar School, Stratford-upon-Avon.

Edward III Anonymous history play, entered in the *Stationers' Register in 1595, published 1596, first ascribed to Shakespeare in 1656. There is strong support for Shakespeare's authorship of certain scenes, and some scholars ascribe the whole play to Shakespeare. It is included in the second edition of the Oxford Shakespeare (2005), and considered by Melchiori as part of a sextet with the second tetralogy and *The* **Merry Wives of Windsor*. Professional productions were staged by Theatr Clwyd in 1987, and the Royal Shakespeare Company in 2002.

electronic texts A number of editions of Shakespeare are available on CD-ROM or online. They have the benefit of powerful and complex searchability but the current lack of sophisticated software and tendency to reproduce out-of-copyright texts, and hence out-of-date scholarship, means the potential of electronic texts has yet to be realized.

Elgar, Sir Edward (1857–1934) English composer whose 'symphonic study', *Falstaff* (1913), is one of the greatest orchestral works inspired by Shakespeare.

Elizabeth I, Queen of England (1533–1603) Though thrifty, she was a great patron of literature and drama. Her enjoyment of plays helped the theatre companies against the opposition of the City fathers. Shakespeare's company often performed for her at Court. Two phrases in *A* **Midsummer Night's Dream*, 'a fair vestal, thronèd by the west', and 'the imperial vot'ress' (ii. i. 158, 163) are often interpreted as allusions to her. She appears on stage, as an infant, at the climax of *All is True (Henry VIII)*, written some ten years after her death.

She was sensitive about comparisons between herself and Richard II, and Shakespeare's company was in trouble about performing *Richard II* on the eve of the *Essex rebellion, in 1601. For the legend that The *Merry Wives of Windsor* was written at her command, *see* DENNIS, JOHN.

Elizabethan Stage Society *See* POEL, WILLIAM.

Emerson, Ralph Waldo (1803–82) The American transcendentalist had scruples about the morality of Shakespeare's plays, but his essay 'Shakspere; or, the Poet' in *Representative Men* (1850) also reveals great admiration for him.

English Shakespeare Company Co-founded in 1985 by Michael *Bogdanov and Michael *Pennington to produce large-scale touring productions. Their first programme was the ambitious twenty-three-hour *Wars of the Roses* 1986–9, which included eight history plays. Other productions include: The *Comedy of Errors, *Coriolanus, The *Winter's Tale, The *Merchant of Venice (all 1990), *Twelfth Night (1991), *Macbeth, The *Tempest (both 1992), *Romeo and Juliet (1993). In 1994 the company ceased touring work to concentrate on educational programmes, but returned to the stage in 1997 with a production of A *Midsummer Night's Dream aimed at children. (*See* Michael Bogdanov and Michael Pennington's *The English Shakespeare Company: The Story of the Wars of the Roses 1986–89*, 1990.)

epilogue Conventionally an apology and request for applause spoken at the end of a performance by a main character. Shakespeare's plays with epilogues are A *Midsummer Night's Dream, *As You Like It, *Henry V, *Twelfth Night (a song), *All's Well that Ends Well, *Troilus and Cressida, *Pericles, The *Tempest, 2 *Henry IV, and *All is True (Henry VIII).

epitaph, Shakespeare's The gravestone traditionally believed to be Shakespeare's, in the chancel of *Holy Trinity Church, Stratford-upon-Avon, close to his *monument, is shown opposite.

The curse refers to the practice of removing bones to a charnel house in order to make more burial space available in the church.

There is a late seventeenth-century tradition that Shakespeare wrote his own epitaph. The gravestone is, according to *Halliwell-Phillipps, a mid-eighteenth-century replacement for the original one, which had decayed. It is oddly shorter than those to each side of it.

Essex, Robert Devereux, 2nd Earl of (1566–1601) A favourite of Queen *Elizabeth. He married Sir Philip *Sidney's widow in 1590, and was a naval commander and Earl Marshal. He commanded the English troops in Ireland in 1599, and this appears to be the occasion of one of Shakespeare's few explicitly *topical allusions, in the Chorus to Act V of *Henry V:

> Were now the General of our gracious Empress—
> As in good time he may—from Ireland coming,
> Bringing rebellion broachèd on his sword,
> How many would the peaceful city quit
> To welcome him! (ll. 30–4)

In fact the expedition failed, and Elizabeth banished Essex from Court. He plotted a rebellion, on the eve of which his followers arranged a special performance by the *Lord Chamberlain's Men of *Richard II*, hoping that the play about the deposition of a monarch who was often associated with Elizabeth would arouse support. The rebellion failed, and Essex was executed on 25 February 1601.

The previous evening, Shakespeare's company played before the Queen.

Evans, Dame Edith (1888–1976) English actress, especially distinguished in Restoration comedy, *Shaw, and high comedy roles. She played Cressida in the first professional English stage performance of *Troilus and Cressida*, directed by William *Poel for the Elizabethan Stage Society in 1912. Her other performances in Shakespeare included Helena in A *Midsummer Night's Dream* (*Drury Lane, 1924), Juliet's Nurse (*Old Vic, 1926, New York, 1934, New Theatre, 1935, Stratford-upon-Avon, 1961), Rosalind (Old Vic, 1936, New, 1937), Katherina (New, 1937), Cleopatra (Piccadilly, 1946), Queen Katherine (Old Vic, 1958), Countess of Rousillon and Volumnia (Stratford-upon-Avon, 1959), and Queen Margaret (Stratford-upon-Avon, 1961).

Evans, Maurice (1901–89) English actor, naturalized American in 1941. His Shakespeare roles included Richard II (*Old Vic, 1934, New York, 1937, etc.), Hamlet (Old Vic, 1934, New York, 1938, etc.), Romeo (New York, 1935, etc.).

Every Body Mistaken *See* COMEDY OF ERRORS, THE.

Eyre, Sir Richard (1943–) Director with the *National Theatre from 1981, artistic director 1988–97. Shakespeare productions include *Hamlet* (1979) with Jonathan Pryce as the ghost and Hamlet (Royal Court), *Hamlet* (1989), *Richard III* (1990), *Macbeth* (1993), *King Lear* (1997), all *Royal National Theatre. As an administrator at the RNT he encouraged young and international directors to experiment with Shakespeare, resulting in Deborah *Warner casting Fiona Shaw as Richard II, and Robert *Lepage's 'mudbath' A *Midsummer Night's Dream*.

F

facsimiles The best available photographic facsimile of the First *Folio is *The Norton Facsimile of the First Folio of Shakespeare* (1968, 2nd edn. 1996), prepared by Charlton Hinman. It is made from the best-printed pages from thirty different copies.

A series of facsimiles of the *quarto editions of Shakespeare's plays initiated by the *Shakespeare Association in 1939 was later taken over by Oxford University Press. A one-volume collection edited by Michael J. B. Allen and Kenneth *Muir appeared in 1981.

fair copy A final, corrected (but not necessarily entirely correct) manuscript such as a dramatist might submit to a theatre company, as distinct from the draft or *'foul papers'.

Fairies, The *See* MIDSUMMER NIGHT'S DREAM, A; SMITH, JOHN CHRISTOPHER.

Fairy Queen, The An adaptation of *A *Midsummer Night's Dream* presented by Thomas *Betterton at *Dorset Garden Theatre in 1692. It has a fine musical score by Henry *Purcell, but the words set to music are not by Shakespeare.

Fairy Tale, A *See* MIDSUMMER NIGHT'S DREAM, A.

Falstaff Shakespeare's greatest character appears in three plays: *1 *Henry IV, 2 *Henry IV*, and *The *Merry Wives of Windsor*; his death is described in *Henry V*, II. iii. Shakespeare derived some hints for him from Sir John *Oldcastle in the anonymous *Famous Victories of Henry V*, and there is evidence within the plays that Falstaff originally had that name and that it was changed because of objections by Oldcastle's descendants, the Lords Cobham.

Falstaff has always been a popular character, and has been a source of inspiration to creative artists. There are, for example, famous tributes by Dr *Johnson, William *Hazlitt, and J. B. Priestley; a novel by Robert Nye (1976); and many paintings and sculptures. He is the central figure of operas by *Nicolai, *Verdi, and *Vaughan Williams, and the subject of a fine symphonic study (1913) by Edward *Elgar. Orson

*Welles's *Chimes at Midnight* (Dublin, 1960, filmed 1966) created a life of Falstaff by drawing on the four plays in which he appears or is mentioned. He is also the subject of much popular art: china figurines, inn-signs, and so on, showing the extent to which he has passed into folk mythology.

Famous Victories of Henry V, The An anonymous chronicle play, registered 14 May 1594, surviving in an edition of 1598, perhaps written by 1588; a possible source for Shakespeare's 1 and 2 *Henry IV* and *Henry V*.

Faucit, Helena (1817–98) English actress who played many Shakespeare roles. She married Sir Theodore Martin, and wrote *On Some of Shakespeare's Female Characters* (1885; enlarged edition, 1891), which includes some remarkable memories of her performances, especially as Hermione, with W. C. *Macready.

Fauré, Gabriel (1845–1924) The French composer wrote a suite, *Shylock* (1889), for a French version of *The *Merchant of Venice*; it has two songs and four orchestral pieces.

Feminism A term applied to a broad range of critical practices unified by an interest in the plays' presentation of women and gender issues.

Field, Richard (1561–1624) Printer of *Venus and Adonis* in 1593, *The *Rape of Lucrece* in 1594, and *Love's Martyr* (which includes 'The *Phoenix and the Turtle') in 1601. He was born in Stratford-upon-Avon, so may well have had some personal acquaintance with Shakespeare. In *Cymbeline* (IV. ii. 379) Imogen, as Fidele, calls her dead master by a version of his name—Richard Du Champ.

films All of Shakespeare's plays have been filmed and in a wide range of styles. The commercial success of Kenneth *Branagh's *Henry V (1989) led to a resurgence of Shakespeare films in the mainstream film industry. Information about some of the more important films is given under the names of the directors and actors concerned, including Grigori *Kozintsev, Laurence *Olivier, Orson *Welles, Franco *Zeffirelli, and Kenneth *Branagh.

There are studies by Robert Hamilton Ball, *Shakespeare on Silent Film* (1968), Jack Jorgens, *Shakespeare on Film* (1977), Kenneth S. Rothwell, *A History of Shakespeare on Screen* (2nd edition, 2004) and a comprehensive filmography by Kenneth S. Rothwell and Annabelle Melzer, *Shakespeare on Screen* (1990).

Finzi, Gerald (1901–56) The English composer wrote a fine Shake-spearian song-cycle, *Let us Garlands Bring* (1942).

Fitton, Mary (*c*.1578–1647) One of Queen *Elizabeth's maids of honour; she became the mistress of William *Herbert, Earl of Pembroke, and has sometimes been thought to be the *Dark Lady of the Sonnets.

Fletcher, John (1579–1625) English playwright who collaborated with Shakespeare in, probably, *The *Two Noble Kinsmen*, *Cardenio*, and *All is True* (*Henry VIII*), and succeeded him as principal dramatist to the *King's Men, collaborating with other dramatists including Francis *Beaumont.

Florio, John (1553?–1625) English-born translator, of Italian descent, educated at Oxford, tutor of Henry *Wriothesley, 3rd Earl of Southampton. Shakespeare knew his translation of *Montaigne, and may have known him.

Florizel and Perdita An adaptation by David *Garrick of *The *Winter's Tale*, made in 1756, which uses mainly the last two acts of the play. It held the stage for the rest of the century, and influenced later versions, including J. P. *Kemble's.

Flower, Charles Edward (1830–92) Founder and benefactor of the *Shakespeare Memorial Theatre at Stratford-upon-Avon, which opened in 1879. His descendants have continued to be actively concerned with the theatre's business.

Flower portrait of Shakespeare The earliest painting of Shakespeare, resembling, and probably deriving from, the *Droeshout engraving. It is painted over a fifteenth-century Italian Madonna and Child. Mrs Charles Flower gave it to the Picture Gallery of the Stratford-upon-Avon theatre, where it now hangs.

Folger Shakespeare Library A research library founded in Washington by the American oil millionaire and book collector, Henry Clay Folger (1857–1930), it is rich in materials for Shake-spearian research, especially editions of the plays.

Folio, the First A folio is a book made of sheets of paper folded only once, and thus of large size. The first collected edition of Shakespeare's plays is the First Folio, of 1623. It was put together by his colleagues, John *Heminges and Henry *Condell, 'without

The Flower portrait

ambition either of self-profit or fame, only to keep the memory of so worthy a friend and fellow alive as was our Shakespeare'.

The volume was printed and published by William and Isaac *Jaggard, with Edward Blount as an additional publisher. It includes sixteen plays not previously printed, and two others (3 *Henry VI* and *The *Taming of the Shrew*) previously printed only in doubtful texts. It also provides superior texts of some of the previously printed plays. *Pericles* is omitted. To make the plays more readable and literary the editors organized them by genre and added act and scene divisions. Probably about 1,000 copies of the Folio were printed; between 230 and 240 survive. It sold originally for about £1.

Heminges and Condell supplied an Address 'To the great variety of readers', and dedicated the volume to William and Philip *Herbert, Earls of Pembroke and Montgomery. The preliminary matter includes the commendatory poem by Ben *Jonson.

The principal studies of the First Folio are W. W. *Greg's *The Shakespeare First Folio* (1955) and Charlton Hinman's *The Printing and Proof-Reading of the First Folio of Shakespeare* (1963). Several facsimiles have

The Workes of William Shakespeare,

containing all his Comedies, Histories, and
Tragedies: Truely set forth, according to their first
ORIGINALL

The Names of the Principall Actors
in all these Playes.

William Shakespeare.	Samuel Gilburne.
Richard Burbadge.	Robert Armin.
John Hemmings.	William Ostler.
Augustine Phillips.	Nathan Field.
William Kempt.	John Underwood.
Thomas Poope.	Nicholas Tooley.
George Bryan.	William Eccleftone.
Henry Condell.	Joseph Taylor.
William Slye.	Robert Benfield.
Richard Cowly.	Robert Goughe.
John Lowine.	Richard Robinson.
Samuell Crosse.	John Shancke.
Alexander Cooke.	John Rice.

A page from the First Folio (1623), listing the principal members of Shakespeare's company, the Lord Chamberlain's/King's Men

been published. The most important for scholarly purposes is *The Norton Facsimile* (1968, 2nd edn. 1996), prepared by Charlton Hinman and using the best pages from thirty different copies.

Folios, the Second, Third, and Fourth The First *Folio was reprinted in 1632, 1663, and 1685. These reprints have no independent authority. *Pericles and six apocryphal plays, The *London Prodigal, *Thomas, Lord Cromwell, Sir John *Oldcastle, The *Puritan, A *Yorkshire Tragedy*, and *Locrine*, were added in the second issue (1664) of the Third Folio.

Fool A type-character, related to the domestic fools kept in royal and noble households. There were wise fools—intelligent men employed as entertainers—and natural fools—idiots kept for amusement. Shakespeare's fools are mostly 'wise'; they include Touchstone, Feste, Lavache, Thersites, and Lear's Fool. Useful studies include Enid Welsford's *The Fool* (1935), which covers the type from classical to modern times, and R. H. Goldsmith's *Wise Fools in Shakespeare* (1955). *See also* CLOWN.

Forbes-Robertson, Sir Johnston (1853–1937) English actor, best known as Romeo, Macbeth, Othello, and Hamlet, whom he played in an early silent film (1913). His stage production of *Hamlet (1897) restored passages that had frequently been omitted, including much of the concluding episode, after Hamlet's death, and is the subject of a classic review by Bernard *Shaw.

forgeries *See* IRELAND, WILLIAM HENRY, AND COLLIER, JOHN PAYNE.

Forman, Simon (1552–1611) English doctor and astrologer; he kept a 'Bocke of Plaies', containing accounts of visits to performances of *Macbeth on 20 April 1611, The *Winter's Tale on 15 May 1611, *Cymbeline (undated), and a play about Richard II which seems not to be Shakespeare's. He made partial summaries of the plots, and drew morals. His voluminous casebooks, written partly in code, include the references to Emilia *Lanier on which A. L. Rowse based his theory that she was the *Dark Lady of the Sonnets.

Forrest, Edwin (1806–72) American tragedian, of heroic build, notable principally as Othello, Lear, and Coriolanus. He also frequently played Hamlet, Macbeth, and Richard III. He had a notorious feud with the English actor W. C. *Macready which culminated in the Astor Place Riot of 1849, in New York, in which thirty-one people were killed. The rivalry was the subject of *Two Shakespearean Actors*, a play by Richard Nelson performed by the *Royal Shakespeare Company in 1990.

Fortune Theatre Built in Finsbury, London, by the *Admiral's Men in 1600. The contract survives, and gives the external and internal dimensions, with much other information, but unfortunately says that the stage was to be 'contrived and fashioned like unto the stage of the said playhouse called the Globe', for which we have no detailed information. The Fortune was square, the walls eighty feet long on the outside, fifty-five feet on the inside, and forty-two feet high. It was popular till it burned down in 1621.

foul papers A dramatist's original, manuscript drafts, as distinct from a *fair copy.

Fratricide Punished As *Der Bestrafte Brudermord*, a German version of *Hamlet surviving in a text of 1710, of uncertain relationship to the original play.

Freeman, Thomas (*c*.1590–?) English poet. His collection of epigrams *Run and a Great Cast* (1614) includes a sonnet addressed to Shakespeare, with the lines:

> Virtue's or vice's theme to thee all one is;
> Who loves chaste life, there's *Lucrece* for a teacher;
> Who list read lust there's *Venus and Adonis*,
> True model of a most lascivious lecher.
> . . .
>> Then let thine own works thine own worth upraise,
>> And help t'adorn thee with deservèd bays.

Freud, Sigmund (1856–1939) The great Austrian psychiatrist used characters of Shakespeare as illustrations in his writings, and wrote papers on some of them. He doubted Shakespeare's authorship of the works.

Fuller, Thomas (1608–61) His *Worthies of England* (pub. 1662) includes early comment on Shakespeare, including a comparison between Shakespeare, the 'English man of War', and *Jonson, the 'Spanish great galleon'.

Fulman, William *See* DAVIES, RICHARD.

Funeral Elegy, A A poem of 578 lines privately published in 1612 by Thomas *Thorpe as 'A Funeral Elegy: in memory of the late virtuous Master William Peter of Whipton near Exeter'. The title-page says it is 'By W.S.', and the same initials appear at the end of the dedication. William Peter was a Devonshire gentleman of independent means stabbed to death in a dispute over a horse after a hard day's drinking. In 1989 Donald Foster conducted a detailed investigation into its authorship in *Elegy by W.S.: A Study in Attribution*, concluding that its author was either Shakespeare or William Strachey. During 1996 Foster came out firmly in favour of the attribution to Shakespeare, basing his case on further stylistic analysis. Even those who believe in the attribution admit that the poem is tedious, but it is printed in the New *Riverside, the revised *Bevington, and the *Norton editions. In 2002, Foster and his supporters conceded that the poem is probably by the dramatist John Ford.

Furness, Horace Howard (1833–1912) An American scholar who founded the New Variorum edition of Shakespeare with his own edition of *Romeo and Juliet* in 1871 (*see* VARIORUM). The work was continued by his son, H. H. Furness jun. (1865–1930). In 1936 the editorship was assumed by a committee of the Modern Language Association of America, and work continues. The volumes in the series are uneven in quality, and some are seriously out of date, but they gather together much information that is not easily found elsewhere.

Fuseli, Henry (Johann Heinrich Füssli; 1724–1825) Swiss painter who came to England in 1764. He did many paintings illustrative of Shakespeare's plays, some of actors, including David *Garrick, and some highly imaginative. He contributed to *Boydell's Shakespeare Gallery.

G

Garrick, David (1717–79) English actor, playwright, and manager of *Drury Lane Theatre from 1747 to 1776. Throughout his career he was specially associated with Shakespeare, and did much to revive his popularity. His greatest roles included Benedick, Richard III, Hamlet, Romeo, King Lear, and Macbeth.

He restored many passages of the plays that had been traditionally omitted, while making new adaptations such as *Catherine and Petruchio* (from The *Taming of the Shrew*), *Florizel and Perdita* (from The *Winter's Tale*), and his own version of *Hamlet*. He wrote a dying speech for Macbeth and a final duologue between Romeo and Juliet. In 1769 he organized a remarkable Jubilee at Stratford-upon-Avon, helping to establish the town as a centre of Shakespearian pilgrimage.

There are a biography by Carola Oman (1958), an important study by Kalman Burnim, *David Garrick, Director* (1961), and several accounts of the Jubilee including Johanne M. Stochholm's *Garrick's Folly* (1964).

Gascoigne, George (*c*.1539–77) A versatile English writer; *see* SUPPOSES.

Gastrell, the Revd Francis As a retired vicar, he bought the rebuilt *New Place in 1756. He had the *mulberry tree cut down in 1758, because of persistent souvenir hunters, and demolished the house in the following year because of a disagreement over the rates.

Genest, the Revd John (1764–1839) English author of *Some Account of the English Stage from the Restoration in 1660 to 1830* (10 vols., Bath, 1832), an important early work of reference.

Gentleman, Francis (1728–84) *See* BELL, JOHN.

George III, King of England (1738–1820) Fanny Burney recorded his opinion of Shakespeare in 1785: 'Was there ever such stuff as great part of Shakespeare? only one must not say so! But what think you?—What? Is there not sad stuff? What?—What? I know it's not to be said! but it's true. Only it's Shakespeare, and nobody dare abuse him.'

German, Sir Edward (1862–1936) The English composer wrote incidental music for several Shakespeare plays, including *Henry VIII* (*Lyceum, 1892), from which the dances are often performed.

Gesta Grayorum Records of Gray's Inn printed in 1688, which include an account of the Christmas revels of 1594 when 'A Comedy of Errors, like to Plautus his *Menaechmi*, was played by the players.' This was almost certainly Shakespeare's play performed by his company. The exceptional shortness of the play has led to the conjecture that it was written for this occasion.

ghost characters Characters such as the 'Innogen' described in the first stage direction in both the *quarto and *Folio texts of *Much Ado About Nothing* as Leonato's wife, mentioned again in the first stage direction of Act III, who says nothing, takes no part in the action, and is neither addressed nor mentioned by any other character.

Gielgud, Sir John (1904–2000) English actor and director, a member of the Terry family, especially renowned for his speaking of verse. His many Shakespeare roles included Romeo (*Old Vic, 1929, New, 1935), Hamlet (Old Vic, 1929, Queen's, 1930, New, 1934, St James, 1936, *Lyceum, 1939, *Haymarket, 1944), Richard II (Old Vic, 1929, Queen's, 1937, etc.), King Lear (Old Vic, 1940, Stratford-upon-Avon, 1950, etc.), Prospero (Old Vic, 1940, Stratford-upon-Avon, 1957, *National Theatre Company, 1974), Angelo (Stratford-upon-Avon, 1950), Benedick (Stratford-upon-Avon, 1950, etc.), Leontes (Phoenix, 1951), Othello (Stratford-upon-Avon, 1961), and Julius Caesar (National Theatre, 1977). He frequently appeared in a solo anthology of selections from Shakespeare, *Ages of Man*, and in films of Shakespeare's plays, including Prospero in Peter Greenaway's 1991 film *Prospero's Books*. He returned to Shakespeare on radio with the Renaissance Theatre Company to play the Ghost in *Hamlet* (1992), Friar Laurence (1993), and King Lear (1994).

Gilbert, Sir William Schwenck (1836–1911) *See* ROSENCRANTZ AND GUILDENSTERN.

Gildon, Charles (1665–1724) English critic and dramatist. He simplified *Davenant's adaptation of *Measure for Measure, The Law Against Lovers*, as *Measure for Measure; or Beauty the Best Advocate* (1700), interpolating *Purcell's opera *Dido and Aeneas* between the acts. In 1710 he issued a volume of Shakespeare's poems fraudulently made to look like a seventh volume of *Rowe's edition of the *Works* (1709).

Girlhood of Shakespeare's Heroines, The A book by Mary Cowden Clarke (1809–98), published in three volumes (1851–2), often maligned as an extreme instance of the critical tendency to treat Shakespeare's characters as real people, but in fact an imaginative work of fiction based on these characters. With her distinguished husband, Charles (1787–1877), she edited the plays (1864–8).

Globe edition *See* CAMBRIDGE SHAKESPEARE.

Globe Playhouse Trust Formed by the actor and director Sam *Wanamaker in 1971 with the prime object of rebuilding a Globe playhouse on Bankside, London. *See* INTERNATIONAL SHAKESPEARE GLOBE CENTRE.

SIR HENRY WOTTON *(1568–1639): letter on the burning of the Globe, 1613*

I will entertain you at the present with what hath happened this week at the Bankside. The King's players had a new play called *All is True*, representing some principal pieces of the reign of Henry VIII, which was set forth with many extraordinary circumstances of pomp and majesty, even to the matting of the stage; the Knights of the Order, with their Georges and Garter, the Guards with their embroidered coats and the like, sufficient in truth within a while to make greatness very familiar, if not ridiculous. Now, King Henry making a masque at the Cardinal Wolsey's house, and certain chambers being shot off at his entry, some of the paper or other stuff wherewith one of them was stopped did light on the thatch, where being thought at first but an idle smoke, and their eyes more attentive to the show, it kindled inwardly and ran round like a train [i.e. ignited fuse], consuming within less than an hour the whole house to the very grounds. This was the fatal period of that virtuous fabric, wherein yet nothing did perish but wood and straw and a few forsaken cloaks; only one man had his breeches set on fire, that would perhaps have broiled him if he had not by the benefit of a provident wit put it out with bottle ale.

Globe Theatre Built on Bankside, London, by the *Lord Chamberlain's Men in 1598 from timbers of the dismantled *Theatre. Shakespeare was a principal shareholder, and here most, if not all, of his plays written from 1599 were performed. Thomas *Platter saw a play about Julius Caesar, probably Shakespeare's, there on 21 September 1599. It was accidentally destroyed by fire on 29 June 1613 during a performance of *All is True (Henry VIII)*; various accounts survive, including one by Sir Henry *Wotton.

It was immediately rebuilt, and was open again by 30 June 1614. A contemporary, John Chamberlain, described the new theatre as 'the fairest that ever was in England'. It can be seen in *Hollar's panorama. This building was, for safety, tiled instead of thatched. It was pulled down in 1644. The remains of the Globe survive. Preliminary investigation during the early 1990s uncovered a limited amount of evidence, but detailed investigation remains to be carried out. For reconstruction of the Globe *see* INTERNATIONAL SHAKESPEARE GLOBE CENTRE.

Golding, Arthur (1536?–1605?) Translator whose version of *Ovid's *Metamorphoses* (1567) in fourteeners (fourteen-syllabled lines) was used by Shakespeare, particularly in The *Tempest*, where Prospero's speech 'Ye elves of hills, brooks, standing lakes, and groves' (v. i. 33–57), in particular, is indebted to it.

good quarto An edition of a play in *quarto printed from an authoritative manuscript, as distinct from a *bad quarto.

Gounod, Charles (1818–93) The French composer's opera *Roméo et Juliette*, based on Shakespeare's play, was written in 1867 and revised for the Paris Opéra in 1888, with the addition of a ballet.

Gower, John (c.1330–1408) English poet whose long poem *Confessio Amantis* includes a version of the tale of *Apollonius of Tyre, which may have been a source for Shakespeare's use of this story in the framework plot of The *Comedy of Errors* and in *Pericles, in which Gower is himself represented, and his style imitated, in the figure of the *Chorus.

Gower memorial Lord Ronald Gower, a sculptor, made and presented to Stratford-upon-Avon a group of bronze statues commemorative of Shakespeare which stood on the lawn south of the theatre from 1888 to 1933, when it was moved to its present position by the canal basin.

A seated figure of Shakespeare mounted on a plinth is surrounded by figures of Henry V (as History), *Falstaff (as Comedy), Lady Macbeth (as Tragedy), and Hamlet (as Philosophy). Behind each figure is a plinth with a mask bearing symbolic vegetation. Henry V has English roses and French lilies, Falstaff, hops and grapes, Hamlet, ivy and cypress, and Lady Macbeth, poppies and peonies.

'Grafton' portrait of Shakespeare A portrait of someone aged twenty-four in 1588. This, and a vague resemblance to the *Droeshout engraving, are all that connect it with Shakespeare. It was found in an inn in County Durham, and had for long been in a farmhouse in the village of Grafton, Northants. It now hangs in the John Rylands Library, Manchester.

Grammar School, Stratford-upon-Avon Known in Shakespeare's day as the King's New School; now the King Edward the Sixth School for Boys. The early schoolroom is next to the *Guild Chapel, above the former Guildhall. It was a good school, with well-qualified masters. Names of sixteenth-century pupils do not survive. Shakespeare probably went to it from the age of 7 or 8, leaving when he was about 15 or less. His principal master would have been Thomas *Jenkins.

The curriculum was mainly classical. Works of literature including Roman comedies, *Ovid's *Metamorphoses*, and other books known to have influenced Shakespeare were studied. Shakespeare portrays a Latin lesson in The *Merry Wives of Windsor, iv. i.

Granville-Barker, Harley (1877–1946) English actor, director, playwright, and scholar. He played Richard II for William *Poel, and his famous productions of The *Winter's Tale, *Twelfth Night (both 1912) and A *Midsummer Night's Dream (1914) at the Savoy Theatre, London, carried over into the professional theatre some of Poel's ideals of a return to the basic principles of Elizabethan staging. He was more of a textual purist than Poel, though less austere in the visual aspects of his staging. After these productions he virtually retired from the theatre, but his *Prefaces* to many of Shakespeare's plays (1927 onwards) have done much to increase understanding of the principles of Shakespeare's stagecraft, in both theatre and study.

Greene, Robert (1558–92) English writer, educated at Cambridge. His romantic comedies *James IV* (c.1590–1) and *Friar Bacon and Friar Bungay* (c.1589–92) may have influenced Shakespeare, and his prose romance

penneſt on ſo meane a ſtay. Baſe minded men all thꝛee
of you, if by my miſerie you be not warnd: foꝛ vnto none
of you (like mee) ſought thoſe burres to cleaue : thoſe
Puppets (J meane) that ſpake from our mouths, thoſe
Anticks garniſht in our colours. Is it not ſtrange, that
J, to whom they all haue beene beholding: is it not like
that you, to whome they all haue beene beholding, ſhall
(were yee in that caſe as J am now) bee both at once of
them foꝛſaken : Yes truſt them not : foꝛ there is an vp-
ſtart Crow, beautified with our feathers, that with his
Tygers hart wrapt in a Players hyde, ſuppoſes he is as
well able to bombaſt out a blanke verſe as the beſt of
you : and beeing an abſolute Iohannes fac totum, is in
his owne conceit the onely Shake-ſcene in a countrey.

*Robert Greene's attack
on Shakespeare (1592)*

Pandosto (1588?) is the main source of *The *Winter's Tale*. The earliest undoubted allusion to Shakespeare in London, and the earliest in print, is in *Greene's Groatsworth of Wit* (1592), written in the last months of his life and published posthumously: 'there is an upstart crow beautified with our feathers that, with his "tiger's heart wrapped in a player's hide", supposes he is as well able to bombast out a blank verse as the best of you; and, being an absolute *Johannes Factotum*, is in his own conceit the only Shake-scene in a country.' This parodies a line from *3 *Henry VI*, I. iv. 138: 'O tiger's heart wrapped in a woman's hide!' The passage, enigmatic like much Elizabethan literary satire, shows resentment that the actor Shakespeare is offering competition to established playwrights; it has also been interpreted as an accusation of plagiarism. The book was prepared for the press by Henry *Chettle, who apologized for the Shakespeare reference in his *Kind-heart's Dream* (1592), though he has been suspected of writing the *Groatsworth* himself.

Greene, Thomas *See* WELCOMBE ENCLOSURES.

Greet, Sir Ben (1857–1936) English actor–manager. In 1886 he gave the first of his many open-air performances of Shakespeare plays, forming a company with which he toured England and America for many years. In 1914 his company became the nucleus of the Shakespeare company at the *Old Vic Theatre, London, where, with Lilian *Baylis, he presented many of the plays from 1915 to 1918. After this he gave many performances of Shakespeare for schoolchildren in the London area, and also worked in both Paris and America.

Greg, Sir Walter Wilson (1875–1959) English bibliographer, Shakespeare scholar, author of *The Shakespeare First Folio* (1955), *The Editorial Problem in Shakespeare* (1942), and major bibliographical studies of the drama of Shakespeare's time.

groundlings Hamlet's word for the spectators who spent one penny to stand on the ground in the open space around the apron stages of Elizabethan theatres: 'O, it offends me to the soul to hear a robustious periwig-pated fellow tear a passion to tatters, to very rags, to split the ears of the groundlings, who, for the most part, are capable of nothing but inexplicable dumb shows and noise.' (III. ii. 8–13).

Guild Chapel, Stratford-upon-Avon The fifteenth-century chapel of the Guild of the Holy Cross, dating from the thirteenth century and dissolved in 1547. It lies across the road from the site of *New Place, and next to the *Grammar School.

Guthrie, Sir Tyrone (1900–71) English director of plays at Stratford-upon-Avon and the *Old Vic, specially associated with the Festival Theatre at *Stratford, Ontario; he directed many Shakespeare plays in a brilliant and idiosyncratic fashion.

H

Hackett, James Henry (1800–71) American actor, distinguished as an imitator. He played Richard III in imitation of Edmund *Kean, and noted Kean's playing of the role in detail. He was the leading American *Falstaff of his time. In 1863 he published *Notes and Comments upon Certain Plays and Actors of Shakespeare*.

Hall, Elizabeth (1608–70) Shakespeare's granddaughter, only child of John and Susanna *Hall, baptized 21 February 1608. Shakespeare bequeathed to her almost all of his plate. She married Thomas *Nash in 1626. When her father died, in 1635, they moved into *New Place.

Her husband died in 1647. He left New Place and other property to his cousin, Edward Nash, but Elizabeth and her mother contested the will and retained the property.

She married John (later Sir John) Bernard on 5 June 1649, in which year her mother died. Some time afterwards the Bernards moved to his estate in Abington, Northamptonshire, where she died in 1670. She directed that New Place be offered for sale to Edward Nash, but he did not buy it, and it was sold in 1675 to Sir Edward Walker, passing from him into the Clopton family.

Elizabeth had no children. With her death, Shakespeare's direct family came to an end.

Hall, John (1575–1635) Entered Queens' College, Cambridge, 1589; BA, 1593; MA, 1597; studied medicine in France; settled in Stratford-upon-Avon about 1600. He married Shakespeare's elder daughter, *Susanna, on 5 June 1607. Their daughter, *Elizabeth, was baptized on 21 February 1608.

He was a distinguished physician, and had to pay £10 on refusing a knighthood from Charles I in 1626. One of his medical diaries, written in Latin, was translated and printed in 1657 as *Select Observations on English Bodies*. He was a devout Christian, with Puritan sympathies, presented *Holy Trinity Church with a carved pulpit, and was a churchwarden.

The Halls are said to have lived in *Hall's Croft; they certainly lived in *New Place after Shakespeare's death. John is buried in the chancel of Holy Trinity Church, and his gravestone is now close to that of his father-in-law.

Hall, Sir Peter (1930–) Director of the *Royal Shakespeare Company 1960–8, *National Theatre 1973–88, and of the *Old Vic 1996–7. He has directed many Shakespeare productions, including, at Stratford-upon-Avon, *Love's Labour's Lost (1956), *Cymbeline (1957), *Twelfth Night (1958, etc.), A *Midsummer Night's Dream and *Coriolanus (1959), The *Two Gentlemen of Verona and (with John *Barton) *Troilus and Cressida (1960), *Romeo and Juliet (1961), The *Wars of the Roses (with John Barton, 1963), *Richard II, 1 and 2 *Henry IV, *Henry V (1964); *Hamlet (1965), *Macbeth (1967), *All's Well that Ends Well (1992), and *Julius Caesar (1995), as well as The *Tempest (*National Theatre Company, 1973), and, at the *National Theatre, *Hamlet (1975), *Othello (1980), *Coriolanus (1984), *Antony and Cleopatra (1987), Cymbeline, The *Winter's Tale, The *Tempest (1988). Formed his own company in 1989 and directed The *Merchant of Venice (1989) with Dustin Hoffman as Shylock, and Hamlet (1994). In his season in charge of the Old Vic, he directed *King Lear (1997) and since then has continued to direct Shakespeare in England and America.

Halle, Edward (c.1498–1547) English author of The Union of the Two Noble and Illustre Families of Lancaster and York, completed and published after his death by Richard Grafton in 1548, much of which *Holinshed incorporated in his Chronicles. Halle's influence on Shakespeare's early history plays is probably greater than Holinshed's.

Halliwell, later **Halliwell-Phillipps, James Orchard** (1820–89) English bibliophile and scholar, author of a Life of William Shakespeare (1848), Outlines of the Life of Shakespeare (1881, final revision 1887), editor of the Works (16 vols., 1853–65). He published many other writings concerned with Shakespeare.

Hall's Croft A fine Tudor house in Old Town, Stratford-upon-Avon, maintained since 1949 as a showplace by the *Shakespeare Birthplace Trust. Tradition says that Shakespeare's daughter, *Susanna, and her husband John *Hall lived there, but the present name of the house has not been traced before the mid-nineteenth century.

Hamlet Shakespeare's tragedy was entered in the *Stationers' Register on 26 July 1602 and first printed in 1603, advertised as having been 'divers times acted by his Highness' servants in the City of London, as also in the two Universities of Cambridge and Oxford, and elsewhere'.

HENRY FIELDING *(1707–54): Mr Partridge sees Garrick as Hamlet; from* Tom Jones *(1749)*

Jones asked [Mr Partridge], 'Which of the players he had liked best?'To this he answered, with some appearance of indignation at the question,'The king, without doubt.'—'Indeed, Mr. Partridge,' says Mrs. Miller.'You are not of the same opinion with the town; for they are all agreed that Hamlet is acted by the best player who ever was on the stage.'—'He the best player!' cries Partridge, with a contemptuous sneer;'why, I could act as well as he myself. I am sure, if I had seen a ghost, I should have looked in the very same manner, and done just as he did.And then, to be sure, in that scene, as you called it, between him and his mother, where you told me he acted so fine, why, Lord help me, any man, that is, any good man, that had such a mother, would have done exactly the same. I know you are only joking with me; but indeed, madam, though I was never at a play in London, yet I have seen acting before in the country: and the king for my money; he speaks all his words distinctly, half as loud again as the other.—Any body may see he is an actor.'

This is a *bad quarto, probably put together from the memories of a few of the actors. A good text appeared in 1604, said to be 'enlarged to almost as much again as it was, according to the true and perfect copy', and probably printed from Shakespeare's manuscript. The version in the *Folio is somewhat shorter, and probably derives from a *prompt copy. From the early eighteenth century until the 1980s, editors regularly conflated the 1604 quarto with the *Folio. The *Oxford Shakespeare bases the text on the *Folio, printing lines found only in the 1604 quarto as 'additional passages'.

Hamlet was probably written about 1600–1, based on a lost play known as the *Ur-Hamlet. Richard *Burbage was almost certainly the first Hamlet, and many allusions to the play vouch for its contemporary success. *Davenant revived it in 1661, omitting much but not radically revising it. Thomas *Betterton, aged 26, played Hamlet, and continued to do so for nearly fifty years. David *Garrick took the role from 1742 till his retirement in 1776. In 1772 he played in his own radical revision, designed to rescue 'that noble play from all the

ANON: *teaching* Hamlet *by the 'look-and-tell' method; from* Time-Life (20 July 1962) . . .

See Hamlet run. Run, Hamlet, Run.

He is going to his mother's room.

'I have something to tell you mother,'

says Hamlet. 'Uncle Claudius is bad. He gave my father poison. Poison is not good. I do not like poison. Do you like poison?'

'Oh, no, indeed!' says his mother. 'I do not like poison.'

'Oh, there is Uncle Claudius,' says Hamlet. 'He is hiding behind the curtain.

Why is he hiding behind the curtain?

Shall I stab him? What fun it would be to stab him through the curtain.'

See Hamlet draw his sword. See Hamlet stab. Stab; Hamlet, stab.

See Uncle Claudius' blood.

See Uncle Claudius' blood gushing.

Gush, blood, gush.

See Uncle Claudius fall. How funny he looks, stabbed.

Ha, ha, ha.

But it is not Uncle Claudius. It is Polonius. Polonius is Ophelia's father.

'You are naughty, Hamlet,' says Hamlet's mother. 'You have stabbed Polonius.'

But Hamlet's mother is not cross. She is a good mother.

Hamlet loves his mother very much. Hamlet loves his mother very, very much.

Does Hamlet love his mother a little too much?

Perhaps.

See Hamlet run. Run, Hamlet, Run.

'I am on my way to find Uncle Claudius,' Hamlet says.

On the way he meets a man. 'I am Laertes,' says the man.

'Let us draw our swords. Let us duel.'

See Hamlet and Laertes duel. See Laertes stab Hamlet. See Hamlet stab Laertes. See Hamlet's mother drink poison. See Hamlet stab King Claudius.

See everybody wounded and bleeding and dying and dead.

What fun they are having!

Wouldn't you like to have fun like that?

rubbish of the fifth act'. It was not published, and the manuscript was lost until 1934.

J. P. *Kemble was the most famous Hamlet of the Romantic period, succeeded by Edmund *Kean and W. C. *Macready. During the nineteenth century the play was much shortened, and the curtain generally went down on Hamlet's own last line. The Frenchman Charles Fechter gave his naturalistic interpretation in London in 1861. Henry *Irving's production achieved an unparalleled run of 200 performances at the *Lyceum in 1874–5. J. *Forbes-Robertson restored Fortinbras to the text in 1897, and F. R. *Benson gave a complete text at the Lyceum in 1900. Barry *Jackson presented the play in *modern dress in 1925. John *Gielgud, perhaps the greatest Hamlet of the twentieth century, first played the part at the *Old Vic in 1930. Laurence *Olivier acted in Tyrone *Guthrie's production in 1937; his film of a heavily abbreviated text appeared ten years later. In recent years Kenneth *Branagh has been a notable Hamlet, playing the role three times, twice on stage, including a full-text version for the RSC in 1992, and once on film in his 1996 full-text version lasting over four hours. The play was also filmed by Franco *Zeffirelli in 1990, starring Mel Gibson.

The most famous American Hamlets have been Edwin *Booth, who played the role from 1853 to 1891, and John Barrymore (1922).

Only a few of the most distinguished performers of Hamlet are mentioned here. The role has appealed, not only to most actors, but also to many actresses. The play has been the world's most popular tragedy, above all because of its vivid portrayal of the struggles of its young and vulnerable hero to come to terms with his own destiny. It has provoked an enormous amount of critical comment and has inspired many other works of art, including operas by Ambroise *Thomas (1868) and Humphrey Searle (1968), music by *Tchaikovsky, *Berlioz, and Liszt, a ballet by Robert Helpmann, and many paintings. Grigori *Kozintsev's film (1964) had music by *Shostakovitch.

Hands, Terry (1941–) English theatre director, since 1967 Associate Director of the *Royal Shakespeare Company, and Joint Artistic Director of the Royal Shakespeare Company 1978–86, sole Artistic Director 1986–91. He has directed many of Shakespeare's plays, including *Henry IV*, *Henry V* (both 1975), all three Parts of *Henry VI* and *Coriolanus* (1977), all with Alan *Howard, *The *Merry Wives of Windsor* (1968, etc.), *Much Ado About Nothing* (1982),

Coriolanus, *Romeo and Juliet* (1989), *Love's Labour's Lost* (1990). After a period working in France, he returned to the *Royal National Theatre to revive his production of *The Merry Wives of Windsor* (1995). He became Director of Clwyd Theatr Wales in 1997.

handwriting, Shakespeare's The only certain examples are six *signatures, along with the words 'by me' before the last signature on the will. But three pages of *Sir Thomas More* may also be in Shakespeare's hand.

Hanmer, Sir Thomas (1677–1746) A country gentleman, Speaker of the House of Commons in 1714, and the fourth editor of Shakespeare. His six-volume edition (1743–4) is of little textual importance, but is finely printed and handsomely illustrated by Hubert Gravelot and Francis *Hayman.

Harsnett, Samuel (1561–1631) Scholar; Archbishop of York, 1629–31; his *A Declaration of Egregious Popish Impostures* (1603) is echoed in *King Lear* and The *Tempest*.

Hart, William *See* SHAKESPEARE, JOAN.

Harvey, Gabriel (1545?–1630?) English scholar, barrister, and controversialist. A note written, probably between 1598 and 1601, in his copy of an edition of Chaucer, alludes to Shakespeare: 'The younger sort takes much delight in Shakespeare's *Venus and Adonis*; but his *Lucrece*, and his tragedy of *Hamlet, Prince of Denmark*, have it in them to please the wiser sort . . .'

Hathaway, Anne (1555 or 1556–1623) Shakespeare's wife, whom he married on 27 November 1582, when she was 26, and by whom he had three children. Her family were landowners in Shottery, a village close to Stratford-upon-Avon, and lived in Hewland, an Elizabethan farmhouse bought by Anne's brother, Bartholomew, in 1610, and known since the late eighteenth century as *Anne Hathaway's Cottage. We know scarcely anything about Shakespeare's relations with his wife. Their children were *Susanna and the twins *Hamnet and *Judith. Anne appears to have remained in Stratford while Shakespeare worked in London, but he retained interests in his home town (*see* e.g. NEW PLACE) and may have returned regularly.

In his will, Shakespeare left Anne only his second-best bed. The exact significance of this is uncertain. Sometimes it has been interpreted as a derisory gesture. But it may be that, by local custom, Anne would have automatically had a life interest in one-third of the estate, as well as the right to continue to live in *New Place, and thus, presumably, to occupy the best bed if she wished.

She died on 6 August 1623 and is buried in *Holy Trinity Church, next to her husband. The inscription on the gravestone states that when she died she was 'of the age of 67 years'; this is the only evidence as to her date of birth.

Haydn, Franz Josef (1732–1809) The great Austrian composer wrote a well-known setting for voice and piano of 'She never told her love', from *Twelfth Night*.

Hayman, Francis (1708–86) An English artist and scene painter who designed most of the illustrations for *Hanmer's edition of Shakespeare (1743–4)

Haymarket Theatre, London Built in 1720, it came to be known as 'the Little Theatre in the Hay'. In 1766 it became a Theatre Royal, and plays could legally be presented there in the summer months. It was demolished in 1820, and the present building on the site opened in 1821. Herbert Beerbohm *Tree presented elaborate Shakespeare productions there from 1887 to 1897, and John *Gielgud acted there in *Hamlet and other plays in 1944–5.

Hazlitt, William (1778–1830) English essayist and critic. His reviews of Edmund *Kean's early London performances include some of his best writing on the theatre. His *The Characters of Shakespeare's Plays* (1817), which incorporates passages from his reviews, has had great popularity.

heavens The cover or canopy over the stages in some Elizabethan theatres, sometimes supported by pillars. Descents could be made from it, and it may have been painted to represent the sky.

hell-mouth The trap-door in the stages of Elizabethan theatres, deriving its name from the use to which it was put in medieval miracle plays.

Heminges, John (d. 1630) An actor in Shakespeare's company through most, if not all, of Shakespeare's career, and in later years apparently their business manager. Shakespeare left him 26s. 8d. to buy a mourning ring. With Henry *Condell, he was responsible for the preparation of the First *Folio.

Henry IV, Part One The second play in Shakespeare's second historical tetralogy was entered in the *Stationers' Register on 25 February 1598, and printed twice the same year. Only an eight-page fragment of the first edition survives. The *quarto was reprinted in 1599, 1604, 1608, 1613, and 1622. The 1613 edition, from which the oaths had been removed (*see* CENSORSHIP), was reprinted in the First *Folio. The play was probably written about 1596–7. It takes up the historical story from the end of *Richard II*, and is based on *Holinshed's *Chronicles* with material from The *Famous Victories of Henry V*, in which Shakespeare found the name Sir John *Oldcastle, which he originally gave to *Falstaff. The change of name, restored in the *Oxford Shakespeare (1986), seems to be the result of protests from Oldcastle's descendant, William Brooke, Lord Cobham. It is the first Shakespeare history play to use the techniques of comedy.

The play has always been successful, mainly because of Falstaff. It was popular before 1640 (*see* DIGGES, LEONARD), and was adapted as a *droll, *The Bouncing Knight*, while the theatres were closed. Thomas *Betterton, who played Hotspur in 1682, appeared as Falstaff in 1700. James *Quin took on the role in 1722 and played it till his retirement in 1751. J. P. *Kemble revived the play carefully in 1803–4 at *Covent Garden, playing Hotspur, a role which W. C. *Macready took from 1815 to 1847. Samuel *Phelps played both Hotspur and, later, Falstaff.

The play's popularity waned during the Victorian period, but Beerbohm *Tree revived it at the *Haymarket in 1896, and later, playing Falstaff. Robert *Atkins was much associated with it, as producer and actor, playing Falstaff, from the 1920s to the 1950s. Ralph *Richardson was a great Falstaff in an *Old Vic production at the New Theatre in 1945, with Laurence *Olivier as Hotspur. Orson *Welles played the role on both stage and film. The play has been given at Stratford-upon-Avon as part of a cycle of English histories in 1951, 1964, and 1975, and as part of the *English Shakespeare Company's cycle of history plays, 1986–9. The Royal Shakespeare Company performed both parts in 1982 and 1991, with Robert *Stephens as a memorable Falstaff in the latter. A conflated version of the two plays was directed by John *Caird for the BBC in 1995.

Henry IV, Part Two The third play in Shakespeare's second historical tetralogy was entered in the *Stationers' Register on 23 August 1600 and printed in the same year. Act III, scene i was accidentally omitted, but included in a second issue. The play was not reprinted until 1623, in the First *Folio, which includes several additional passages. It was probably written about 1597–8. Like Part One, it is based mainly on *Holinshed's *Chronicles*, with additional material from *The *Famous Victories of Henry V.*

The play has been generally less popular than Part One; sometimes the two plays have been conflated, usually with emphasis on *Falstaff. James *Quin played Falstaff in both Parts. Theophilus *Cibber presented his adaptation, *The Humourists*, in 1754, playing Pistol. An elaborate production at *Covent Garden in 1761–2 celebrated the coronation of George III, and there was another coronation production, for George IV, at Covent Garden in 1821. Samuel *Phelps played both the King and Shallow at *Sadler's Wells in 1853, and later. F. R. *Benson played Part Two more often than Part One. Barry *Jackson presented both parts in a single day at Birmingham Repertory Theatre on 23 April 1922. The *Old Vic production of 1945 had Ralph *Richardson as a great Falstaff and Laurence *Olivier as Shallow. It has been played at Stratford-upon-Avon as part of a cycle of histories in 1951, 1964, and 1975, and as part of the *English Shakespeare Company's cycle of history plays, 1986–9. The Royal Shakespeare Company performed both parts in 1982 and 1991, with Robert *Stephens as a memorable Falstaff in the latter. A conflated version of the two plays was directed by John *Caird for the BBC in 1995.

The relative unpopularity of Part Two may be the result of its having a less clearly defined structure than Part One, but it offers a more profound, if more pessimistic, portrayal of human beings under the pressures of war and time, and the Gloucestershire scenes are among Shakespeare's greatest dramatic achievements.

Henry V The fourth play in Shakespeare's second historical tetralogy was entered in the *Stationers' Register on 4 August 1600 and printed in a *bad quarto the same year. This text was reissued in 1602 and (falsely dated 1608) in 1619 (*see* JAGGARD, WILLIAM). A good text appeared in the First *Folio (1623). A line in the *Chorus to Act V seems to refer to the Earl of *Essex's campaign in Ireland, which would date its composition between 27 March and 28 September 1599. It is based mainly on *Holinshed's *Chronicles*.

Aaron Hill's radical adaptation, omitting the comic scenes and adding romantic complications, was played at *Drury Lane in 1723. Shakespeare's play seems to have been revived first at Goodman's Fields in 1735, and was played frequently in London after that. J. P. *Kemble played the King with great success in his own revision from 1789 to 1811; W. C. *Macready took over from 1819 to 1839. His 1839 version was pictorially spectacular, as was Charles *Kean's production at the Princess's in 1859, in which his wife played the Chorus as Clio, the muse of history. He interpolated a pageant of Henry's entry into London after Agincourt. F. R. *Benson and Lewis Waller were successful as Henry in the early twentieth century. The play has had special appeal in time of war. Laurence *Olivier's popular film appeared in 1944. The play has been given at Stratford-upon-Avon as part of a cycle of history plays in 1901, 1906, 1951, 1964, 1975, and 1977, and has frequently been played independently. At 24, Kenneth *Branagh was the youngest recorded Henry at Stratford-upon-Avon in 1984. His film of 1989 was a great success and did much to generate mainstream movie interest in filming Shakespeare's plays.

Until comparatively recent times, *Henry V* was regarded as a great patriotic play. Modern criticism, perhaps defensively, has discerned ironic attitudes in Shakespeare's presentation of the hero.

Henry VI, Part One The first play in Shakespeare's first historical tetralogy was first printed in the First *Folio (1623). Its authorship has often been disputed, and even scholars who regard it as mainly by Shakespeare have argued that another writer, perhaps George *Peele or Thomas *Nashe, may have had a hand in it. Its date is uncertain; some scholars have thought that it may have been written later than Parts Two and Three. There is an apparent allusion to it in *Pierce Penniless*, by Thomas *Nashe, published in 1592. It is firmly based on *Holinshed's *Chronicles* and *Halle's *Union of the Two Noble and Illustre Families of Lancaster and York*. One of the characters is Joan of Arc, portrayed here, as in Holinshed, as a loose-living witch. The patriotic tone of the play may well be related to the defeat of the Spanish Armada in 1588.

This play may be the 'Harey the vj' listed by *Henslowe as having been performed by Strange's Men at the Rose on 3 March 1592, and played thirteen times more that year and twice again the following January. Only one revival in the eighteenth century is recorded, at *Covent Garden on 13 March 1738, and only one in the nineteenth, in 1899, at Stratford-upon-Avon, where F. R. *Benson gave it again, along with the other two Parts, in 1906. Robert *Atkins produced it at the *Old Vic on 29 January 1923 only, with the first part of Part Two. It was given successfully as part of a complete cycle of the histories in California at the Pasadena Community Playhouse in 1935, and, directed by Douglas Seale, at the Birmingham Repertory Theatre and the Old Vic in 1953, as part of the trilogy. This production was repeated at the Old Vic in 1957. Much of the play was included in Peter *Hall's *The Wars of the Roses* (1963), and in Adrian *Noble's *The *Plantagenets* (1988). Terry *Hands directed all three parts in an important revival at Stratford-upon-Avon in 1977, and Michael *Bogdanov directed all the history plays in the two tetralogies for the *English Shakespeare Company (1986, filmed 1989). Michael Boyd directed all three parts in the Swan Theatre in 2000.

Henry VI, Part Two The second play in Shakespeare's first historical tetralogy first appeared in a corrupt text in 1594 (*see* 'CONTENTION' PLAYS). The title by which it is now generally known may derive from the editors of the First *Folio. It is usually dated 1590–1, and is freely based on *Holinshed's *Chronicles* and *Halle's *Union of the Two Noble and Illustre Families of Lancaster and York*. For its later history, *see* HENRY VI, PART THREE.

Henry VI, Part Three The third play in Shakespeare's first historical tetralogy was first printed in a corrupt text in 1595 (*see* 'CONTENTION' PLAYS). As with 2 *Henry VI, the title may derive from the editors of the First *Folio. It is alluded to in Robert *Greene's *Groatsworth of Wit*, written by September 1592, and is usually dated shortly before this. It is based on *Holinshed's *Chronicles* and *Halle's *Union of the Two Noble and Illustre Families of Lancaster and York*, and is so closely related to Part Two that the plays were probably intended to be given consecutively.

John *Crowne adapted the first three acts of Part Two as *Henry the Sixth, the First Part*, and parts of both plays in *The Misery of Civil War*, both in 1680 (acted 1681). Ambrose Philips's *Humphrey, Duke of Gloucester*, given at *Drury Lane in 1723, uses only about thirty lines of Part Two. Theophilus *Cibber's *Historical Tragedy of the Civil Wars in the Reign of King Henry VI*, given once only at Drury Lane in the same year, draws on both Parts, as well as on Crowne and on *Henry V. J. H. Merivale also drew on both Parts in his *Richard, Duke of York* in which Edmund *Kean appeared at Drury Lane in 1817–18.

Shakespeare's Part Two was given at the Surrey Theatre, London, in 1864. F. R. *Benson gave it at Stratford-upon-Avon in 1899, 1901, and 1909, and included all three Parts in a history cycle of seven plays in 1906. Robert *Atkins reduced the three plays to two at the *Old Vic in 1923. Douglas Seale directed all three at the Birmingham Repertory Theatre in 1951–3, and they were repeated with great success at the Old Vic in 1957. Much of the play was included in Peter *Hall's *The

Wars of the Roses (1963), and in Adrian *Noble's The *Plantagenets (1988). Terry *Hands directed all three parts in an important revival at Stratford-upon-Avon in 1977, and Michael *Bogdanov directed all the history plays in the two tetralogies for the *English Shakespeare Company (1986, filmed 1989). The plays were included in the BBC television series *An *Age of Kings*. There was a rare independent revival in 1994 when Katie Mitchell directed a touring production for the *Royal Shakespeare Company.

Henry VIII *See* ALL IS TRUE.

Henslowe, Philip (d. 1616) English theatre manager, stepfather of Edward *Alleyn's wife, associated especially with the *Admiral's

---

JANE AUSTEN *(1775–1815): Henry Crawford and Edmund Tilney discuss* Henry the Eighth; *from* Mansfield Park *(1814)*

'That play must be a favourite with you,' said he; 'you read as if you knew it well.'

'It will be a favourite, I believe, from this hour,' replied Crawford; 'but I do not think I have had a volume of Shakespeare in my hand before since I was fifteen. I once saw Henry the Eighth acted,—or I have heard of it from somebody who did—I am not certain which. But Shakespeare one gets acquainted with without knowing how. It is a part of an Englishman's constitution. His thoughts and beauties are so spread abroad that one touches them everywhere; one is intimate with him by instinct. No man of any brain can open at a good part of one of his plays without falling into the flow of his meaning immediately.'

'No doubt one is familiar with Shakespeare in a degree,' said Edmund, 'from one's earliest years. His celebrated passages are quoted by everybody: they are in half the books we open, and we all talk Shakespeare, use his similes, and describe with his descriptions; but this is totally distinct from giving his sense as you gave it. To know him in bits and scraps is common enough; to know him pretty thoroughly is, perhaps, not uncommon; but to read him well aloud is no everyday talent.'

'Sir, you do me honour,' was Crawford's answer, with a bow of mock gravity.

Men. His papers, including the *Diary* (really an account or memoran-
dum book), are a uniquely valuable source of information about
theatre practice in his time. They include detailed lists of performances and takings from 1592 to 1603, records of transactions
with and for actors, playwrights, and the *Master of the Revels,
notes about costumes and properties, etc. They could only be more
valuable if they related to Shakespeare's company. There are editions
by W. W. *Greg (3 vols., 1904–9), and by R. A. Foakes and R. T. Rickert
(1961).

Herbert, Philip, Earl of Montgomery, later 4th Earl of Pembroke
(1584–1650) Dedicatee, with his brother, *William, of the First
*Folio.

Herbert, William, 3rd Earl of Pembroke (1580–1630) Dedicatee, with
his brother, *Philip, of the First *Folio; sometimes identified as the
Mr W. H. of the *Sonnets.

Heywood, Thomas (*c*.1570–1641) English dramatist, poet, and prose-
writer; *see* THE PASSIONATE PILGRIM.

Histories The *Folio distinguishes ten of Shakespeare's plays as
Histories. These are the English history plays: *King John, *Richard II, 1*
and 2 *Henry IV, *Henry V, 1, 2,* and 3 *Henry VI, *Richard III,* and *All
is True (Henry VIII).* Shakespeare also drew on British history for
*Macbeth, *Cymbeline,* and *King Lear.* The plays about Roman history
are grouped with the *Tragedies.

Eight of Shakespeare's English history plays fall naturally into two
groups. In 1, 2, and 3 *Henry VI* and *Richard III* he dramatizes a con-
secutive sequence of events, and in *Richard II, 1* and *2 *Henry IV,* and
Henry V, which he wrote later, he does the same with an earlier
historical period. Each group of four plays is often referred to as a
tetralogy, though the degree to which Shakespeare thought of them
as sequences is disputed. In performance, the first two tetralogies
are often most effective when played as a cycle of plays; this is
particularly true of *Richard III* where Richard's dominance is tem-
pered by Margaret.

Hogarth, William (1697–1764) The English artist's best-known illustration of Shakespeare is his fine oil-painting of David *Garrick as
Richard III (1745). There are also an early drawing, 'Falstaff Examining
his Recruits' (*c*.1728), and a painting of 'A Scene from *The Tempest*'
(*c*.1735).

Holinshed, Raphael (*c*.1529–*c*.1580) English chronicler whose pub-lisher asked him to compile a history of the world. What he produced in 1577 was *The Chronicles of England, Scotland, and Ireland*. He wrote the history of England (borrowing extensively from Edward *Halle), and included a 'Description of England' by William Harrison, as well as material by other writers.

Shakespeare drew on Holinshed, probably in the greatly enlarged edition of 1587, for his *history plays, and for *Macbeth*, *Cymbeline*, and *King Lear*. Richard Hosley has edited *Shakespeare's Holinshed* (1968).

Holland, Hugh (d. 1633) English poet; author of a commendatory poem in the First *Folio.

Hollar, Wenceslaus (1607–77) An engraver from Prague whose 'Long View' of London from the Bankside was etched in Antwerp in 1647 and based on sketches made while he lived in London from about 1636 to 1642 or later. It is the most detailed panorama of early London, and includes a representation of the second *Globe Theatre, its name mistakenly reversed with that of the Bear-baiting house.

Holm, Ian (1931–) British actor whose Shakespeare roles include Puck, Lear's Fool (both 1959, * Shakespeare Memorial Theatre), Puck, Troilus (both 1962), Ariel, Richard III (1963), Hal in both parts of *Henry IV*, Henry V (1964, 1966), Malvolio (1966), Romeo (1967, all Royal Shakespeare Company), King Lear (1997, *Royal National Theatre); also played Fluellen in *Branagh's film of *Henry V* (1989).

Part of Hollar's Long View of London *(1647), showing the second Globe Theatre and the Beargarden, with their names interchanged*

Holst, Gustav (1874–1934) The English composer wrote an opera, *At the Boar's Head* (1925), based on 1 and 2 **Henry IV*, and using much folk-music.

Holy Trinity Church Parish church of Stratford-upon-Avon, dating mainly from the fourteenth century; the steeple is an eighteenth-century addition. In this fine church Shakespeare was baptized and buried.

Howard, Alan (1937–) British actor and player of many major Shakespeare roles with the *Royal Shakespeare Company 1966–80, particularly in partnership with the director Terry *Hands. These roles included Orsino (1966), Jaques (1967), Achilles, Benedick, Edgar (1968), Theseus and Oberon (doubled), Hamlet (1970), Prince Hal, Henry V (1975), Henry VI, Coriolanus (1977), Richard II, Richard III (1980). He returned to classical acting in 1993 to play Macbeth for the *Royal National Theatre, and played King Lear for the *Old Vic in 1997.

Humourists, The *See* HENRY IV, PART TWO.

Hunsdon, Lord *See* LORD CHAMBERLAIN'S MEN.

Huntington Library Henry E. Huntington (1850–1927) endowed a library and art gallery at San Marino, California, as a public trust. The library is rich in Renaissance, including Shakespearian, research materials.

hut A room above the canopy or *'heavens' in at least some Elizabethan theatres, in which stage hands could operate machinery for ascents and descents and create sound effects. Alongside it appears to have been a platform from which three trumpet calls were sounded to announce a performance, and a flag flew above it during a performance.

Hutt, William (1920–) Canadian actor and director who has been associated with the *Stratford, Ontario Festival since its opening in 1953. Roles he has played there included Polonius (1957), Jaques (1959), Prospero (1962, 1976), Pandarus (1963), Richard II (1964), Brutus (1965), Enobarbus (1967), Duke Vincentio (1969, etc.), Lear (1972, 1988, 1996), *Falstaff (1978), Prospero (1976), Titus (1978, 1980), Feste (1980), and Ghost and First Gravedigger (1994). He has also directed for the company.

I

illustrations of Shakespeare's plays The only illustration of a Shakespeare play surviving from his own time is in the *Longleat manuscript. Some information about the many later drawings and paintings inspired by the plays is given under the names of individual artists.

image cluster Certain images seem regularly to have led Shakespeare's mind along a train of associated ones. Walter *Whiter, in his *Specimen of a Commentary on Shakespeare* (1794), showed that flattery suggested dogs, which suggested sweetmeats. The phenomenon was more fully discussed by E. A. Armstrong in his *Shakespeare's Imagination: A Study of the Psychology of Association and Inspiration* (1946), and is used by Kenneth *Muir as evidence of authorship in his *Shakespeare as Collaborator* (1960).

imagery Both the verse and the prose in Shakespeare's plays contain images which can serve various purposes, and the imagery can also extend to visual and auditory effects.

The study of Shakespeare's imagery goes back to the late eighteenth century (*see* WHITER, WALTER), but first became prominent in the 1930s, under the influence of the movement known as the New Criticism, and forming a reaction against study of the plays centred on character criticism.

Caroline *Spurgeon's pioneering *Shakespeare's Imagery and What it Tells Us* (1935) identified prominent image patterns in a number of the plays, and, less happily, extends the investigation to an attempt to define Shakespeare's personality and temperament through deductions from his imagery.

W. H. *Clemen's *The Development of Shakespeare's Imagery* (1936, translated 1951) is a more truly critical study, revealing how recurrent imagery can convey meaning, and also showing how metaphor takes over from simile as a vehicle of imagery in Shakespeare's later plays.

Many other critics have used the study of imagery as an instrument in the critical examination of the plays, notably G. Wilson *Knight.

BERNARD LEVIN *(1928–2004) on Shakespeare's impact on the English language; from* Enthusiasms *(1983)*

If you cannot understand my argument, and declare 'It's Greek to me', you are quoting Shakespeare; if you claim to be more sinned against than sinning, you are quoting Shakespeare; if you recall your salad days, you are quoting Shakespeare; if you act more in sorrow than in anger, if your wish is father to the thought, if your lost property has vanished into thin air, you are quoting Shakespeare; if you have ever refused to budge an inch or suffered from green-eyed jealousy, if you have played fast and loose, if you have been tongue-tied, a tower of strength, hoodwinked or in a pickle, if you have knitted your brows, made a virtue of necessity, insisted on fair play, slept not one wink, stood on ceremony, danced attendance (on your lord and master), laughed yourself into stitches, had short shrift, cold comfort or too much of a good thing, if you have seen better days or lived in a fool's paradise— why, be that as it may, the more fool you, for it is a foregone conclusion that you are (as good luck would have it) quoting Shakespeare; if you think it is early days and clear out bag and baggage, if you think it is high time and that that is the long and short of it, if you believe that the game is up and that truth will out even if it involves your own flesh and blood, if you lie low till the crack of doom because you suspect foul play, if you have your teeth set on edge (at one fell swoop) without rhyme or reason, then—to give the devil his due—if the truth were known (for surely you have a tongue in your head) you are quoting Shakespeare; even if you bid me good riddance and send me packing, if you wish I was dead as a doornail, if you think I am an eyesore, a laughing stock, the devil incarnate, a stony-hearted villain, bloody-minded or a blinking idiot, then—by Jove! O Lord! Tut, tut! for goodness' sake! what the dickens! but me no buts—it is all one to me, for you are quoting Shakespeare.

Induction Part of a play which lies outside, but leads into, the main action. The most obvious example in Shakespeare is the opening episode of *The *Taming of the Shrew*. The First *Folio also gives this label to Rumour's speech which introduces 2 *Henry IV*.

Ingratitude of a Commonwealth, The *See* CORIOLANUS.

Injured Princess, The, or The Fatal Wager *See* CYMBELINE.

inner stage Many plays of Shakespeare's time call for an area at the back of the stage where characters may be revealed, from which a bed may be put forth (as in *Othello*, v. ii), or which could suggest at least the opening of a cave (as in *Cymbeline*, III. iii). Some historians have believed that there was an inner stage area at the back of the main acting area, and the term 'inner stage' (not found in Elizabethan times) was created to describe it. The general current belief is that while some theatres, at least, may have had a large door or a curtain at the back of the stage which could open to reveal an area where characters or properties could be revealed, this was no more than an extension of the main platform, on which all the main action would take place. An alternative theory suggests that one or more curtained booths were set against the back wall, and that they could open to reveal characters or properties.

Inns of Court Four London law colleges: Gray's Inn, the *Middle Temple, the Inner Temple, and Lincoln's Inn. The first two particularly were famous for their masques and revels. *The *Comedy of Errors* was played at Gray's Inn in 1594, and *Twelfth Night* at the Middle Temple in 1602. It has been conjectured of more than one Shakespeare play that it was specifically written to be performed at an Inn of Court, but there is no external evidence.

inn yards The rectangular yards of inns, surrounded by galleries or balconies, were sometimes used for theatrical performances during the sixteenth century. A stage could be set up against one wall, and some inns were taken over entirely for this purpose. A City of London regulation of 1576 referred to 'evil practices of incontinency in great inns having chambers and secret places adjoining to their open stages and galleries.' This may have encouraged James *Burbage to build the *Theatre in 1576, but performances continued to be given in inns from time to time.

International Shakespeare Association An association founded after the first *World Shakespeare Congress in Vancouver in 1971, to further the development of Shakespearian interests and to plan other World Congresses. The Association has organized six Congresses: in Washington, DC (1976), Stratford-upon-Avon (1981), Berlin (1986),

Tokyo (1991), Los Angeles (1996) and Valencia (2001). Occasional papers are published for members and smaller conferences held between the Congresses. The headquarters of the Association is at the *Shakespeare Centre, Stratford-upon-Avon.

International Shakespeare Globe Centre The name given to the reconstruction of the Globe Theatre and its associated activities at Bankside, London. The reconstruction is a remarkable achievement based on pictorial evidence, clues provided by play texts, archaeological research, and knowledge of Elizabethan building techniques. Despite this research, there is no consensus on the exact dimensions of the original theatre and stage. The Globe became a producing theatre in 1996 under the artistic directorship of Mark *Rylance who appeared in The *Two Gentlemen of Verona. The first full season in 1997 provided a combination of plays both by Shakespeare and other contemporary dramatists, including *Henry V, The *Winter's Tale, A Chaste Maid in Cheapside, and The Maid's Tragedy. The ISGC also has an education department providing a variety of lectures, tours, and workshops for students.

Invader of his Country, The See DENNIS, JOHN, AND CORIOLANUS.

Ireland, William Henry (1775–1835) A London lawyer's clerk who forged many documents purporting to relate to Shakespeare, including a letter to Anne *Hathaway with a lock of her hair. He also wrote a Shakespeare play, Vortigern. The papers were published late in 1795 (dated 1796), deceiving many eminent persons, but in March 1796 Edmond *Malone published an Inquiry demonstrating that they were inauthentic. A few days later, Vortigern was given its single performance, at *Drury Lane. Later that year, Ireland published An Authentic Account of the Shakespear Manuscripts, admitting his responsibility. A rare revival of Vortigern was staged at the Bridewell Theatre, London, in 1997.

Irving, Sir Henry (1838–1905) The greatest actor–manager of his time: his first major success was as Hamlet in a production of 1874. From 1878 to 1902 he owned and managed the *Lyceum Theatre, London, appearing in many Shakespearian roles, including Richard III, Hamlet, Shylock, Othello, Iago, Romeo, Benedick, Macbeth, Wolsey, Lear, Iachimo, and Coriolanus. His leading lady was Ellen *Terry, and his productions were prepared with great care for visual effect. He was at his best in roles requiring the presentation of intellectuality,

WASHINGTON IRVING *(1783–1859) visits Shakespeare's Birthplace; from* Stratford-upon-Avon: *from* The Sketch-Book *(1819–20)*

The house is shown by a garrulous old lady, in a frosty red face, lighted up by a cold blue anxious eye, and garnished with artificial locks of flaxen hair, curling from under an exceedingly dirty cap. She was peculiarly assiduous in exhibiting the relics with which this, like all other celebrated shrines, abounds. There was the shattered stock of the very matchlock with which Shakspeare shot the deer, on his poaching exploits. There, too, was his tobacco-box, which proves that he was a rival smoker of Sir Walter Raleigh; the sword also with which he played Hamlet; and the identical lantern with which Friar Laurence discovered Romeo and Juliet at the tomb! There was an ample supply also of Shakespeare's mulberry-tree, which seems to have as extraordinary powers of self-multiplication as the wood of the true cross; of which there is enough extant to build a ship of the line.

such as Hamlet and Iago. In 1895 he became the first actor to be knighted. See Alan Hughes, *Henry Irving, Shakespearean* (1981).

Irving, Washington (1783–1859) American writer whose *Sketch-Book* (1819–20) includes an account of a visit to Shakespeare's *Birthplace.

italic hand A style of handwriting beginning to come into use in Shakespeare's time; it eventually displaced the *secretary hand, and is closer to modern handwriting.

J

Jackson, Sir Barry (1879–1961) Founder in 1913 of the Birmingham Repertory Theatre, where the many Shakespeare productions included influential *modern-dress versions of *Cymbeline* (1923), *Hamlet* (1925–6), and *Macbeth* (1928). He directed the Shakespeare Memorial Theatre at Stratford-upon-Avon from 1945 to 1948.

Jackson, Glenda (1936–) British actress known for strong, forceful interpretations of Shakespeare heroines. Shakespeare roles include Princess of France, Ophelia (1965), Cleopatra (1978, all *RSC), Lady Macbeth (1988, New York). Gave up her career in acting to become a Labour MP in 1992.

Jacobi, Sir Derek (1938–) British actor whose poetic voice has led to comparisons with John *Gielgud. Shakespeare roles include Touchstone (1967), King of Navarre (1968, both *Old Vic), Aguecheek, Pericles (both 1973), Hamlet, Octavius Caesar (all 1977, *Prospect Theatre Company), Benedick, Prospero (both 1982, *Royal Shakespeare Company), Richard II, Richard III (both 1988, Phoenix Theatre), Macbeth (1993, RSC). In 1988 directed *Hamlet* for the Renaissance Theatre Company, and appeared as the Chorus and Claudius in the films of *Henry V* (1989) and *Hamlet* (1996).

Jaggard, William (1569–1623) Printer, with his son Isaac (1595–1627), of the First *Folio (1623), and also (independently) of The *Passionate Pilgrim* (1599). In 1619, with Thomas Pavier, he issued a collection of ten Shakespearian and pseudo-Shakespearian plays. After they started to appear, the Lord Chamberlain ordered the Stationers' Company not to reprint any of the *King's Men's plays without the actors' consent, and this is probably why some of the editions are falsely dated 1600.

James I, King of England (1566–1625) The only child of Mary Queen of Scots, he became James VI of Scotland in 1567 and in 1589 married Princess Anne of Denmark. He succeeded Queen *Elizabeth I in March 1603, and gave his royal patent to Shakespeare's company, the *Lord Chamberlain's Men, making them the King's Men. In 1604

Shakespeare was one of nine members of the company to whom James gave four-and-a-half yards of red cloth for livery to walk in the Coronation procession.

Many of Shakespeare's plays were acted at Court during James's reign, and *Macbeth seems especially relevant to James's interests. Attempts have been made to identify him and members of his family more or less closely with characters in a number of Shakespeare's other plays, but the evidence is speculative.

Janssen, Gheerart (fl. 1600–23) Son of a Dutch sculptor who emigrated from Amsterdam to London about 1567. The family had a workshop in Southwark, London, and Gheerart made Shakespeare's *monument.

Jenkins, Thomas Schoolmaster of Stratford-upon-Avon *Grammar School, 1575–9.

jig A satirical, song-and-dance entertainment customarily performed as an after-piece at certain theatres in Shakespeare's time. In 1612 the Middlesex justices of the peace made an order suppressing jigs because they provoked breaches of the peace. Very few examples survive.

Johnson, Charles *See* As You Like It.

Johnson, Robert (*c*.1583–1633) Lutenist and composer who wrote music for many of the *King's Men's masques and plays. His only Shakespeare settings known to have survived are of 'Full Fathom Five' and 'Where the Bee Sucks', from The *Tempest*, and appear to have been

---

Dr Samuel Johnson *(1709–84) in praise of Shakespeare; Prologue spoken by David Garrick at the opening of Drury Lane Theatre, 1747*

When Learning's triumph o'er her barb'rous foes
First rear'd the stage, immortal Shakespeare rose;
Each change of many-coloured life he drew,
Exhausted worlds, and then imagined new:
Existence saw him spurn her bounded reign,
And panting Time toil'd after him in vain:
His powerful strokes presiding truth impress'd,
And unresisted passion storm'd the breast.

THOMAS FULLER *(1608–61): Shakespeare and Jonson; from* The History of the Worthies of England *(1662)*

Many were the wit-combats betwixt him and Ben Jonson; which two I behold like a Spanish great galleon and an English man of war: Master Jonson (like the former) was built far higher in learning; solid, but slow in his performances. Shakespeare, with the English man of war, lesser in bulk, but lighter in sailing, could turn with all tides, tack about, and take advantage of all winds, by the quickness of his wit and invention.

---

written for a Court performance in 1612 or 1613 during the celebrations of Princess Elizabeth's marriage.

Johnson, Samuel (1709–84) The great English essayist, biographer, poet, editor, lexicographer, and conversationalist first published proposals for a new edition of Shakespeare in 1745, then again in 1756, but his edition, with its famous Preface, did not appear until 1765. A useful compilation of his Shakespeare criticism is the Penguin *Samuel Johnson on Shakespeare*, edited by Henry Woudhuysen (1989).

Jonson, Ben (1572–1637) Shakespeare's most distinguished contemporary playwright. There are some certain and some possible allusions to Shakespeare in a number of his plays. His *Conversations with William Drummond*, of 1618–19, include informal comments, such as 'That Shakespeare wanted art'. The First *Folio includes his lines 'To the Reader', placed opposite the portrait of Shakespeare, and his famous verse elegy 'To the Memory of my Beloved, the Author Master William Shakespeare, and what he hath left us', in which he refers to Shakespeare's 'small Latin and less Greek', but declares 'He was not of an age, but for all time!' In his 'Ode to Himself', written *c*.1629, he alludes to the 'mouldy tale' of *Pericles*, and in notebooks, published as *Timber: or Discoveries Made upon Men and Matter*, wrote 'the players have often mentioned it as an honour to Shakespeare that in his writing, whatsoever he penned, he never blotted out line. My answer hath been, would he had blotted a thousand . . . I loved the man, and do honour his memory (on this side idolatry) as much as any. He was, indeed, honest, and of an open and free nature; had an excellent fancy, brave notions, and gentle expressions, wherein he flowed with that facility, that sometime it was necessary he should be stopped . . . But he redeemed his vices with his virtues. There was ever more in him to be praised than to be pardoned.' Shakespeare is known to have acted in Jonson's plays *Every Man in his Humour* (1598) and *Sejanus* (1603).

Jordan, Dorothea (1762–1816) Irish actress who became the mistress of the Duke of Clarence, later King William IV. She excelled in comedy, and her best Shakespeare performances were as Rosalind, Viola, and Imogen. There is an excellent biography by Claire Tomalin (1995).

Jordan, John (1746–1809) A self-educated wheelwright, poet, and antiquarian, born at Tiddington, near Stratford-upon-Avon, who collected (and elaborated) anecdotes about Shakespeare (*see* VILLAGES, THE SHAKESPEARE), and concerned himself with the Shakespeare properties. He appears to be responsible for the identification of *Mary Arden's House, and assisted Edmond *Malone with his investigations into the *'spiritual testament' of John *Shakespeare.

Jubilee *See* GARRICK, DAVID.

Julius Caesar Shakespeare's Roman tragedy, based fairly closely on the translation of *Plutarch by Sir Thomas *North, was first printed in the First *Folio (1623), but there is an apparent reference to a performance of it at the *Globe on 21 September 1599 in a notebook of Thomas *Platter. It has been a popular play in the theatre. After the Restoration, it was played, with little alteration, by the *King's Company. Thomas *Betterton played Brutus frequently from 1684 to 1709. An adaptation published in 1719 and acted at *Drury Lane continued to influence performances for a century.

Though David *Garrick did not put the play on while he was manager of Drury Lane, it was played regularly at *Covent Garden until 1767, after which there were only eight more London performances until 1780, and then none until J. P. *Kemble's revival at Covent Garden in 1812, with Kemble as Brutus. W. C. *Macready played first Cassius then Brutus, and Samuel *Phelps was a distinguished Brutus.

Performances by the Duke of Saxe-Meiningen's company at Drury Lane in 1881 were famous for the handling of the crowd scenes. Beerbohm *Tree played Mark Antony in a spectacular production at Her Majesty's in 1898, many times revived. During the twentieth century, *Julius Caesar* has been played frequently at Stratford-upon-

Avon and the *Old Vic. A *modern-dress version at the Embassy Theatre, London, in 1939 set it in Mussolini's Italy. John *Gielgud was a powerful Cassius at Stratford-upon-Avon in 1950 and in Joseph Mankiewicz's film (1952), which also had James Mason as Brutus and Marlon Brando as Mark Antony. Gielgud also played Caesar at the *National Theatre in 1977. In America in the later part of the nineteenth century Edwin *Booth and Laurence Barrett frequently played together as Brutus and Cassius. Orson *Welles used modern dress in his successful New York production (1937), in which he played Brutus. There have been frequent revivals at Stratford-upon-Avon, including David Thacker's 1993 touring promenade production, and Peter *Hall's 1995 production which used amateur actors for the crowd scenes.

Julius Caesar is a powerful, male-dominated drama of the political life in which Shakespeare returns to a consideration of the functions and responsibilities of rulers and of the consequences of usurpation such as had preoccupied him in the English history plays. Its demonstration of the uses and abuses of rhetoric is part of his constant concern with language. At the same time, the inward portrayal of Brutus looks forward to the even more profound examinations of men under stress that were to follow in the great tragedies.

K

Kean, Charles (1811–68) Son of *Edmund, educated at Eton; married Ellen Tree. In 1850 he began to manage the Princess's Theatre, where for nine years he presented and acted in spectacular productions of Shakespeare's plays with great attention to accuracy of historical detail.

Kean, Edmund (1787?–1833) One of the greatest of English actors. His first triumph was as Shylock at *Drury Lane in 1814, when William *Hazlitt luckily happened to be present. His Shakespeare roles also included Hamlet, Richard III, Macbeth, Othello, and Lear. He lived recklessly, and in his later years became unreliable. Coleridge said 'to see him act is like reading Shakespeare by flashes of lightning'.

Keeling, William Captain of the *Dragon*, an East India Company ship which in 1607, along with *Hector* and *Consent*, journeyed to the East Indies. His journal tells of performances of Shakespeare's plays on the High Seas, off Sierra Leone: 5 September: 'I sent the interpreter, according to his desire, aboard the *Hector* where he broke fast, and after came aboard me, where we gave the tragedy of *Hamlet*'; 30 September: 'Captain Hawkins [of the *Hector*] dined with me, where my companions acted *King Richard the Second*'; 31 March 1608: 'I invited Captain Hawkins to a fish dinner, and had *Hamlet* acted aboard me; which I permit to keep my people from idleness and unlawful games, or sleep.'

Kemble, Charles (1775–1854) English actor, brother of *John Philip, who played a wide range of Shakespeare roles. He followed his brother as manager of *Covent Garden where in 1823, with the help of J. R. *Planché, he put on a production of *King John* which inaugurated the fashion for accuracy in historical detail.

Kemble, Frances (Fanny) Anne (1809–93) *Charles's daughter, who at the age of nineteen had a great success at *Covent Garden as Juliet to her father's Mercutio. She played Portia, Beatrice, Lady Macbeth, and other leading roles. In 1832 she went with her father to America where she married Pierce Butler, a plantation owner. She divorced him because of her aversion to slavery in 1848, and in later years gave many readings in England and America, as well as writing several books.

Kemble, John Philip (1757–1823) Brother of Sarah *Siddons, manager of *Drury Lane from 1788 to 1802, and of *Covent Garden from 1803 till his retirement in 1817. He produced and acted in many of Shakespeare's plays, and was best in stately and declamatory roles. He was successful as Hamlet, King John, Macbeth, Othello, Brutus, and Coriolanus.

Kemp, Will Actor with the Lord Chamberlain's Men from 1594 to 1599; listed as one of the 'principal actors' in the First *Folio. Famous as a comedian; his name appears in the stage directions to the second *quarto of *Romeo and Juliet as Peter, and in the 1600 quarto of *Much Ado About Nothing as Dogberry, suggesting that Shakespeare wrote these parts for him. In 1600, for a bet, he morris-danced from London to Norwich, nearly one hundred miles, and wrote a book about it. There is no record of him after 1603.

Kesselstadt death mask A death mask once in the possession of the Kesselstadt family, who lived in and near Cologne. The mask was found in a junk-shop at Mainz in 1849, and was said to resemble a picture dated 1637, traditionally supposed to represent Shakespeare lying in state, which also had belonged to the Kesselstadt family. Otherwise the mask has nothing to connect it with Shakespeare beyond the fact that it is dated 1616. The date is probably false: no other death masks of non-royal persons are known to have been made at that time.

Will Kemp: from the title-page of Kemp's Nine Days' Wonder, Performed in a Dance from London to Norwich, *published in 1600*

Killigrew, Thomas (1612–83) Like Sir William *Davenant, he was a dramatist and theatre manager who was active before the closing of the theatres, in 1642, and who was granted a patent in 1660 enabling him to form an acting company and to manage a theatre. Killigrew established the King's Men, playing for a short time in Vere Street, then, in 1663, in the Theatre Royal, *Drury Lane. The right to perform Shakespeare's plays was divided between Killigrew and Davenant (*see* PATENT THEATRES).

King John Shakespeare's play was first printed in the First *Folio (1623), probably from his manuscript. It was mentioned by Francis *Meres in 1598, and probably dates from a few years earlier. In structure, though not in language, it is closely based on an anonymous play, The *Troublesome Reign of John, King of England*, printed in 1591. Shakespeare greatly reduced the anti-Catholic bias of his source.

The first recorded production of *King John* was at *Covent Garden in 1737, but censored oaths in the *Folio suggest it was staged during Shakespeare's lifetime. In the same year, Colley *Cibber adapted it as *Papal Tyranny in the Reign of King John*, reverting to the anti-Catholic position of the source play. Cibber's version was performed at Covent Garden in 1745, when it was of topical interest because of Jacobite risings. David *Garrick played Shakespeare's *King John* at *Drury Lane five nights later. In 1800 Richard Valpy, headmaster of Reading School, prepared a version which incorporated some of Cibber's alterations, and this had a few performances at Covent Garden in 1803.

King John was popular in the nineteenth century. John Philip *Kemble appeared frequently as the King from 1783 to 1817, often with Sarah *Siddons as a great Constance. A production at Covent Garden in 1823 is important because Charles *Kemble, who played the Bastard, commissioned J. R. *Planché to design historically accurate costumes and settings. This inaugurated the trend in methods of staging Shakespeare which was rapidly to become dominant for the rest of the century. W. C. *Macready mounted the play spectacularly in 1842. Samuel *Phelps staged it at *Sadler's Wells in 1844, and again at Drury Lane, with great success, in 1865. The archaeological style of production reached its peak with Charles *Kean at the Princess's Theatre in the 1850s; he gave *King John* in 1852 and 1858. Beerbohm *Tree's spectacular production at Her Majesty's in 1899 included an elaborate dumb-show of the signing of Magna Carta, an episode that Shakespeare failed to provide. Tree's portrayal of John's death became the first film of a Shakespeare performance, in 1899.

King John's theatrical popularity has waned during the twentieth century, though there have been a number of productions in Stratford-upon-Avon, London, and elsewhere. The *Old Vic had Ralph *Richardson as the Bastard in 1931, Ernest Milton as the King and Sybil *Thorndike as Constance in 1941, and Richard *Burton as the Bastard in 1953. Peter *Brook directed Paul *Scofield as the Bastard in Birmingham in 1945. At Stratford-upon-Avon, Robert Helpmann played the King in 1948, and Robert Harris in 1957, with Alec Clunes as the Bastard. There also, in 1974, John *Barton directed his radical adaptation, omitting about 1,200 lines of Shakespeare, and incorporating many lines from *The Troublesome Reign* and many more of his own composition. Deborah *Warner's full text production (Stratford-upon-Avon, 1988) demonstrated the play could succeed without embellishment. Gregory Doran directed a successful production in the Swan Theatre in 2001.

The changing fortunes of the play are an interesting index to fluctuations in taste. So is the relative importance accorded to the King and the Bastard. Prince Arthur has often been played by a girl. Constance's lament over his absence (III. iv. 93–105)—not over his death—has often been interpreted as a reflection of Shakespeare's grief for the death of his son, *Hamnet, in August 1596, but this requires a later date for the play's composition than is suggested by stylistic evidence.

King Lear Shakespeare's tragedy was entered in the *Stationers' Register on 26 November 1607 'as it was played before the King's Majesty at Whitehall upon St Stephen's Night at Christmas last by his Majesty's servants playing usually at the Globe on the Bankside.' It was printed in 1608 'for Nathaniel Butter . . . to be sold at his shop in Paul's Churchyard at the sign of the Pied Bull near St Austin's Gate.' This text, known as the *Pied Bull Quarto, was reprinted with corrections and additions in 1619 (*see* JAGGARD, WILLIAM). The First *Folio text contains 100 lines not in Q1, which contains about 300 not in the Folio. Editors have traditionally conflated these texts, but many modern scholars believe that the Quarto represents Shakespeare's first version of the play, written about 1605–6, and the Folio his revision, of about 1609–10. The *Oxford Shakespeare prints texts based on both.

The play's sources include an anonymous play, *The True Chronicle History of* *King Leir (printed in 1605), *Sidney's *Arcadia* (for the Gloucester plot), and Samuel *Harsnett's *A Declaration of Egregious Popish Impostures*, published in 1603.

A performance in Yorkshire in 1610 is recorded. In 1681, Nahum *Tate's adaptation was performed, with Thomas *Betterton as Lear, and published. Tate makes Edgar and Cordelia lovers, omits the Fool altogether, and gives the play a happy ending, with Lear, Kent, and Gloucester going into peaceful retirement. Tate's play kept Shakespeare's off the stage for a century and a half, though revisions by David *Garrick (1756) and George *Colman (1768) brought it closer to the original without restoring either the Fool or the tragic ending. Garrick was a great Lear. J. P. *Kemble played the part well from 1788, and Edmund *Kean was successful in 1820. In 1823 he acted in a version which restored the tragic ending, but it was not well received, and he soon reverted to Tate.

W. C. *Macready played Lear from 1834, restoring parts of Shakespeare, and in 1838 played in a text purged of Tate's rewritings, and including the Fool (played by a woman), though rearranged and abbreviated. Samuel *Phelps played Lear finely, in a much purer text and with a man as the Fool, at *Sadler's Wells in 1845 and later. Charles *Kean's version (1858) was, as usual, retrogressive. Henry *Irving's Lear at the *Lyceum (1892) cut much of the text and was not one of his most successful productions.

In the early years of the twentieth century, the play had comparatively few major productions. John *Gielgud played Lear in 1931, 1940 (co-directed by Harley *Granville-Barker, whose *Preface* (1927) had a great influence), and 1955. Donald *Wolfit was greatly admired in the role during the 1940s and '50s. Laurence *Olivier played Lear at the New Theatre for the *Old Vic in 1946 and for television in 1983. Peter *Brook's Stratford-upon-Avon production of 1962, filmed in 1970, had Paul *Scofield as a fine Lear. Robert *Stephens gave a fine performance as Lear in his last Shakespeare role (Stratford-upon-Avon, 1993), and 1997 saw two major revivals with Ian *Holm and Alan *Howard taking the lead at the *Royal National Theatre and Old Vic.

The first really distinguished American interpreter of the role was Edwin *Forrest, who played it over forty-five years from 1826. Edwin *Booth played first in Tate's adaptation, but gave impressive performances in the original play from 1870. Robert Mantell played Lear successfully from 1905, and Morris Carnovsky impressed at Stratford,

Connecticut in 1963 and 1965. Grigori *Kozintsev's film version (1970) made a profound impression.

Reduced by Tate, and often regarded as unplayable, partly perhaps under the influence of Charles *Lamb's essay, 'On the Tragedies of Shakespeare Considered with Reference to their Fitness for Stage Representation' (1811), *King Lear*'s true stature has only been appreciated during the twentieth century, when, partly under the influence of Granville-Barker's *Preface*, it has come to be recognized as perhaps Shakespeare's most profound examination of the human condition.

King Leir, The True Chronicle History of A play entered in the *Stationers' Register in 1594 and published anonymously in 1605; a source of *King Lear*.

King's Men *See* LORD CHAMBERLAIN'S MEN; *also* KILLIGREW, THOMAS.

Kirkman, Francis *See* DROLLS.

Kiss Me, Kate A musical by Cole Porter (1893–1964) based on *The *Taming of the Shrew*.

Kittredge, George Lyman (1860–1941) Harvard scholar, revered by his pupils, versatile in his interests, who edited the whole of Shakespeare (1936) and published *Sixteen Plays* (1946) with excellent annotation.

Knight, G. Wilson (1897–1985) Professor of English at the Universities of Toronto and Leeds, author of studies of seminal importance in the criticism of Shakespeare's plays, including *The Wheel of Fire* (1930, enlarged 1949), *The Imperial Theme* (1931), *The Shakespearian Tempest* (1932), *The Sovereign Flower* (1958), and *Shakespeare and Religion: Essays of Forty Years* (1967).

Knight of the Burning Pestle, The *See* BEAUMONT, FRANCIS.

Komisarjevsky, Theodore (1882–1954) Russian theatre director who emigrated to England in 1919 and directed some of Shakespeare's plays in a modern, fantasticated style at Stratford-upon-Avon and elsewhere. His best-known Stratford-upon-Avon productions were a 'steel' *Macbeth* (1933), *King Lear* with Randle Ayrton (1936), and *The *Comedy of Errors* (1938–9). See Ralph Berry, 'Komisarjevsky at Stratford-upon-Avon', *Shakespeare Survey 36* (1983).

Kozintsev, Grigori (1905–73) Russian film director, best known in the West for his book *Shakespeare: Time and Conscience* (1967), and for his films of *Hamlet* (1964) and *King Lear* (1970).

Kurosawa, Akira (1910–98) Japanese film director best known in the West for his adaptations of *Macbeth* (The *Throne of Blood*, 1957), and *King Lear* (Ran, 1985). There is also an adaptation of *Hamlet* (The Bad Sleep Well, 1963).

Kyd, Thomas (1558–94) Author of the popular and influential play *The Spanish Tragedy* (c.1587); the *Ur-Hamlet* is sometimes attributed to him.

L

Lamb, Charles (1775–1834) Author with his sister, Mary, of the well-known *Tales from Shakespeare* (1807); his criticism includes the essay 'On the Tragedies of Shakespeare Considered with Reference to their Fitness for Stage Representation' (1811), arguing that the plays suffer in performance, a view which may be related to the conditions of performance in his time.

Lampe, John Frederick (*c.*1703–51) German musician who wrote a new version of *The Comick Masque of Pyramus and Thisbe*, by Richard *Leveridge, which was performed at *Covent Garden in 1745.

Langham, Michael (1919–) Artistic Director of *Stratford, Ontario, Shakespeare Festival 1956–67, Artistic Director of Guthrie Theatre, Minneapolis, 1971–7. He has often attempted to create a Canadian identity by playing Shakespeare in modern dress and making contemporary analogies. His productions include *Henry V, *Hamlet, (both 1956, *Shakespeare Memorial Theatre), *Love's Labour's Lost (1961), *Troilus and Cressida (1963), *Timon of Athens (1963, 1992), The *Merchant of Venice (1988; all Stratford, Ontario).

Lanier, Emilia (*c.*1569–1645) English-born poet; daughter of a musician, Baptista Bassano; wife of a composer, Alphonso Lanier. According to an entry in the notebooks of Simon *Forman in 1597, she had been the mistress of Lord Hunsdon (*see* LORD CHAMBERLAIN'S MEN). A. L. Rowse has claimed her as the *Dark Lady of the Sonnets. For an edition of her works see *The Poems of Aemilia Lanyer*, edited by Susanne Woods (Oxford, 1993).

Late Plays A term given to *Pericles, *Cymbeline, The *Winter's Tale, and The *Tempest, sometimes extended to include *All is True (Henry VIII) and The *Two Noble Kinsmen. Sometimes also called the Last Plays.

Law Against Lovers, The William *Davenant's adaptation of *Measure for Measure, which includes Beatrice and Benedick from *Much Ado About Nothing, performed in 1662 and not known to have been revived, though it was itself adapted by Charles *Gildon.

Leopold Shakespeare A popular one-volume edition published in 1877 with an introduction by F. J. Furnivall and the text prepared by the German scholar Nikolaus Delius, dedicated to Prince Leopold, Queen Victoria's youngest son.

Lepage, Robert (1957–) Canadian director whose experimental productions have included a bilingual *Roméo et Juliette* (1992), a Shakespeare collage *Shakespeare Rapid Eye Movement* (1993), and *Elsinore* (1996), a one-man multi-media reworking of *Hamlet.* He became the first North American to direct at the *Royal National Theatre with A *Midsummer Night's Dream* (1992). His other productions include *Macbeth*, and *Coriolan* (Théâtre Repère, Paris, 1993).

Leveridge, Richard (*c.*1670–1758) English singer and composer who probably wrote some of the once-popular incidental music for *Macbeth* attributed to Matthew *Locke, and who also composed several settings of lyrics by Shakespeare, as well as a burlesque of Italian opera, *The Comick Masque of Pyramus and Thisbe*, based on *A *Midsummer Night's Dream* and performed at *Lincoln's Inn Fields in 1716.

Lichtenberg, Georg Christoph (1742–99) A German scientist and philosopher who made two visits to England, in 1770 and 1774–5. His published letters from England to his friends at home include some vivid accounts of visits to the theatre, and especially of performances by *Garrick.

Liebesverbot, Das *See* WAGNER, RICHARD.

Lincoln's Inn Fields Theatre, London Originally Lisle's Tennis Court, built in 1656 and converted into a theatre by Sir William *Davenant in 1661, for the Duke's Men. It was the first public theatre to have a proscenium arch and to use variable scenery. On 28 August 1661, *Pepys saw *Hamlet there, 'done with scenes very well, but above all Betterton did the prince's part beyond imagination.' Davenant died in 1668, but his widow, along with Henry Harris and Thomas *Betterton, continued to manage the theatre until the *Dorset Gardens Theatre opened in 1671. Lincoln's Inn Fields became a tennis-court again, except for its use as a theatre by *Killigrew's company in 1672–4, until 1695, when Betterton returned there. The building ceased to be used as a theatre in 1732, but was not demolished till 1848.

Linley, Thomas, the younger (1756–78) English composer, friend of Mozart, who died at the age of 22. His compositions include a fine '*Ode on the Fairies, Aeriel Beings, and Witches of Shakespeare*', performed at *Drury Lane in 1776, and incidental music for a production of *The *Tempest* at Drury Lane in 1777.

location of scenes With very few exceptions, the early editions of Shakespeare's plays do not indicate the locality of the action. Later editions frequently added indications, often influenced by pictorial and representational methods of staging. The current editorial trend is to omit scene locations.

Locke, Matthew (*c*.1630–77) English composer of music for productions of *Macbeth* in the late seventeenth century, though some of the music for this play traditionally ascribed to him is probably by Richard *Leveridge (*c*.1670–1758). Locke also wrote music for *The *Tempest* (1674) and a setting of 'Orpheus with his lute', from *Henry VIII* (published in 1673).

Locrine An anonymous tragedy, entered in the *Stationers' Register in 1594, published in 1595 as 'newly set forth, overseen and corrected by W.S.', and attributed to Shakespeare in the seventeenth century (*see* APOCRYPHAL WORKS).

Lodge, Thomas (*c*.1557–1625) English author of *Rosalynde*; his *Wit's Misery* (1596) refers to an *Ur-Hamlet*: 'the vizard of the ghost which cried so miserably at the Theatre, like an oyster-wife, "Hamlet, revenge!"'

London Prodigal, The An anonymous play published in 1605 as by Shakespeare and included in the second issue of the Third *Folio, no longer ascribed to Shakespeare.

Longleat manuscript A single leaf in the library of the Marquess of Bath at Longleat, signed by Henry Peacham (*c*.1576–1643), a teacher and artist. Usually dated 1594 or 1595, it bears a transcript of forty lines from various parts of *Titus Andronicus* and a drawing roughly illustrating the first scene.

The drawing is of exceptional interest as the first illustration to a Shakespeare play. Whether it is based on performance, public or private, is not known. Aaron is shown as a negro; the major characters wear Roman costume, but the attendants are clearly Elizabethan. The manuscript is discussed by, among others, J. Dover *Wilson in

The Longleat drawing of Titus Andronicus, *showing a mixture of sixteenth-century and classical costumes*

Shakespeare Survey 1 (1948) and E. M. Waith in his Oxford edition (1984).

Lopez, Roderigo A Jewish physician to Queen *Elizabeth, hanged for conspiracy in a plot against her in 1594. Graziano's statement that Shylock's 'currish spirit/Governed a wolf . . . hanged for human slaughter' (*Merchant of Venice*, IV. i. 132–3), is sometimes interpreted as an allusion to him.

Lord Chamberlain A senior official of the royal household, immediately superior to the *Master of the Revels, in charge of all Court entertainments. *See* LORD CHAMBERLAIN'S MEN.

Lord Chamberlain's Men A theatre company formed in 1594 under the patronage of Henry Carey, 1st Lord Hunsdon, Lord Chamberlain from 1585 till his death in 1596. Shakespeare may have been an original member; he was prominent within it by March 1595, and remained with it as shareholder and playwright for the rest of his career.

In its early years, the company performed mainly at the *Theatre, then at the Curtain. It was known as Hunsdon's Men between July 1596 and March 1597, when the second Lord Hunsdon was appointed Lord Chamberlain. By 1599 it occupied the *Globe Theatre, and for the next ten years was the leading London company, with unusually stable membership, and with Richard *Burbage as its principal actor.

In 1603, when *James I succeeded *Elizabeth, he gave the company a royal patent, and it became the King's Men. From 1603 to 1616 it played an average of twelve performances a year at Court. James supplied nine members, including Shakespeare, with four-and-a-half yards of red cloth each to make liveries to wear in his coronation procession.

In late 1608 the company bought the *Blackfriars Theatre, and probably started using it as their winter house in 1609. The Globe burned down in 1613, and was rebuilt the following year. The company continued to be successful till the closing of the theatres, in 1642.

Lords' Room An area in some Elizabethan theatres reserved for distinguished patrons; once thought to be the gallery above the stage, it is more likely to have been part of the gallery on stage level.

lost years, Shakespeare's Nothing is known of Shakespeare between the birth of his twins in 1585 and Robert *Greene's reference to him in London in 1592. There are many legends such as John *Aubrey's report that he was 'a schoolmaster in the country', and there has been much speculation. Considering how much he had written by 1598, it seems likely that he began to write some years before 1592.

Love Betrayed *See* TWELFTH NIGHT.

Love in a Forest *See* AS YOU LIKE IT.

Lover's Complaint, A A poem published in the first edition of Shakespeare's *Sonnets (1609) and there stated to be his; its authenticity, once doubted, is now generally accepted.

Love's Labour's Lost Shakespeare's early comedy was first printed in *quarto, in 1598, probably from his manuscript. It was reprinted in the First *Folio, in 1623. The text includes several passages in both revised and unrevised form, but the revisions may have been made at the time of composition rather than later. Some editions print both forms, rather confusingly. The play's date is uncertain, but probably not later than 1594. No direct source is known, though the three Lords have the same names as commanders in the contemporary French civil wars, and there are other *topical allusions, some of them no longer explicable. The play may have been written for a private audience, but it was performed in the public theatres. It appears to have been played at Court at Christmas 1597 and early in 1605.

An unperformed adaptation, *The Students*, was published in 1762, but the play was not revived till 1839, when Elizabeth *Vestris put it on at *Covent Garden. Samuel *Phelps gave it at *Sadler's Wells in 1857, but only for nine performances.

Despite a number of revivals, and although *Granville-Barker's *Preface* of 1930 had drawn attention to its theatrical qualities, the play had little success till Peter *Brook directed it at Stratford-upon-Avon in 1946 and 1947. Hugh Hunt directed a successful production with the *Old Vic Company in 1949, with Michael *Redgrave as Berowne. Despite the difficulty of the language it has been one of the most frequently produced Shakespeare plays at Stratford-upon-Avon in recent years, including Terry *Hands's last Shakespeare production for the *Royal Shakespeare Company in 1990. The simplicity of setting makes it suitable for open-air performance, and it has often been given in the Open-Air Theatre, *Regent's Park. Kenneth *Branagh adapted and directed a film version in 1999.

Love's Labour's Lost is about artificiality of behaviour, and its language, too, is often full of artifice. This makes it difficult to read. But its design is eminently theatrical, and its disturbingly original final episodes can be profoundly moving in performance.

Love's Labour's Won Listed by Francis *Meres among Shakespeare's plays, and also in a bookseller's list of 1603, discovered in 1953. It may be an alternative title for another play—perhaps The *Taming of the Shrew (not otherwise listed by Meres), though the bookseller has 'taming of a shrew' in his list—or a lost play.

Love's Martyr The volume of poems in which 'The *Phoenix and the Turtle' first appeared, in 1601; the title poem is by Robert Chester (c.1566–1640).

Lucian (c.120–180) Greek writer of satirical dialogues, one of which influenced *Timon of Athens*.

Lucy, Sir Thomas (1532–1600) Landowner of Charlecote, near Stratford-upon-Avon. Late seventeenth-century gossip first recorded by Richard *Davies said that Shakespeare was prosecuted for stealing deer from his grounds, wrote a satirical ballad in revenge, was prosecuted again, and had to leave Stratford-upon-Avon, later caricaturing Lucy in The *Merry Wives of Windsor, I. i.

Lyceum Theatre London theatre best known for the tenancy of Sir Henry *Irving from 1878 to 1902, during which he staged and, with Ellen *Terry, appeared in many Shakespeare productions.

Lyly, John (c.1554–1606) English writer and dramatist; his prose romances Euphues, or the Anatomy of Wit (1579) and Euphues and his England (1580), written in a highly elaborate and artificial style, were fashionable and influential for over a decade. His comedies, written for Court performance by boys' companies, mostly between 1584 and 1590, developed prose as a dramatic instrument and influenced Shakespeare.

M

Macbeth Shakespeare's tragedy was first printed in the First *Folio (1623), and is usually dated *c.*1606. Freely based on *Holinshed's *Chronicles*, it is Shakespeare's shortest tragedy, and some scholars believe the surviving text to be an abbreviation prepared for a special performance, possibly at Court. The authenticity of the Hecate scenes (III. v, II. i) has often been doubted. These include the first lines of two songs found also in Thomas *Middleton's play *The Witch*, and Middleton has been proposed as the author of the scenes, but the question is disputed. The passage describing Edward the Confessor's touching for the King's Evil (IV. iii) may be a compliment to King *James I, the patron of Shakespeare's company, who himself carried out this practice. James traced his ancestors back to Banquo and had a special interest in witchcraft, about which he wrote a book, *Demonology* (1597).

Possible allusions to early performances appear in *The *Puritan (*c.*1606), perhaps by Middleton, and in *Beaumont's *Knight of the Burning Pestle* (*c.*1607); Simon *Forman saw *Macbeth* in 1611.

Macbeth was soon revived after the Restoration, usually, perhaps always, in an adaptation by William *Davenant which gives a balletic quality to the witches, who sing, dance, and fly; increases the importance of Lady Macduff (partly, no doubt, because actresses were now taking the female roles); modernizes the language and brings it into greater conformity with contemporary ideas of decorum; and adds explicit moralization. Thomas *Betterton and his wife excelled in the leading roles. The witches were normally played by men until well into the nineteenth century, and occasionally afterwards.

James *Quin played Macbeth frequently between 1717 and 1751. David *Garrick's revival in 1744 restored much of Shakespeare's play, but still omitted the Porter and the murder of Lady Macduff's children and retained the singing and dancing witches, as well as adding a new dying speech for Macbeth. Garrick and Mrs *Pritchard excelled as Macbeth and Lady Macbeth. Charles *Macklin introduced Scottish costume in 1773. J. P. *Kemble played Macbeth frequently from 1788 to 1817, often with Sarah *Siddons as the greatest of all

MARK TWAIN *(1835–1910): 'the most celebrated thing in Shakespeare';
from* Huckleberry Finn *(1884)*

To be, or not to be; that is the bare bodkin
That makes calamity of so long life:
For who would fardels bear, till Birnam Wood do come to
    Dunsinane.
But that the fear of something after death,
Murders the innocent sleep,
Great nature's second course,
And makes us rather sling the arrows of outrageous fortune
Than fly to others that we know not of.
There's the respect must give us pause:
Wake Duncan with thy knocking! I would thou couldst,
For who would bear the whips and scorns of time,
The oppressor's wrong, the proud man's contumely,
The law's delay, and the quietus which his pangs might take,
In the dead waste and middle of the night, when churchyards
    yawn
In customary suits of solemn black.
But that the undiscovered country from whose bourne no
    traveller returns
Breathes forth contagion on the world,
And thus the native hue of resolution, like the poor cat i' the
    adage,
Is sicklied o'er with care,
And all the clouds that lowered o'er our housetops,
With this regard their currents turn awry,
And lose the name of action.
'Tis a consummation devoutly to be wished. But soft you, the
    fair Ophelia:
Ope not thy ponderous and marble jaws.
But get thee to a nunnery—go!

Lady Macbeths. Edmund *Kean was a more dynamic Macbeth from 1814.

W. C. *Macready first played the role in 1820, improving on Kemble's text, and Samuel *Phelps, in his production of 1847, abandoned

Davenant's revisions, which however were reintroduced by Charles *Kean at the Princess's in a spectacular production of 1857. Henry *Irving, who at the *Lyceum in 1888 had Ellen *Terry as Lady Macbeth, was not greatly admired as Macbeth, though he also produced the play in 1875 and 1895. Barry *Jackson produced a *modern-dress version in 1928. John *Gielgud first played Macbeth in 1930, and Laurence *Olivier in 1937, both at the *Old Vic. Gielgud played it again in 1942, and Olivier, at Stratford-upon-Avon, in 1955. Trevor *Nunn directed a highly successful, somewhat compressed studio production in Stratford-upon-Avon (1976), with Ian *McKellen and Judi *Dench. Adrian *Noble directed the play for the *Royal Shakespeare Company in 1986 (Stratford-upon-Avon) with Jonathan Pryce and Sinead Cusack, and *Ninagawa staged a lavish revival in 1987 employing kabuki and noh techniques (*National Theatre).

Though it has a reputation in the theatre for bringing bad luck, and is often disappointing in performance, *Macbeth has been one of Shakespeare's most frequently acted plays. It has been directed on film by, among others, Orson *Welles (1949) and *Roman Polanski (1971). There are operatic versions by *Verdi (1847, revised 1865) and *Bloch (1910).

McKellen, Sir Ian (1939–) English actor who excels in portraying intelligent, amoral villains. His Shakespeare roles include Richard II (*Prospect Players, 1968–70), Hamlet (Prospect Players, 1971), Edgar (Actors' Company, 1973), Romeo, Leontes, and Macbeth (Stratford-upon-Avon, 1976), Coriolanus (*National Theatre, 1984), *Acting Shakespeare* (1980–3, one-man show), Iago (Stratford-upon-Avon, 1989), Richard III, Kent (both 1990, *Royal National Theatre). Also starred in and directed a film based on the 1990 *Richard III* (1996). *See also* SIR THOMAS MORE.

Macklin, Charles (1699–1797) Irish actor and dramatist, best known for his interpretation of Shylock first seen in 1741, described as 'the Jew that Shakespeare drew', and played seriously instead of comically, as had been customary. He last played the role in 1789, when he was about 90. In 1754 he gave the first series of public lectures on Shakespeare.

Macready, William Charles (1793–1873) English actor, manager of *Covent Garden Theatre 1837–9, and of *Drury Lane, 1841–3. He played most of the leading tragic roles, and helped in the restoration of Shakespeare's text in place of the traditional adaptations. In 1838 he restored *King Lear* in place of *Tate's version. He retired in 1851. His revealing personal diaries have been published, and there is a good biography by Alan S. Downer (*The Eminent Tragedian: William Charles Macready*, 1966).

Maddermarket Theatre A sixteenth-century house in Norwich which Nugent *Monck, under the influence of William *Poel, converted into an Elizabethan-style theatre in 1921. All Shakespeare's plays have been performed there, by amateur companies.

Malone, Edmond (1741–1812) Irish scholar, a pioneer in the study of the chronology of Shakespeare's plays, author of an important *History of the Stage* (1780), first editor of the *Sonnets, editor of the *Works* (1790). When he died he was working on a revised edition, completed by James Boswell the younger, published in 1821 and known as the *Third Variorum* or *Boswell's Malone*. He exposed the forgeries of William *Ireland.

Manningham, John (d. 1622) An English lawyer and diarist. On 13 March 1602 he recorded the anecdote about Shakespeare and Burbage printed below.

    On 2 Feb. 1602. Manningham saw *Twelfth Night* at the *Middle Temple: 'At our feast we had a play called *Twelfth Night, or What You Will*, much like *The Comedy of Errors*, or *Menaechmi* in Plautus, but most like and near to that in Italian called *Inganni*. A good practice in it to make

---

JOHN MANNINGHAM *(died 1622): an anecdote about Shakespeare*

Upon a time when Burbage played Richard the Third there was a citizen grew so far in liking with him, that before she went from the play she appointed him to come that night unto her by the name of Richard the Third. Shakespeare, overhearing their conclusion, went before, was entertained and at his game ere Burbage came. Then message being brought that Richard the Third was at the door, Shakespeare caused return to be made that William the Conqueror was before Richard the Third.

    Manningham informatively adds, 'Shakespeare's name William.'

the steward believe his lady widow was in love with him, by counter-feiting a letter as from his lady in general terms, telling him what she liked best in him, and prescribing his gesture in smiling, his apparel, etc., and then when he came to practise making him believe they took him to be mad.'

manuscripts, Shakespeare's No Shakespeare manuscripts are known except for the *signatures and the three pages of *Sir Thomas More* believed to be in his hand.

Marina *See* PERICLES.

Marlowe, Christopher (1564–93) English poet and playwright, leading dramatist of the *Admiral's Men. Born in the same year as Shake-speare, he seems to have developed earlier. His best plays are *Tamburlaine* (in two parts), *Dr Faustus*, and *Edward II*. Their dating is uncertain, as is that of Shakespeare's carly plays, so it is difficult to be sure which influenced the other. *Tamburlaine* (c.1587), at least, probably predates any Shakespeare play.

Marlowe's narrative poem *Hero and Leander* is of the same kind as Shakespeare's *Venus and Adonis*. It is the only contemporary work from which Shakespeare quotes directly and consciously (as distinct from works which are used as sources). This is in *As You Like It*, when Phebe says:

> Dead shepherd, now I find thy saw of might:
> 'Who ever loved that loved not at first sight?' (III. v. 82–3)

Marlowe Society A Cambridge University dramatic society, founded in 1908. Under George *Rylands, and the auspices of the British Council, past and present members, many of whom have become leading actors, along with professional players, have recorded complete texts of all Shakespeare's works.

Marowitz, Charles (1934–) American director and playwright. After working as assistant to Peter *Brook in the early 1960s Marowitz began a series of radical adaptations of Shakespeare plays. These include *Hamlet* (1965), *A Macbeth* (1969), *Othello* (1972), *The Shrew* (1973), *Variations on Measure for Measure* (1975), *Variations on the Merchant of Venice* (1977).

marriage, Shakespeare's On 27 November 1582, a special licence was issued by the Bishop of Worcester for the marriage of 'Willelmum

Shaxpere et Annam Whateley de Temple Grafton.' On the following day Fulk Sandells and John Richardson, friends of the bride's family, entered into a bond of £40 exempting the Bishop and his officers from liability if the marriage of 'William Shagspere . . . and Anne Hathwey of Stratford', which was to take place 'with once asking of the bannes of matrimony', should prove invalid.

This procedure was normal. Banns were forbidden between the beginning of Advent and the end of Epiphany, in 1582–3 between 2 December and 13 January. Shakespeare's could have been read on 30 November, and he could have married at any time after that. Anne's pregnancy explains why he would not have wished to wait till the banns could have been asked three times.

The licence presents a problem in naming 'Annam Whateley de Temple Grafton.' We know from other evidence that Shakespeare's bride was Anne *Hathaway. Errors in names are not uncommon in the registers; and Anne Hathaway may have been living at Temple Grafton, which is three-and-a-half miles west of Shottery. It is not known where the marriage took place; there is a late-recorded tradition that it was at Luddington, a small village near Stratford-upon-Avon.

Martin, Frank (1890–1974) The Swiss composer wrote an opera, *Der Sturm* (1956), based on The *Tempest*.

Mary Arden's House A farmhouse in Wilmcote, near Stratford, which belonged to Shakespeare's parents, now maintained by the Shakespeare Birthplace Trust. It was for long thought to be the house now known as Palmer's Farm; the correct identification dates from 2003.

masque A form of entertainment, in its early stages, during the fourteenth century, related to 'mumming': friends with masks, musicians, and torches would unexpectedly visit a house, dancing, sometimes presenting gifts, and inviting spectators to join in the dance. Later, spectacular elements were elaborated, resulting in courtly entertainments of great formality, with speeches and allegorical shows or 'devices'.

The masque reached its height at *James I's court in the work of Inigo Jones, who devised and designed them, and Ben *Jonson, who wrote them. Only at this period did literary and dramatic elements become of real importance. Shakespeare did not write independent masques, but there are masques and masque-like entertainments in a number of his plays, including *Love's Labour's Lost, *Romeo and Juliet, *Much Ado About Nothing, *Timon of Athens, and *All is True (Henry VIII). The less developed stages of the form usually suited his dramatic purposes better than the more highly developed, to which however Prospero's masque in The *Tempest is closer.

massed entries *See* CRANE, RALPH.

Master of the Revels A Court official, under the *Lord Chamberlain, with responsibility for the Court Revels, which traditionally lasted from All Saints' Day (1 November) to the beginning of Lent, with performances of masques and plays centring on the twelve days of Christmas. Plays performed in public theatres were often given at Court, and in the later sixteenth century the Master became the official licenser and censor of plays, at first for performance, and, from 1607, for printing.

Measure for Measure Shakespeare's comedy, first printed in the First *Folio (1623), was performed at Court on 26 December 1604, and is usually dated in that year. It is based on George *Whetstone's two-part play *Promos and Cassandra* (1578). William *Davenant's adaptation, *The Law Against Lovers*, in which Angelo repents and marries Isabella, and which introduces Benedick from *Much Ado About Nothing, was performed at *Lincoln's Inn Fields in 1662. Charles *Gildon's *Measure for Measure, or Beauty the Best Advocate* was played during the 1699/1700 season at the same theatre, with Thomas *Betterton as Angelo; it omitted most of the comedy and added *Purcell's opera *Dido and Aeneas*. Shakespeare's play was performed at *Drury Lane in 1738, when James *Quin played the Duke, as he did in 1742, and later at *Covent Garden. Susannah Cibber was admired as Isabella, a role Sarah *Siddons first played at Bath in 1779. She often acted with her brother, John Philip *Kemble, as the Duke. Samuel *Phelps played the Duke in his revival at *Sadler's Wells in 1846.

The play dwindled in popularity in the later part of the nineteenth century, and in the early years of this century there were objections to its performance on grounds of obscenity. William *Poel produced it in London in 1893 and in Manchester and Stratford-upon-Avon in 1908. Tyrone *Guthrie directed it several times, as at the *Old Vic in 1933 with Charles Laughton as Angelo, Flora Robson as Isabella, and James Mason as Claudio. Mason played Angelo for Guthrie at *Stratford, Ontario in 1954. Peter *Brook's Stratford-upon-Avon production of 1950 had John *Gielgud as a moving Angelo. Judi *Dench was Isabella at Stratford-upon-Avon in 1962, and John *Barton directed the play there in 1970. Juliet *Stevenson was a strong Isabella in Adrian *Noble's production (Stratford, 1983), and David Thacker directed the play for *BBC television in 1994.

Measure for Measure's critical reputation has fluctuated. Its profound examination of moral issues distinguishes it from most of Shakespeare's other comedies, and, along with *All's Well that Ends Well* and *Troilus and Cressida*, it is often set apart from them as a *'problem play'. The conflict between Isabella and Angelo has great theatrical power and the play rarely fails to excite and disturb audiences.

mechanicals (i.e. labouring men), term given to Bottom and his fellows in A *Midsummer Night's Dream.

Menaechmi *See* PLAUTUS.

Mendelssohn, Felix (1809–47) German composer whose overture to A *Midsummer Night's Dream* was written in 1826, when he was 17. The remainder of his score, perhaps the finest sequence of incidental music ever written for a Shakespeare play, appeared in 1843, and it was used in virtually every production of A *Midsummer Night's Dream* until Harley *Granville-Barker's production of 1914, and occasionally since.

Mendes, Sam (1965–) Versatile British director and artistic director of the Donmar Warehouse, 1992– . His Shakespeare productions include *Troilus and Cressida* (1990), *Richard III* (1992), The *Tempest* (1993, all *Royal Shakespeare Company), and *Othello* (1997, *Royal National Theatre) and *Twelfth Night* (Donmar and Broadway, 2002).

Merchant of Venice, The Shakespeare's comedy, entered on the *Stationers' Register on 22 July 1598, was first printed in 1600 in an exceptionally good text. A reprint of 1619 was falsely dated 1600 (*see* JAGGARD, WILLIAM). The First *Folio text (1623) was based on a corrected copy of the first *quarto. The main plot is based on a tale in a compilation by Ser Giovanni Fiorentino called *Il Pecorone*. Both the casket story and the pound-of-flesh story were well known. Shakespeare may have been influenced by a lost play, *The Jew*, known from an allusion of 1579, and he must have known *Marlowe's play *The Jew of Malta*. *The Merchant of Venice* is usually dated 1594–5, partly on the strength of a supposed allusion to the execution in June 1594 of Roderigo *Lopez.

Court performances on 10 and 12 February 1605 are recorded. An adaptation, *The Jew of Venice*, by George Granville, later Lord Lansdowne, was acted in 1701, with Thomas *Betterton as Bassanio. Shylock was played for broad comedy. This adaptation was frequently revived. Shakespeare's play was restored at *Drury Lane in 1741, with Charles *Macklin as a serious Shylock. He continued to play the role for almost fifty years. The play became popular, often with musical interpolations. J. P. *Kemble first played Shylock in 1784, and continued in it for twenty years, often with Sarah *Siddons as Portia.

Edmund *Kean made a triumphant London début as Shylock, acclaimed by William *Hazlitt, at Drury Lane in 1814, wearing a black wig instead of the traditional red one. His son *Charles put on a spectacular production at the Princess's in 1858. Ellen *Terry had a great success as Portia in the Bancrofts' beautifully designed production at the Prince of Wales' Theatre in 1875. She continued in the role in Henry *Irving's *Lyceum production of 1879. Irving played Shylock, one of his greatest roles, with nobility and pathos. At this time, the fifth act was sometimes entirely omitted. Donald *Wolfit was a distinguished Shylock during the 1940s, and Laurence *Olivier played the role in Jonathan *Miller's *National Theatre production in 1970. Dustin Hoffman was a celebrated Shylock in Peter *Hall's production (Phoenix, 1988). Antony *Sher played Shylock as a bitter outsider (Stratford, 1987), whereas David Calder was a fully assimilated city businessman in David Thacker's modern-dress production set in Thatcherite Britain (Stratford, 1993). Peter Sellars employed multi-media resources for his 1994 production seen at the Barbican. Henry Goodman played Shylock in Trevor *Nunn's elegant 1930s production (National, 1999).

Though the relative importance of the play's varied elements has often caused critical and theatrical problems, it has had great appeal for both its romantic and its dramatic qualities, and Shylock, for all the uncertainties about his interpretation, has been recognized as one of Shakespeare's great characters.

Meres, Francis (1565–1647) English author of a book called *Palladis Tamia: Wit's Treasury*, printed in 1598. Its chief importance lies in a list of plays by Shakespeare, which for some of them is the only objective evidence as to their date. The passage runs: 'As Plautus and Seneca are accounted the best for comedy and tragedy among the Latins, so

Francis Meres's praise of Shakespeare, 1598

Shakespeare among the English is the most excellent in both kinds for the stage; for comedy, witness his *Gentlemen of Verona*, his *Errors*, his *Love Labour's Lost*, his *Love Labour's Won*, his *Midsummer's Night Dream*, and his *Merchant of Venice*; for tragedy, his *Richard II*, *Richard III*, *Henry IV*, *King John*, *Titus Andronicus*, and his *Romeo and Juliet*.' The reference to *Love Labour's Won creates a puzzle.

Meres makes other allusions to Shakespeare, some simply in lists of writers; the two most interesting are 'As the soul of Euphorbus was thought to live in Pythagoras, so the sweet witty soul of Ovid lives in mellifluous and honey-tongued Shakespeare, witness his *Venus and Adonis*, his *Lucrece*, his sugared sonnets among his private friends, etc.'; and 'As Epius Stolo said, that the Muses would speak with Plautus' tongue, if they would speak Latin, so I say that the Muses would speak with Shakespeare's fine-filed phrase if they would speak English.'

Mermaid Tavern, The In Bread Street, Cheapside, London. The story that Shakespeare joined in convivial meetings there with other poets may be no more than a romantic legend, but the host, William Johnson, was a trustee in Shakespeare's purchase of the *Blackfriars Gatehouse.

Merry Conceits of Bottom the Weaver, The *See* MIDSUMMER NIGHT'S DREAM, A.

Merry Wives of Windsor, The Shakespeare's comedy was entered in the *Stationers' Register on 18 January 1602 and published in that year in a *bad quarto. A better text appeared in the First *Folio (1623). A passage in Act V printed only in the Folio and alluding to the ceremony of the feast of the Knights of the Garter has obvious topical reference. It has been argued that the play was written for the Garter ceremony of 23 April 1597, when the patron of Shakespeare's company, Lord Hunsdon (*see* LORD CHAMBERLAIN'S MEN, and MOMPEL-GARD, FREDERICK, COUNT OF) was installed, and later revised for public performance about 1601, and that the Folio text is that of the first performance, and the quarto based on that of the revision. The difficulty with the theory is that the play uses several characters who are also in one or more of Shakespeare's later history plays, that 2 *Henry IV* and *Henry V* were probably not written by 23 April 1597, and that some critics feel it unlikely that Shakespeare transferred characters from the comedy to the history plays rather than the other way around. G. R. Hibbard, in the *New Penguin edition, suggests that the play incorporates part of a short entertainment written for the 1597 ceremony.

A legend that the play was written rapidly because Queen *Elizabeth expressed the desire to see *Falstaff in love was first recorded by John *Dennis. No definite source is known, though the plot uses traditional elements. The play contains proportionally more prose in relation to verse than any other by Shakespeare, and it is his only comedy to have what is essentially (in spite of Falstaff's historical origins) a contemporary English setting.

Court performances are recorded in 1604 and 1638. *Pepys saw it three times between 1660 and 1667, with little pleasure. John Dennis's adaptation, *The Comical Gallant*, was played at *Drury Lane in 1702, but the original play was reinstated within a few years, and was popular. James *Quin (from 1720) and John Henderson (from 1777) were specially successful as Falstaff.

A musical adaptation by Frederick *Reynolds, the music arranged by Henry *Bishop, was played at Drury Lane in 1824, and some of the music was included in later revivals up to Charles *Kean's production at the Princess's in 1851. Samuel *Phelps was a good Falstaff in 1874. Beerbohm *Tree played the role several times, in

1902 with Madge Kendal and Ellen *Terry as Mistress Ford and Mistress Page.

There have been numerous London and Stratford-upon-Avon productions during the twentieth century. Ian *Richardson was a brilliant Ford in Terry Hands's Stratford-upon-Avon production (1968, etc.), with Brewster Mason as a dignified Falstaff. The play has also been popular in America, with James *Hackett as a successful Falstaff for nearly forty years, from 1832 in London, 1838 in New York. He had a highly moral view of the character. Michael *Langham's production at *Stratford, Ontario in 1956 had Douglas Campbell as Falstaff. Bill *Alexander effectively captured the spirit of nostalgia by setting the play in the 1950s (Stratford, 1985), and *Northern Broadsides set the play in Yorkshire, renaming it *The Merry Wives* (1993).

The Merry Wives of Windsor has been much less successful with critics than with audiences, and its Falstaff has suffered by comparison with the presentation of the character in 1 and 2 *Henry IV*. The play forms the basis of *Nicolai's opera *The Merry Wives of Windsor*, *Verdi's *Falstaff*, and *Vaughan Williams's *Sir John in Love*. Artists have often illustrated it, especially the episodes of Falstaff and the buck-basket and Falstaff at Herne's Oak.

Middle Temple An *Inn of Court in which John *Manningham saw a performance of *Twelfth Night* on 2 February 1602. Donald *Wolfit and his company gave the play in a special performance there in 1951.

Middleton, Thomas (*c*.1570–1627) English dramatist. His play *The Witch* includes the full texts of two songs mentioned in the stage directions to the scenes in *Macbeth* involving Hecate, which have long been suspected of being interpolations by Middleton. He may have adapted the play, and there is also good reason to suppose that he collaborated with Shakespeare on *Timon of Athens*; his hand has also been found in *Measure for Measure*.

Midsummer Night's Dream, A Shakespeare's comedy was first printed in *quarto in 1600, probably from his manuscript. The edition was reprinted in 1619, falsely dated 1600 (*see* JAGGARD, WILLIAM). The play was printed again in the First *Folio (1623), from a copy of the 1619 edition which seems to have been marked up from a theatre *prompt-book. It was mentioned by Francis *Meres in 1598. It is usually dated about 1594 because the bad weather of that year is thought to be reflected in Titania's lines at II. i. 81–117, though there is no certainty that these are topical. Nor is there any external evidence for the theory that the play was written for a wedding; the title-page of the first quarto says that it had been 'sundry times publicly acted'. Shakespeare invented the plot, with help from Chaucer's 'Knight's Tale', *Ovid's *Metamorphoses*, and English folklore.

The only recorded early performance was at Court in 1604, as *A Play of Robin Goodfellow*. A *droll, *The Merry Conceits of Bottom the Weaver*, based on the mechanicals' scenes, was printed in 1661. In 1662, *Pepys found *A Midsummer Night's Dream* 'the most insipid ridiculous play that ever I saw in my life'. Thomas *Betterton produced a spectacular operatic adaptation, *The Fairy Queen*, with music by Henry *Purcell, in 1692, and musical adaptations during the eighteenth century included Richard *Leveridge's *Comic Masque of Pyramus and Thisbe* (1716), revised by J. F. *Lampe as *Pyramus and Thisbe* in 1745. Charles Johnson grafted the play-within-the-play into *As You Like It* to make *Love in a Forest* (1723).

The clowns are omitted from the musical version, sometimes attributed to *Garrick, *The Fairies* (1755), which introduced many additional songs (*see* SMITH, J. C.); George *Colman abbreviated it as *A Fairy Tale* (1763). J. P. *Kemble gave Frederick *Reynolds's musical version at *Covent Garden in 1816, provoking an indignant attack by William *Hazlitt, concluding that 'Poetry and the stage do not agree together'.

*Mendelssohn's famous overture, written in 1826, was used by Elizabeth *Vestris in the first successful production of Shakespeare's original play since the Restoration, given at Covent Garden in 1840. Even better was Samuel *Phelps's production at *Sadler's Wells in 1853, in which he played Bottom. Charles *Kean's, at the Princess's in 1856, sacrificed poetry and drama to spectacle. Beerbohm *Tree's elaborate version of 1900, revived in 1911, at Her Majesty's, represents a culmination of the pictorial method of staging Shakespeare. *Granville-Barker's controversial Savoy production of 1914 swept away the traditional accretions.

Subsequent productions have included heavily pictorial ones, such as Basil Dean's at *Drury Lane in 1924, Max *Reinhardt's in 1927, etc., and Tyrone *Guthrie's at the *Old Vic in 1937, and more austere ones such as Harcourt Williams's at the Old Vic in 1929 and 1931 and Peter *Brook's revolutionary Stratford-upon-Avon one of 1970. John *Caird directed a riotous staging, with punk fairies and junkyard forest (Stratford, 1989), and Robert *Lepage directed a nightmarish production, with a mudbath in the forest (*Royal National Theatre, 1992). *Northern Broadsides toured a refreshingly simple and effective production in 1994. The play has frequently been performed in the open air, especially at *Regent's Park, and has been filmed, notably by Max Reinhardt (1935), turned into a ballet by Frederick Ashton (*The Dream*, 1964), and made into an opera by Benjamin *Britten (1960). During the twentieth century it has been one of Shakespeare's most popular plays, even though directors have rarely achieved an ideal balance of its varied elements.

Miller, Jonathan (1934–) Associate Director with *National Theatre 1973–5, Artistic Director of *Old Vic 1987–90. His Shakespeare productions include *King Lear* (Nottingham, 1969), *The *Merchant of Venice* (with Laurence *Olivier, National, 1970), *The *Tempest* (Mermaid, 1970), *Hamlet* (Greenwich, 1974), *Measure for Measure* (1974, National Theatre), *All's Well that Ends Well* (Greenwich, 1975), *Hamlet* (Donmar Warehouse, 1982), *The Taming of the Shrew* (*Royal Shakespeare Company, 1987), *The Tempest* (1988), *King Lear* (1989, both *Old Vic), *A Midsummer Night's Dream* (Almeida, 1996). He was responsible for a number of productions in the *BBC Television Shakespeare series.

Milton, John (1608–74) English poet; his first published poem was his sonnet 'An Epitaph on the Admirable Dramatic Poet, W. Shakespeare', printed anonymously in the Second *Folio (1632), and retitled 'On Shakespeare, 1630' in his first collected edition of 1645.

Mirren, Dame Helen (1946–) British actress with *Royal Shakespeare Company 1967–83. Shakespeare roles include Cressida (1968), Hermia (1969, on film), Ophelia, Lady Anne, Julia (1970), Lady Macbeth (1974), Queen Margaret in *1*, *2*, and *3 *Henry VI* (1977), Cleopatra (1982, all RSC), Isabella (1979, Riverside Studios), Rosalind (1978), Titania (1981), Imogen (1982, all *BBC Television Shakespeare), and Cleopatra (National, 1998).

Mirror for Magistrates, A A collection of nineteen verse 'tragedies' by William Baldwin and others, published in 1559, in each of which the ghost of a dead figure in English history tells his story in the form of a 'complaint'. An edition of 1563 adds eight more lives, and includes an Induction by Thomas Sackville. Later editions adding new material appeared in 1574, 1587, and 1610. The work aims to provide

> JOHN MILTON *(1608–74): 'An Epitaph on the Admirable Dramatic Poet,*
> *W. Shakespeare'; published in the second edition of the Folio, 1632*
>
> What needs my Shakespeare for his honour'd bones,
> The labour of an age in pilèd stones?
> Or that his hallow'd relics should be hid
> Under a star-ypointing pyramid?
> Dear son of Memory, great heir of Fame,
> What need'st thou such weak witness of thy name?
> Thou, in our wonder and astonishment,
> Hast built thyself a life-long monument.
> For whilst, to the shame of slow-endeavouring art,
> Thy easy numbers flow; and that each heart
> Hath, from the leaves of thy unvalued book,
> Those Delphic lines with deep impression took;
> Then thou, our fancy of itself bereaving,
> Dost make us marble with too much conceiving;
> And, so sepulchr'd, in such pomp dost lie,
> That kings, for such a tomb should wish to die.

instructive examples ('mirrors') for rulers ('magistrates'). Shakespeare may have been influenced by it in his history plays.

mirror scenes A term given to scenes such as that of the gardeners (III. iv) in *Richard II* which may be held to mirror the basic concerns of a play rather than to further its action.

Misery of Civil War, The *See* CROWNE, JOHN, and HENRY VI, PART 3.

Mnouchkine, Ariane (1939–) Influential French director. Founder and artistic director of Théâtre du Soleil 1964– , a collaborative ensemble company drawing on an international range of theatre techniques. Shakespeare productions include A *Midsummer Night's Dream* (1968), and a 1981 season of *Richard II*, *Twelfth Night*, *Henry IV* which toured for three years.

modern-dress productions In Shakespeare's time, and till the end of the eighteenth century, his plays were regularly performed largely, if not entirely, in costumes of the time. Barry *Jackson's production of *Cymbeline*, in 1923, seems to have been the first revival of this practice, which has continued to be pursued from time to time, and can be justified mainly by the argument that modern costumes are more meaningful as indications of, e.g., social status than those of the past, which can seem merely like fancy dress.

modern spelling Almost all editions of Shakespeare's plays from the First *Folio onwards have brought the spelling into conformity with current practice. It is sometimes difficult to distinguish between variant spellings and variant forms, so that e.g. some editors modernize *murther* to *murder*, others retain *murther* on the grounds that it is a different word.

Moiseiwitsch, Tanya (1914–2002) Theatre designer whose work includes 1 and 2 *Henry IV* at Stratford-upon-Avon, 1951, and many Shakespeare productions at the Festival Theatre, *Stratford, Ontario (which she helped to design) and elsewhere.

Mompelgard, Frederick, Count of He visited England in 1592, and had trouble with his post-horses. He became Duke of Württemberg in 1593. He coveted the title of Knight of the Garter, which he claimed *Elizabeth had offered him. She eventually gave him it in 1597, but omitted to tell him so. The episode appears to be alluded to in The *Merry Wives of Windsor*, which may have been written for the Garter ceremony of 1597, at which the Duke was installed in his absence. The play includes a horse-stealing episode, with a reference to 'cozen Garmombles' (IV. v. 72, quarto text only), which may be a joke on his name, with other possible allusions.

Monck, Nugent (1877–1958) *See* MADDERMARKET THEATRE.

Montaigne, Michel de (1533–92) French writer of essays, a form which he virtually invented. A translation into English by John *Florio was published in 1603 and was known to Shakespeare, who drew on it in The *Tempest* and possibly elsewhere.

Montemayor, Jorge de (c.1521–61) *See* DIANA.

monument, Shakespeare's An effigy in the north wall of the chancel of *Holy Trinity Church, Stratford-upon-Avon, made by Gheerart *Janssen; one of the only two authentic portrayals of Shakespeare. (*See* PORTRAITS OF SHAKESPEARE.) It bears two inscriptions. One is in Latin:

> Iudicio Pylium, Genio Socratem, Arte Maronem:
> Terra tegit, populus maeret, Olympus habet.

*Shakespeare's monument in Holy
Trinity Church, Stratford-upon-Avon*

i.e. 'In judgement a Nestor, in genius a Socrates, in art a Virgil; the
earth covers him, the people mourn him, Olympus has him.'

The other inscription reads:

> Stay, passenger, why goest thou by so fast?
> Read, if thou canst, whom envious death hath placed
> Within this monument: Shakespeare, with whom
> Quick nature died; whose name doth deck this tomb,
> Far more than cost, sith all that he hath writ
> Leaves living art but page to serve his wit.

Obiit anno domini 1616
Aetatis 53 Die 23 Apr[ilis]

(On the reported day of his death, Shakespeare was in his fifty-
third year.) The monument was erected by 1623, during Anne
Shakespeare's lifetime. It was repaired in 1749. In 1790 the original
lead pen was replaced by a quill, which is renewed annually on 23
April.

More, Sir (St.) Thomas *See* SIR THOMAS MORE.

Morgan, McNamara (d. 1762) Irish barrister whose adaptation of *The *Winter's Tale* as *The Sheep-Shearing; or, Florizel and Perdita*, was acted at *Covent Garden in 1754.

Morgann, Maurice (1726–1802) A British civil servant whose *Essay on the Dramatic Character of Falstaff* (1777) is an early and distinguished example of character criticism.

Morley, Thomas (1557–*c*.1603) English musician, author of *A Plain and Easy Introduction to Practical Music* (1597), composer of tunes to which 'It was a Lover and his lass' (*As You Like It*) and 'O mistress mine' (*Twelfth Night*) can be sung, though it is not sure whether he wrote the music to the words, or Shakespeare wrote the words to the music.

motto, Shakespeare's *See* ARMS, SHAKESPEARE'S.

Mountjoy, Christopher A French Huguenot tire-maker, who lived in London in a house at the corner of Silver and Monkwell Streets, in Cripplegate ward. His daughter, Mary, married his apprentice, Stephen Belott, on 19 November 1604. In 1612 Belott brought a suit against Mountjoy alleging that he had not honoured his financial obligations in relation to the marriage. Shakespeare had lodged in the household, and was called as a witness on 11 May 1612. He is described in the deposition as a 'gentleman' of Stratford-upon-Avon. He said that he had known the parties for ten years, that Belott was 'a very good and industrious servant' and was well treated by the Mountjoys, who had begged Shakespeare 'to move and persuade' Belott to marry their daughter, which he did. Shakespeare could not remember the financial provisions, though the plaintiff and defendant were living in the same house 'and they had amongst themselves many conferences about their marriage . . .'. Belott won the suit.

The relevance of this suit to Shakespeare is that it shows he was living with the Mountjoys at some time between 1602 and 1604, and that by 1612 he was living in Stratford-upon-Avon. The deposition also provides one of the few undisputed specimens of his *signature.

Mousetrap, The Hamlet's name (III. ii. 226) for the play-within-the-play with which he hopes to 'catch the conscience of the King'.

Mr W. H. *See* SONNETS.

Mucedorus An anonymous play published in 1598, frequently reprinted, and in the seventeenth century sometimes attributed to Shakespeare.

Much Ado About Nothing Shakespeare's comedy was first printed in *quarto in 1600, probably from the author's manuscript. This edition was reprinted in the First *Folio (1623). The play was not mentioned by *Meres in 1598, and is usually dated 1598–1600. It is based on a traditional story which had been told by Ariosto in his *Orlando Furioso* (1516, translated 1591), and by Bandello, translated into French by *Belleforest. It was played at Court in 1613, and a poem by Leonard *Digges printed in 1640 suggests that it remained popular. William *Davenant adapted it as *The Law Against Lovers* (1662), with little success.

The original play was performed in 1721, and there were further revivals in 1739 and 1746, but it did not fully regain its popularity until David *Garrick first played Benedick, in 1748, after which he revived it regularly until he retired in 1776. His first, and greatest, Beatrice was Mrs *Pritchard.

During the later part of the century Frances Abington and Elizabeth Farren shone as Beatrice. Charles *Kemble succeeded as Benedick from 1803, and the play's popularity during the nineteenth century culminated in Henry *Irving's *Lyceum revival of 1882, in which Ellen *Terry gave her legendary Beatrice, which she went on playing for a quarter of a century.

The most famous twentieth-century production is John *Gielgud's at Stratford-upon-Avon, first given in 1949, when he did not appear in it, but revived in 1950 with himself as Benedick and Peggy *Ashcroft as Beatrice, and repeated several times during the 1950s.

Much Ado About Nothing has proved to be one of Shakespeare's most resilient plays. Twentieth-century productions have frequently updated the action. Hugh Hunt directed it in modern dress in 1947, Douglas Seale, at Stratford-upon-Avon in 1958, in costumes of about 1851, Franco *Zeffirelli, at the *Old Vic in 1965 in a farcical version set in late nineteenth-century Sicily, John *Barton at Stratford-upon-Avon in 1976 in a setting of nineteenth-century British India with Judi *Dench an unusually serious, and wholly credible, Beatrice, and Terry *Hands, also at Stratford-upon-Avon, in 1982. Susan Fleetwood and Roger Allam played Beatrice and Benedick in Bill *Alexander's production (Stratford, 1990), and Kenneth *Branagh directed a lively and successful film in 1993, playing opposite Emma Thompson as Beatrice. The play was enjoyable in all these varied interpretations. Critics have been troubled by the moral ambiguities of the Hero–Claudio plot, but theatrically the sub-plot characters of Beatrice and Benedick, along with Dogberry and the Watch, have always carried the play to success.

Muir, Kenneth (1907–96) Shakespeare scholar and critic, King Alfred Professor of English Literature at the University of Liverpool 1951–74. Editor of *Shakespeare Survey* for fifteen years and of *Macbeth* and *King Lear* for the *Arden Shakespeare.

mulberry tree, Shakespeare's A mulberry tree in the garden of *New Place, cut down by Francis *Gastrell in 1758, said to have been planted by Shakespeare. The wood was sold to a watchmaker, Thomas Sharpe, who carved many souvenirs from it and swore a deathbed affidavit in 1799 that the tree was indeed planted by Shakespeare, and was the source of all the articles claimed to have been made from it.

music based on Shakespeare A great many musical works have been based on, and inspired by, Shakespeare's plays and poems. They include solo songs, part songs, cantatas, operas, incidental music for use in the theatre, concert overtures, symphonic poems, ballet scores, etc. Information about some of this music is given under the names of individual composers.

music room An area in the Elizabethan theatre occupied by the musicians; its precise location is unknown.

N

Nash family Thomas Nash (d. 1587) had two sons, Anthony (d. 1622) and John (d. 1623), to whom Shakespeare left 26*s*. 8*d*. each to buy mourning rings. They witnessed some of his legal agreements. Anthony's son Thomas (1593–1647) married Shakespeare's grand-daughter, Elizabeth *Hall, in 1626. As master of *New Place he entertained Queen Henrietta Maria in 1643. He died in 1647, and is buried next to Shakespeare.

Nashe, Thomas (1567–*c*.1601) Writer whose Preface to Robert *Greene's prose-romance *Menaphon* (1589) includes enigmatic references to the *Ur-Hamlet. His *Pierce Penniless his Supplication to the Devil* (1592) mentions 'brave Talbot' in 1 *Henry VI which assists in the play's dating. It has been suggested that Nashe himself collaborated on the play's composition. Shakespeare appears to have known the work of Nashe, one of the most brilliant stylists of his age.

National Theatre *See* ROYAL NATIONAL THEATRE.

New Arden edition *See* ARDEN EDITION.

New Cambridge edition Name commonly given to the New Shakespeare series, published by Cambridge University Press, which began in 1921; early volumes were edited by J. Dover *Wilson with introductions by Sir Arthur Quiller-Couch, who died in 1944. Wilson then took complete responsibility, but in later years individual volumes were edited by others. The series concluded with the *Sonnets in 1966. In 1983 appeared the first volumes of the New Cambridge Shakespeare under the General Editorship of Professor Philip Brockbank, who was succeeded by Brian Gibbons.

New Penguin edition A one-volume-per-play edition, established under the General Editorship of T. J. B. Spencer in 1967. Each volume has an extended introduction, a freshly-edited, modernized text, a detailed Commentary, and an Account of the Text. The sections for further reading were revised in 1996–7. A major revision, with new introductions, started to appear in 2005.

New Place A house built opposite the *Guild Chapel, on the corner of Chapel Street and Chapel Lane in Stratford-upon-Avon, in the late fifteenth century by Sir Hugh Clopton. John Leland, Henry VIII's antiquary, toured England searching for records in cathedrals and monasteries from 1534 to 1542. In an account of his journey published by Thomas Hearne in 1710–12 as *The Itinerary of John Leland* (9 vols.) he describes New Place as 'a pretty house of brick and timber'.

Shakespeare bought it for £60 on 4 May 1597. In documents relating to the sale, it is said to have ten fireplaces, two barns, two gardens, and two orchards. It is believed to have had a frontage of sixty feet and a depth of seventy feet. In 1598 the Stratford-upon-Avon Corporation paid Shakespeare or his father 10*d*. 'for one load of stone'. This may have been left over from repairs to the house.

A late description survives. In 1767, a Richard Grimmitt, who had been born in 1683, remembered that 'in his youth he had been a playfellow with Edward Clopton Sr., eldest son of Sir John Clopton Kt., and had been often with him in the great house near the Chapel in

George Vertue's drawing of the frontage of New Place, 1737

Stratford, called New Place; that to the best of his remembrance there was a brick wall next the street, with a kind of porch at that end of it next the chapel; when they crossed a small kind of green court before, they entered the house, which was bearing to the left and fronted with brick, with plain windows consisting of common panes of glass set in lead, as at this time.'

This confirms the only visual evidence, a drawing made in 1737 by George Vertue, based on a description from an unknown source. The sketch reproduced here shows 'the outward appearance towards the street'. Vertue explains that 'there was before the House itself . . . a little courtyard, grass growing there—before the real dwelling house, this outside being only a long gallery etc. and for servants.'

New Place remained in Shakespeare's possession till he died. He probably settled his family there soon after buying it. By 4 February 1598 he was named as a householder in Chapel Street ward; a survey of grain and malt lists him as owning eighty bushels of malt, a normal supply for household brewing. In spite of his London commitments, Shakespeare maintained his interest in the property. In 1602 he bought a cottage on the south side of Chapel Lane. He seems to have lived increasingly in Stratford-upon-Avon from 1611. At his death, the house passed to his daughter, *Susanna, and her husband, Dr John *Hall, and then to their daughter and son-in-law, Elizabeth and Thomas *Nash.

New Place was sold in 1675 to Sir Edward Walker, and passed from him to his daughter and, in 1699, into the Clopton family. It was extensively rebuilt by Sir John Clopton, who settled it on his son, Hugh, in 1702 before it was ready for reoccupation. When Sir Hugh died, it passed to his daughters, who sold it to the Reverend Francis *Gastrell in 1756. He demolished it in 1759.

The site of New Place was acquired by the *Shakespeare Birthplace Trust in 1892. The foundations of the house, and a well which presumably stood in the original courtyard, remain. This site, along with a beautifully maintained knot garden and the Great Garden, is open to the public. The house next door, which belonged to Thomas Nash, also belongs to the Trust and is maintained as a museum.

New Shakspere Society Founded in 1873 by F. J. Furnivall, it reprinted primary materials such as Brooke's *Romeus and Juliet* and The *Two Noble Kinsmen, and published scholarly papers read at its meetings. It disbanded in 1894.

New Variorum edition *See* FURNESS, H. H.

New York Shakespeare Festival Developed from the Shakespeare Workshop founded by Joseph Papp (1921–91) in 1953. From 1962 the Festival had a permanent home in the open-air Delacorte Theatre in Central Park, New York, where Papp directed many of the plays, and to which admission was free.

Nicolai, Otto (1810–49) German composer of an opera (1849) based on *The *Merry Wives of Windsor*.

Nicoll, Allardyce (1894–1976) Historian of the drama, founder of *Shakespeare Survey* and the *Shakespeare Institute.

Ninagawa, Yukio (1935–) Japanese director, whose Shakespeare productions, some seen internationally, include *Romeo and Juliet* (1974), *King Lear* (1975, both Nissei Theatre), *Hamlet* (1978), and *Macbeth* (1980, 1990), *King Lear* (1991), *The *Tempest* (1992), *A *Midsummer Night's Dream* (1995, all Point Tokyo Company), and *King Lear* (1999, with Royal Shakespeare Company).

Noble, Adrian (1950–) British director with the *Royal Shakespeare Company since 1981, Artistic Director from 1991 to 2003. Has frequently produced critically acclaimed productions which also appeal to large audiences. His Shakespeare productions include *King Lear* (1982), *Henry V* (1984), *As You Like It* (1985), *Macbeth* (1986), *The *Plantagenets* (1988), *The *Winter's Tale*, *Hamlet* (both 1992), A *Midsummer Night's Dream* (1994, filmed 1995), *Cymbeline* (1997), *The Tempest* (1998), *Pericles* (2002), all with the *Royal Shakespeare Company.

North, Sir Thomas (1535?–1601) Translator whose *Lives of the Noble Grecians and Romans* (1579) from Jacques Amyot's French version of *Plutarch's *Lives* was Shakespeare's main source for his *Roman plays. Shakespeare often follows its wording closely: T. J. B. Spencer's *Shakespeare's Plutarch* (1964) usefully reprints North's version of the lives mainly used by Shakespeare, with the passages directly based on it, as, for example, Enobarbus' famous speech 'the barge she sat in' (*Antony and Cleopatra*, II. ii. 196).

Northern Broadsides Formed in 1992 under the artistic direction of Barrie Rutter, the company specialize in low-budget Shakespeare, playing in non-mainstream theatres and, as their name suggests, using non-standard English. Productions include *Richard III* (1992), *Merry Wives* (1993), *A *Midsummer Night's Dream* (1994), *Antony and Cleopatra* (1995, etc.), *Romeo and Juliet* (1996).

Norton edition A one-volume edition of the Complete Works published under the General Editorship of Stephen Greenblatt in 1997, reprinting, and in some cases adapting, the text of the *Oxford Complete Works (1986). It prints for example a conflated text of *King Lear* as well as the Oxford texts based on *quarto and *Folio, and a conflated text of *Hamlet*. In the American tradition, it includes extensive annotations and other study materials.

Nunn, Sir Trevor (1940–) Artistic Director of the *Royal Shakespeare Company 1968–86, Artistic Director of *Royal National Theatre 1997–2003. Proved successful in classical and popular theatre in both small and large spaces, a talent demonstrated by the 1976 RSC season which included a large-scale musical version of *The *Comedy of Errors* in the Royal Shakespeare Theatre, and a sparse, emotional *Macbeth* in The *Other Place. His Shakespeare productions include *King Lear* and *Much Ado About Nothing* (1968), *The *Winter's Tale* and *Henry VIII* (1969), *Hamlet* (1970), a season of *Roman plays (1972), *Macbeth* (1974, etc.), *Romeo and Juliet* (1976), *All's Well that Ends Well* (1981), 1 and 2 *Henry IV* (Barbican, 1982), *Othello* (1989, filmed 1990), *Measure for Measure* (1991), all for the RSC, *Timon of Athens* (1989) at the Young Vic, *Troilus and Cressida*, *Merchant of Venice* (National, 1999) and *Love's Labour's Lost* (National, 2003). He adapted and directed a film version of *Twelfth Night* (1996).

O

octavo A book made of sheets of paper folded three times, producing sixteen pages (eight leaves) from each sheet. In Shakespeare's time, single plays were usually printed in *quarto, but *The True Tragedy* (*see* 'CONTENTION' PLAYS) of 1595 is in octavo, as are The *Passionate Pilgrim* and numerous reprints of *Venus and Adonis* and The *Rape of Lucrece*. For ease of reference, as in lists of reprints, octavo volumes are sometimes loosely called quartos.

Oldcastle, Sir John (*c.*1375–1417) A Lollard martyr who became Lord Cobham. Shakespeare, following his source play, The *Famous Victories of Henry the Fifth*, originally used this name in 1 *Henry IV* for *Falstaff. Probably because of protests by the current Lord Cobham, Shakespeare altered the name before the play was printed, but traces remain, and the Epilogue to 2 *Henry IV* includes the disclaimer 'Falstaff shall die of a sweat—unless already a be killed with your hard opinions. For Oldcastle died a martyr, and this is not the man.' The *Admiral's Men, a rival company, then put on a successful two-part play called *The True and Honourable History of the Life of Sir John Oldcastle, the Good Lord Cobham* (acted 1599–1600). The second part is lost, but the first was printed anonymously in 1600, reprinted in 1619 with a mistaken ascription to Shakespeare, and included in the second issue of the Third *Folio (1664).

Old Vic Theatre A theatre built in an unfashionable area of London, south of the river, in 1818 as the Royal Coburg, renamed the Victoria in 1833, which gave mainly melodramas till it was taken over in 1880 by Emma Cons, who reopened it as a temperance music-hall, the Royal Victoria Hall and Coffee Tavern. In 1914 her niece, Lilian *Baylis, established it as a home of Shakespeare. By 1923 all the plays had been presented.

It continued as the main London home of Shakespeare with distinguished performances under directors such as Robert *Atkins (1919–25), Harcourt Williams (1929–33), and Tyrone *Guthrie (1933–4, 1936–43), with actors such as Edith *Evans, Laurence

*Olivier, John *Gielgud, Ralph *Richardson, Donald *Wolfit, Peggy *Ashcroft, etc. Lilian Baylis died in 1937.

The theatre was damaged in the war, but the Old Vic company continued its work, mainly at the New Theatre, and it reopened in 1950. In 1953 under Michael *Benthall it embarked on a plan to produce all Shakespeare's plays in five years, culminating in 1958 with *Henry VIII with Gielgud and Edith Evans.

The Old Vic company was disbanded in 1963, and from then till 1976 the theatre was used by the *National Theatre company. The theatre was briefly used as a centre for the *Prospect Theatre Company (1977–81). Peter *Hall became the artistic director in 1997 and embarked on a repertory programme of classical and modern drama, including a production of *King Lear.

Olivier, Lord (Laurence Olivier; 1907–89) One of the greatest English actors and a major figure in the history of the English theatre; Founder Director of the *National Theatre (1963–73). His Shakespeare roles included Romeo (*Old Vic, alternating Mercutio, 1935, New York, 1940), Hamlet, Sir Toby Belch, Henry V (Old Vic, 1937), Macbeth (Old Vic and New, 1937, Stratford-upon-Avon, 1955), Iago (Old Vic, 1938), Coriolanus (Old Vic, 1938, Stratford-upon-Avon, 1959), Richard III (New, 1944, etc.), Hotspur, Justice Shallow (New, 1945–6), King Lear (New, 1946, and television, 1983), Antony in *Antony and Cleopatra (St James's, 1951), Titus Andronicus (Stratford-upon-Avon, 1955, etc.), Malvolio (Stratford-upon-Avon, 1955), Othello (National Theatre company, 1964, filmed 1965), and Shylock (National Theatre company, 1970). He also starred in and directed films of *Henry V (1944), *Hamlet (1948), and *Richard III (1955), and directed a number of Shakespeare's plays on the stage.

operas based on Shakespeare's plays Many operas have been based on Shakespeare; there is an excellent survey by Winton Dean in *Shakespeare in Music*, edited by Phyllis Hartnoll (1964). Information in the present volume is given under the names of individual composers, e.g. BRITTEN, LORD; VERDI, GIUSEPPE.

Oregon Shakespeare Festival Founded by Angus Bowmer in 1935 in Ashland, Oregon, it presents Shakespeare's plays on a stage based on the dimensions given in the contract for the *Fortune Theatre, with amateur and semi-professional performers.

Orff, Carl (1895–1982) German composer whose works include incidental music (1939) for *A *Midsummer Night's Dream.*

Othello Shakespeare's tragedy first appeared in *quarto in 1622; a somewhat different and longer text appeared in the First *Folio (1623). The origin and relationship of these two versions of the play is a matter of scholarly debate. The play was given at Court in November 1604, and was probably written in that or the previous year. It is based on a story by *Cinthio. It was one of Shakespeare's most popular plays throughout the seventeenth and eighteenth centuries, and was played without major revisions. Thomas *Betterton, James *Quin, and Spranger *Barry had particular success as Othello, Charles *Macklin and David *Garrick as Iago. J. P. *Kemble and Mrs *Siddons were popular as Othello and Desdemona for twenty years from 1785. Othello was one of the greatest roles of Edmund *Kean, who played it from 1814 to 1833, when he collapsed during a performance. W. C. *Macready, a fine Iago, played Othello more frequently though less successfully. Samuel *Phelps played both roles during most of his long career, scoring particularly as Othello.

The first distinguished black Othello seems to have been Ira *Aldridge, who played the role in England several times between 1826 and 1865. In America, Edwin *Forrest was the leading Othello during this period. Henry *Irving failed as Othello but Iago became one of his greatest roles; sometimes he alternated with Edwin *Booth in both roles. Paul Robeson played Othello with varying success in several productions between 1930 and 1959. Tyrone *Guthrie's Freudian reading of the play at the *Old Vic in 1938, with Ralph *Richardson as Othello and Laurence *Olivier as Iago, was a failure, though Richardson had succeeded as Iago at the Old Vic in 1932, and Olivier was to give a brilliant, individual interpretation of Othello with the *National Theatre company in 1964, filmed in 1965. Janet *Suzman directed a politically provocative production in South Africa (Market Theatre, 1988), and the intimacy of The *Other Place enabled Trevor *Nunn to direct an emotionally charged and detailed staging with Ian *McKellen as Iago.

Othello has been one of Shakespeare's most frequently performed plays. It offers great opportunities to its performers, and rarely fails to hold its audiences, though *Zeffirelli's Stratford-upon-Avon production (1961) was tedious in its over-emphasis on spectacle, and sometimes actors have been over-ambitious in hoping to succeed in both Othello and Iago. The play has often been filmed, e.g. by Orson *Welles (1951), (in Russian) by Sergei Yutkevitch (1955), and by Oliver Parker (1995) with Kenneth *Branagh as Iago, and is the basis of one of the greatest operas, *Verdi's *Otello*.

Other Place, The Studio theatre for the *Royal Shakespeare Company in Stratford-upon-Avon, opened in 1974 under the artistic directorship of Buzz Goodbody. Many fine Shakespeare productions have been staged, including Goodbody's *Hamlet* (1975) and Trevor *Nunn's *Macbeth* (1976) and *Othello* (1989), and it has also been used to stage rarely seen plays such as *Timon of Athens* (1980), *Pericles* (1979), and *King John* (1988). The original building closed in 1989 and was replaced in 1991 by a new theatre, based on the original dimensions.

OUDS (Oxford University Dramatic Society) Founded in 1885, it has produced many Shakespeare plays. After the Second World War Nevill *Coghill worked with and supported it.

Ovid (Publius Ovidius Naso; 43 BC–AD 18) Roman poet. Shakespeare knew his works well, and used his *Metamorphoses* in both the original and the translation by Arthur *Golding. For The *Rape of Lucrece* he used Ovid's *Fasti*, which had not been translated into English at the time. *Metamorphoses* appears on stage in *Titus Andronicus* IV. i. 42. The standard study is *Shakespeare and Ovid* (1993) by Jonathan Bate.

Oxford, Edward de Vere, 17th Earl of (1550–1604) A courtier and writer who has absurdly been put forward as the author, or part-author, of Shakespeare's plays. The theory was first advanced by J. T. Looney in his *'Shakespeare' Identified in Edward de Vere the Seventeenth Earl of Oxford* in 1920, and has had other adherents including Percy Allen who, in *Talks with Elizabethans Revealing the Mystery of 'William Shakespeare'* (1947), communicated the outcome of his psychic conversations with Oxford, Bacon, and Shakespeare (*see* AUTHORSHIP).

Oxford Shakespeare In 1978 Oxford University Press established a Shakespeare department under the directorship of Stanley Wells with the aim of producing a multi-volume edition (the Oxford Shakespeare), with detailed scholarly and critical apparatus, and also a freshly edited text of the Complete Works, to be issued in both original and modern spelling. The first volumes of the multi-volume edition appeared in 1982; the series appears in paperback in the Oxford World's Classics series.

The Complete Works appeared in 1986, with Stanley Wells and Gary Taylor as General Editors. Its breaks from tradition, based largely on the belief that some of the plays survive in both unrevised and revised texts, and that where possible the more theatrical version is to be preferred, include the printing of two texts of *King Lear, one based on the 1608 quarto, the other on the First *Folio; Folio-based texts of *Hamlet and *Othello; the use of the name 'Oldcastle' instead of 'Falstaff' in 1 *Henry IV; a radical reconstruction of the text of *Pericles; a thorough rethinking of stage directions; and (for the modern-spelling edition) the first attempt at a rational system of modernizing spelling. The editorial decisions are explained in the Textual Companion (1987). The Oxford text forms the basis for the *Norton edition. A second edition, with revised introductions, including Edward III and a complete text of Sir Thomas More, appeared in 2005.

P

Painter, William *See* BOCCACCIO, GIOVANNI.

Palladis Tamia *See* MERES, FRANCIS.

Pandosto *See* GREENE, ROBERT.

Papal Tyranny in the Reign of King John *See* CIBBER, COLLEY; KING JOHN.

Papp, Joseph *See* NEW YORK SHAKESPEARE FESTIVAL.

'Parnassus' Plays Three anonymous satirical plays—*The Pilgrimage to Parnassus*, and *The Return from Parnassus*, Parts I and II—acted at St John's College, Cambridge, probably at Christmas 1598, 1599, and 1601. They are about student life, and contain interesting allusions to Shakespeare and his theatre. A love-sick young courtier quotes part of *Venus and Adonis and exclaims 'O sweet Master Shakespeare! I'll have his picture in my study at the Court! . . . Let this duncified world esteem of Spenser and Chaucer, I'll worship sweet Master Shakespeare, and to honour him will lay his *Venus and Adonis* under my pillow.'

A character suggests that Shakespeare should try 'a graver subject . . . Without love's foolish lazy languishment.' Actors at the *Globe remark 'Few of the university men pen plays well; they smell too much of that writer Ovid . . . Why, here's our fellow Shakespeare puts them all down, ay and Ben Jonson, too. O, that Ben Jonson is a pestilent fellow, he brought up Horace giving the poets a pill, but our fellow Shakespeare hath given him a purge that made him beray his credit.' And Richard *Burbage auditions a student for the role of Richard III.

Pasco, Richard (1926–) English actor, whose Shakespeare roles include Pericles (Birmingham Repertory Theatre, 1954), Henry V, and Berowne (Bristol Old Vic, 1964), Hamlet (Bristol Old Vic, 1965, 1967), and, with the *Royal Shakespeare Company, Buckingham in *Henry VIII* (1969), Orsino (1970), Richard II and Bolingbroke (alternating with Ian *Richardson, 1973–4), Timon (1980), etc.

Passionate Pilgrim, The Only two sheets of the first edition of this collection of poems, probably published in 1599, survive. The second edition, certainly of that year, was published by William *Jaggard as by William Shakespeare. The twenty poems include corrupt versions of Shakespeare's *sonnets 138 and 144, and three extracts from his *Love's Labour's Lost.

Some of the remaining poems are known to be by other poets, and none of them can be confidently attributed to Shakespeare. An edition of 1612 added nine poems by Thomas *Heywood. In an Epistle to his *Apology for Actors*, also of 1612, he protested against the 'manifest injury' done to him by printing his poems 'in a less volume, under the name of another, which may put the world in opinion I might steal them from him . . . But as I must acknowledge my lines not worthy his patronage under whom he hath published them, so the author I know much offended with Master Jaggard that, altogether unknown to him, presumed to make so bold with his name.' Probably as a result, the original title-page of the 1612 edition was replaced with one that did not mention Shakespeare's name.

Pastoralism A literary and dramatic mode deriving from classical literature, including the poems of Theocritus and Virgil, which celebrates the country life of humble folk, especially shepherds and shepherdesses. Common features of it are an opposition between courtly sophistication and rustic innocence, praise of the simple life regulated by the seasons, and nostalgia for a lost Golden Age.

Shakespeare frequently uses these and related conventions, always in a sophisticated and critical manner. His most obviously pastoral works are *As You Like It and The *Winter's Tale.

patent theatres At the Restoration in 1660, Charles II granted patents to Thomas *Killigrew and Sir William *Davenant, giving them the exclusive right to manage theatres at which plays were performed. The theatres which their companies, and their successors', occupied were the patent theatres. The major patent theatres were *Drury Lane, from 1663, and *Covent Garden, from 1732. From 1766, the *Haymarket Theatre had a royal patent during the summer months. The monopoly created by these patents was much resented and abused, and they were finally abolished in 1843.

Pattern of Painful Adventures, The *See* TWINE, LAURENCE.

Pavier, Thomas *See* JAGGARD, WILLIAM.

Payne, Ben Iden (1881–1976) English actor and director, Director of the *Shakespeare Memorial Theatre, Stratford-upon-Avon, 1935–42; he produced many of Shakespeare's plays in Stratford-upon-Avon and elsewhere, including the University of Texas.

Peacham, Henry *See* LONGLEAT MANUSCRIPT.

Peele, George (1556–96) Playwright, one of the *'University Wits'. He was active during Shakespeare's early years in the theatre, and has often been proposed as a possible part-author of *1 *Henry VI* and *Titus Andronicus*.

Pelican Shakespeare A paperback edition, one play per volume, under the General Editorship of Alfred Harbage, with short introductions, and notes on the page. It appeared from 1956 to 1967, with a collected volume in 1969.

Pembroke, Earls of *See* HERBERT, WILLIAM AND PHILIP.

Pennington, Michael (1943–) British actor with the *Royal Shakespeare Company 1964–81, formed *English Shakespeare Company with Michael *Bogdanov in 1985. Shakespeare roles include Angelo in *Measure for Measure* (1974), Mercutio, Hector, Edgar (all 1976), Duke Vincentio, Berowne (both 1978), Hamlet (1980), Timon (1999, all RSC), Coriolanus, Leontes (1990), Macbeth (1992) all English Shakespeare Company, for whom he directed *Twelfth Night* in 1991.

Pepys, Samuel (1633–1703) The great English diarist recorded many visits to Shakespeare plays and adaptations from 1660 to 1669. His library includes a manuscript setting of Hamlet's 'To be or not to be', possibly made for him by his music teacher, Cesare Morelli.

Pericles This play was first printed in *quarto in 1609. It was not included in the First *Folio (1623), but appeared in the second issue (1664) of the Third *Folio. The text is corrupt, and the original play may not have been written entirely by Shakespeare. It was entered in the *Stationers' Register on 20 May 1608, and was probably written shortly before then. It is based on the traditional tale of *Apollonius of Tyre as told by John *Gower in his *Confessio Amantis* (1385–93). Gower appears as the narrator. The story was also told by Laurence *Twine in *The Pattern of Painful Adventures*, entered in 1576, and printed firstly without date, and secondly in 1607. In 1608 appeared a prose tale, *The Painful Adventures of Pericles, Prince of Tyre*, by George *Wilkins, described as 'The True History of the Play of Pericles, as it was lately presented by the worthy and ancient poet, John Gower.' This appears to be based on the original play, as well as on Twine, and can sometimes be used to correct the corrupt text.

The play was popular in its own times. The quarto was reprinted five times by 1635. Several early performances are recorded, and Ben *Jonson, in his 'Ode to Himself' (1629), enviously remarked that 'No doubt some mouldy tale|Like Pericles . . . may keep up the play-club.'

Why *Pericles* was omitted from the Folio is unknown: perhaps for lack of an authentic text. The first two acts of the surviving version are generally felt to be much inferior to the later three. It should be remembered that edited versions necessarily tidy up the original text.

Pericles was the first Shakespeare play to be given after 1642, in 1660 and 1661, with Thomas *Betterton as Pericles. Since then it has been comparatively unsuccessful, no doubt largely because the authentic text was not available. A radical adaptation by George Lillo, *Marina*, was played at *Covent Garden in 1738. Samuel *Phelps's *Sadler's Wells version of 1854 had spectacular scenery. John Coleman made drastic alterations in his unsuccessful Stratford-upon-Avon production of 1900.

Pericles has had greater theatrical success in the twentieth century. Robert *Atkins produced an unexpurgated version at the *Old Vic in 1921, and also at the Open-Air Theatre, *Regent's Park in 1939. Nugent *Monck, who had directed it at the *Maddermarket, Norwich, brought it to Stratford-upon-Avon in 1947, omitting the first act, with Paul *Scofield as Pericles. Richard *Pasco led the cast in Douglas Seale's Birmingham production of 1954. Tony Richardson directed the play at Stratford-upon-Avon in 1958, and Terry *Hands in 1969, with Ian *Richardson as Pericles. The *Prospect Players gave it in 1973, set entirely in a male brothel. David Thacker directed a widely acclaimed production at the *Swan (1989), and Phyllida Lloyd offered a colourful production at the *Royal National Theatre in 1994.

Phelps, Samuel (1804–78) English actor, and manager from 1844 to 1862 of *Sadler's Wells Theatre, London, where he presented and acted in all but six of Shakespeare's plays with great good taste and distinction. He had a concern for the overall values of each play exceptional in his time, and frequently restored the original text in favour of traditional revisions and rearrangements. His *Pericles* (1854) was the first since the Restoration, his *Antony and Cleopatra* (1849) the first for a century. His own best performances included Lear, Othello, and Bottom. His last appearance was as Cardinal Wolsey, in the year of his death.

Phillips, Augustine (d. 1605) An actor, one of the original *Lord Chamberlain's Men (Shakespeare's company) from their formation in 1594; named among the list of the Principal Actors in the First *Folio of Shakespeare's plays. His will, proven in 1605, is a source of information about the company. His bequests included 'a thirty shillings piece in gold' to Shakespeare.

Phillips, Robin (1942–) English actor and director, Artistic Director of the *Stratford Festival, Ontario, from 1975 to 1980.

Phoenix and the Turtle, The Shakespeare's poem was first published, without title but ascribed to him, as one of a group of commendatory poems appended to Robert Chester's *Love's Martyr, or Rosalind's Complaint* (1601). It is a sixty-seven line elegy. The first twenty lines call on the birds to mourn; then comes an anthem for the phoenix and the turtle-dove; and the poem ends with a 'threnos', or lament for the dead, composed by Reason. It probably has irrecoverable allegorical significance.

'Pied Bull' quarto The first edition of *King Lear, published by Nathaniel Butter 'at the sign of the Pied Bull' in 1608. This name distinguishes it from William *Jaggard's reprint of 1619, falsely dated 1608.

pirated texts *See* BAD QUARTOS.

plague In outbreaks of plague the City of London authorities would force the theatres to close to reduce the risk of infection. Theatre companies usually then toured the provinces. During Shakespeare's career there were severe outbreaks in 1593–4, 1603, and 1609.

Planché, James Robinson (1796–1880) English dramatist, antiquary, historian of costume, authority on heraldry; his *History of British Costume* (1834) has been much used by theatre designers, and his work with Charles *Kemble on a production of *King John* in 1823 was influential as the first to set one of Shakespeare's plays in the costumes of the period of the action.

He was associated with Elizabeth *Vestris in her important revivals of *Love's Labour's Lost* and *A *Midsummer Night's Dream* (for which he prepared the texts), and also worked with Benjamin Webster on a remarkable production of *The *Taming of the Shrew* in Elizabethan style in 1844 and 1846.

Planchon, Roger (1931–) French director with Théâtre National Populaire, Villeurbanne. Influenced both by Jan Kott and *Brecht, Planchon directed provocative, experimental productions including *Twelfth Night* (1951), *1* and *2 *Henry IV* (1957), *Troilus and Cressida* (1964), *Antony and Cleopatra*, *Love's Labour's Lost*, *Pericles* (1978, all Villeurbanne).

Plantagenets, The The name given to Adrian *Noble's adaptation of *1*, *2*, and *3 *Henry VI* and *Richard III*, acted at Stratford-upon-Avon in 1988 in three parts, as *Henry VI*, *Edward IV*, and *Richard III*. The text of the adaptation was published (1989).

Platter, Thomas (1574–1628) Swiss doctor who visited London in 1599 and wrote, in German, an account of his travels which includes reference to a visit to a tragedy about Julius Caesar, probably Shakespeare's, at the *Globe, and a description of the Curtain Theatre.

Plautus, Titus Maccius (*c*.254–184 BC) Roman dramatist, author of over twenty surviving comedies based on Greek originals. They were much studied in schools in the sixteenth century, and sometimes acted, exerting an influence on the development of English comedy. His *Menaechmi* is the main source of *The *Comedy of Errors*, to which his *Amphitruo* also contributed. His influence can be detected in other plays by Shakespeare; in *Hamlet* Polonius speaks of the actors for whom 'Seneca cannot be too heavy, nor Plautus too light' (II. ii. 401–2).

play-within-a-play This dramatic convention, popular in Elizabethan times, was a favourite with Shakespeare, who used it with great subtlety. It occurs in his work in varied forms, most prominently in *Love's Labour's Lost*, *The *Taming of the Shrew*, *A *Midsummer Night's Dream*, *Hamlet*, and *The *Tempest*.

Plutarch (*c*.50–130) Greek biographer. *See* NORTH, SIR THOMAS.

Poel, William (1852–1934) Actor and producer, founder (1894) of the Elizabethan Stage Society, with which he produced many of Shakespeare's plays in conditions approximating to those of the

Elizabethan theatre. His first production in this style was in 1881, of the first *quarto of *Hamlet.

He was an eccentric, and far more of a visual than a textual purist, with strong ideas about verse-speaking. His theories about the desirable balance of voices sometimes led him to cast women in such surprising roles as Thersites.

His work constituted a powerful reaction against the nineteenth-century 'spectacular' tradition in Shakespeare production, and has been highly influential. His actors included Nugent Monck (*see* MADDERMARKET THEATRE), Harley *Granville-Barker, and Robert Speaight, author of *William Poel and the Elizabethan Revival* (1954). Edith *Evans played Cressida for him in 1912, in the first professional English stage performance of *Troilus and Cressida.

poems Shakespeare's principal independently printed poems are *Venus and Adonis* (1593), The *Rape of Lucrece* (1594), 'The *Phoenix and the Turtle' (1601), the *Sonnets (1609), and (less certainly by Shakespeare) The *Passionate Pilgrim* (1599) and A *Lover's Complaint* (printed along with the Sonnets in 1609).

Pope, Alexander (1688–1744) English poet, the second editor of Shakespeare (1725). His main contribution is in the division of the scenes, and he is the first editor to consult the early *quartos, though he emended freely on grounds of taste. He included only the plays in the First *Folio. He distinguishes 'Some of the most shining passages . . . by commas in the margin', while 'suspected passages, which are excessively bad' (such as the Porter episode in *Macbeth) 'are degraded to the bottom of the page'.

portraits of Shakespeare The only two portraits with strong claims to authenticity are the *Droeshout engraving and the bust on the *monument. Many paintings have been claimed as portraits of Shakespeare; some are genuine paintings of the time faked to resemble the authentic portraits; some are forgeries; others are genuine portraits of the time of unknown sitters. The subject is treated by David Piper in '*O Sweet Mr Shakespeare: I'll have his picture*' (National Portrait Gallery, 1964). See also: CHANDOS PORTRAIT; CHESTERFIELD PORTRAIT; FLOWER PORTRAIT; GRAFTON PORTRAIT; KESSEL-STADT DEATH MASK; SOEST PORTRAIT; SCHEEMAKERS, PETER.

Princess's Theatre, London *See* KEAN, CHARLES.

> ALEXANDER POPE *(1688–1744) on Shakespeare's characterization; from*
> *the Preface to his edition, 1725*
>
> ---
>
> His *Characters* are so much Nature her self, that 'tis a sort of injury
> to call them by so distant a name as Copies of her. Those of other
> Poets have a constant resemblance, which shews that they receiv'd
> them from one another, and were but multiplyers of the same
> image: each picture like a mock-rainbow is but the reflection of a
> reflection. But every single character in *Shakespear* is as much an
> Individual, as those in Life itself; it is as impossible to find any two
> alike; and such as from their relation or affinity in any respect
> appear most to be Twins, will upon comparison be found remark-
> ably distinct. To this life and variety of Character, we must add the
> wonderful Preservation of it; which is such throughout his plays,
> that had all the Speeches been printed without the very names of
> the Persons, I believe one might have apply'd them with certainty
> to every speaker.

Pritchard, (Mrs) Hannah (1711–68) English actress who frequently
performed with David *Garrick, and was specially distinguished as
Lady Macbeth, Gertrude, and Queen Katherine.

private theatres Roofed and enclosed theatres of Shakespeare's time,
originally occupied by *boy actors. They were smaller and had higher
admission prices than the public theatres, but were nonetheless open
to the public. The main one during Shakespeare's career was the
second *Blackfriars, used by the Children of the Chapel from 1600 to
1608, and by his company, the *King's Men, from 1609 to 1642.

problem plays A term first applied to Shakespeare by F. S. Boas in 1896
to describe *Hamlet, *All's Well that Ends Well, *Troilus and Cressida, and
*Measure for Measure. Since then *Hamlet* has not always been included.

Profanity Act *See* CENSORSHIP.

Prokofiev, Serge (1891–1953) The Russian composer wrote incidental
music (unpublished) for *Hamlet* in 1937, and an important full-length
score for a ballet based on *Romeo and Juliet* (first performed in 1938).

Prologue *See* CHORUS.

Promos and Cassandra *See* WHETSTONE, GEORGE.

prompt-book The 'book', or copy, of a play used during performance by the prompter, and marked with cuts, cues for music, and other indications for performance. The early texts of some of Shakespeare's plays appear to have been printed from prompt copies rather than from the manuscript as it left the author's hands.

pronunciation There are many differences between the pronunciation of Shakespeare's time and modern standard pronunciation, some of them preserved in dialects. The standard study is Fausto Cercignani's *Shakespeare's Works and Elizabethan Pronunciation* (1981).

Prospect Theatre Company Founded in Oxford in 1961, it became a touring company known for producing ensemble productions of classic drama on a small budget. Shakespeare productions included *Richard II* (1968) with Ian *McKellen, *Antony and Cleopatra* and *Hamlet* (1977), *Macbeth* and *The *Merchant of Venice* (1980). It was forced to disband in 1981 after its Arts Council budget was cut.

punctuation Elizabethan punctuation was different from, and freer than, modern. In setting up type, compositors seem to have felt at liberty to alter the punctuation of their manuscripts. The result is that we cannot speak with certainty of Shakespeare's practice.

Purcell, Henry (1659–95) The great composer's music associated with Shakespeare includes a score for The *Fairy Queen*, one (whose authenticity has been questioned) for a 1695 revival of Thomas Shadwell's revision of *Dryden and *Davenant's version of *The *Tempest*, and incidental music (1694) for *Shadwell's *The History of Timon of Athens, the Man-Hater*, based on Shakespeare. Purcell's opera *Dido and Aeneas* was interpolated between the acts of Charles *Gildon's version of *Measure for Measure* (published in 1700). His only settings of Shakespeare's words are for the Shadwell libretto: 'Come unto these yellow sands', sung by Ariel and chorus, and 'Full fathom five', sung by the non-Shakespearian Milcha, with chorus.

Puritan, The, or The Puritan Widow An anonymous play of about 1606, attributed in the eighteenth century to Shakespeare, but now thought to be by Thomas *Middleton. It includes a probable allusion to *Macbeth*: 'Instead of a jester, we'll ha' the ghost i' the white sheet sit at upper end o' the table' (IV. iii. 89–91). *See* APOCRYPHAL WORKS.

Q

quarto A book made from sheets folded twice, making eight pages (four leaves) for each sheet. Most of the early editions of Shakespeare were in quarto.

Quayle, Sir Anthony (1913–89) English actor and producer. He directed the *Shakespeare Memorial Theatre, Stratford-upon-Avon, from 1948 to 1952, and, with Glen Byam *Shaw, from 1952 to 1956. He played *Falstaff (1951), Bottom (1954), Aaron (1955), and other roles.

Queen Mab speech In *Romeo and Juliet*, Mercutio's speech (i. iv. 53–103) in which he talks of Queen Mab, 'the fairies' midwife'.

Quilter, Roger (1877–1953) The English composer wrote several well known settings of Shakespeare lyrics, including his 'Three Shakespeare Songs' ('Come away, death', 'O mistress mine', and 'Blow, blow, thou winter wind'), of 1906.

Quin, James (1693–1766) English actor who played many Shakespeare roles, from 1734 to 1751 mostly at *Covent Garden, rivalling David *Garrick at *Drury Lane. His style was formal and declamatory, quite unlike the more volatile Garrick. His most famous role was *Falstaff. Tobias Smollett writes of him in his novel *Humphrey Clinker* (1771).

Quiney, Richard (d. 1602) Father of *Thomas. As an alderman of Stratford-upon-Avon (which had been hit by bad weather and two severe fires), he regularly visited London for negotiations with the Privy Council on behalf of the Corporation. His correspondence on these occasions includes references to Shakespeare and also the only known letter addressed to Shakespeare. On 24 January 1598, Abraham Sturley, also a member of the Corporation, wrote to Quiney from Stratford-upon-Avon suggesting that, as Shakespeare was considering buying some land 'at Shottery or near about us', it would be worth asking him 'to deal in the matter of our tithes'. On another visit he became short of money, and wrote to Shakespeare asking for the loan of the large sum of £30:

TOBIAS SMOLLETT *(1721–71): Tabitha Bramble sees James Quin as the Ghost of Hamlet's father; from* Humphrey Clinker *(1771)*

'Mr. Gwynn, (said she the other day), I was once vastly entertained with your playing the Ghost of Gimlet at Drury-lane, when you rose up through the stage, with a white face and red eyes, and spoke of *quails upon the frightful porcofine*—Do, pray, spout a little the Ghost of Gimlet.' 'Madam, (said Quin, with a glance of ineffable disdain), the Ghost of Gimlet is laid, never to rise again—' Insensible of this check, she proceeded: 'Well, to be sure, you looked and talked so like a real ghost; and then the cock crowed so natural. I wonder how you could teach him to crow so exact, in the very nick of time; but, I suppose, he's game—An't he game, Mr. Gwynn?' 'Dunghill, Madam.' 'Well, dunghill, or not dunghill, he has got such a clear counter-tenor, that I wish I had such another at Brambleton-hall, to wake the maids of a morning. Do you know where I could find one of his brood?' 'Probably in the work-house of St. Giles's parish, madam; but I protest I know not his particular mew.' My uncle, frying with vexation, cried, 'Good God, sister, how you talk! I have told you twenty times, that this gentleman's name is not Gwynn.—' 'Hoity toity, brother mine, (she replied), no offence, I hope—Gwynn is an honourable name, of true old British extraction—I thought the gentleman had been come of Mrs. Helen Gwynn, who was of his own profession; and if so be that were the case, he might be of King Charles's breed, and have royal blood in his veins—' 'No, madam, (answered Quin, with great solemnity) my mother was not a whore of such distinction.'

'Loving countryman, I am bold of you as of a friend, craving your help with £30 upon Mr Bushell's and my security, or Mr Mytton's with me. Mr Rosswell is not come to London as yet, and I have especial cause. You shall friend me much in helping me out of all the debts I owe in London, I thank God, and much quiet my mind which would not be indebted. I am now towards the Court in hope of answer for the dispatch of my business. You shall neither lose credit nor money by me, the Lord willing, and now but persuade yourself so as I hope and you shall not need to fear but with all hearty thankfulness I will hold

The address of Richard Quiney's letter to Shakespeare

my time and content your friend and if we bargain farther you shall be the paymaster yourself. My time bids me hasten to an end, and so I commit this [to] your care and hope of your help. I fear I shall not be back this night from the Court. Haste. The Lord be with you and with us all. Amen. From the Bell in Carter Lane the 25 October 1598. Yours in all kindness Ryc. Quyney.'

The address is 'H [aste] to my loving good friend and countryman Mr Wm Shakespeare deliver these', and there is a seal.

This letter seems not to have been sent, as it was found among Quiney's papers. A few days afterwards, on 30 October, his father wrote in terms which suggest that Richard was still negotiating with Shakespeare, perhaps for the land mentioned by Sturley: 'if you bargain with Mr Sha. or receive money therefor, bring your money home if you may . . .'. The implication is that Shakespeare was in London. A letter of 4 November from Sturley acknowledges one from Quiney importing 'that our countryman Mr Wm Shak. would procure us money, which I will like of as I shall hear when, and where, and how . . .'.

Eventually Quiney's negotiations were successful: the Queen agreed to relieve 'this town twice afflicted and almost wasted by fire', and Quiney's London expenses were borne by the Exchequer.

Quiney, Thomas (1589–1655?) Husband of Shakespeare's daughter *Judith.

R

Rape of Lucrece, The Shakespeare's narrative poem was first published in 1594, probably from his own manuscript, by Richard *Field, from Stratford-upon-Avon, who had also printed *Venus and Adonis* the previous year. Like the earlier poem, it bears a dedication to Henry *Wriothesley, 3rd Earl of Southampton. It is written in *rhyme royal (seven-line stanzas, rhyming a b a b b c c) and has 1,855 lines. It was reprinted seven times by 1640.

In *The Rape of Lucrece*, as in *Venus and Adonis*, Shakespeare was following the fashion for the Ovidian narrative poem. Its elaborate style and discursive structure form barriers to the modern reader, yet its rhetoric is often powerful, and the portrayal of Tarquin's inner turmoil, the result of an irresistible yet self-destructive urge, adumbrates a dominant theme of Shakespeare's major tragedies, notably *Macbeth*.

Ravenscroft, Edward (c.1640–97) English dramatist; he adapted *Titus Andronicus* in 1678. In the Address to the printed text (1687), he claims to 'have been told by some anciently conversant with the stage that it was not originally his [Shakespeare's], but brought by a private author to be acted, and he only gave some master touches to one or two of the principal parts of characters; this I am apt to believe, because 'tis the most incorrect and indigested piece in all his works; it seems rather a heap of rubbish than a structure.' This is the first suggestion that *Titus Andronicus* is not entirely by Shakespeare.

recurrent imagery *See* IMAGERY.

Redgrave, Sir Michael (1908–85) English actor famous for detailed characterization and combining classical restraint with emotional outbursts. His Shakespeare performances included Orlando (*Old Vic, with Edith *Evans, 1936, etc.), Macbeth (Aldwych, 1947), Berowne and Hamlet (Old Vic, 1949–50), Richard II and Hotspur (Stratford-upon-Avon, 1951), Shylock, King Lear, and Antony (Stratford-upon-Avon, 1953), Benedick and Hamlet (Stratford-upon-Avon, 1958), and Claudius (*National Theatre company, 1963).

TO THE RIGHT
HONOVRABLE, HENRY
VVriothesley, Earle of Southhampton,
and Baron of Titchfield.

HE loue I dedicate to your
Lordship is without end:wher-
of this Pamphlet without beginning is but a superfluous
Moity. The warrant I haue of
your Honourable disposition,
not the worth of my vntutord
Lines makes it assured of acceptance. VVhat I haue
done is yours, what I haue to doe is yours, being
part in all I haue, deuoted yours . VVere my worth
greater, my duety would shew greater, meane time,
as it is, it is bound to your Lordship; To whom I wish
long life still lengthned with all happinesse.

Your Lordships in all duety.

William Shakespeare.

A 2

Shakespeare's dedication of The
Rape of Lucrece *(1594)*

Redgrave, Vanessa (1937–) English actress whose Shakespeare roles include Rosalind, Katherine (both 1961), Imogen (1962, *Royal Shakespeare Company), Viola (1972, Shaw Theatre), Cleopatra (1973), Lady Macbeth (1975, Los Angeles), Katherine (*The *Taming of the Shrew*), Cleopatra (1986, Haymarket). Returned to the stage in 1995 to direct and play the lead in *Antony and Cleopatra* at the Riverside Studios. She played Prospero in *The Tempest* (International Shakespeare Globe Centre, 2000).

Reed, Isaac (1742–1807) English scholar. He revised George *Steevens's edition of Shakespeare in 1785, and assisted Steevens with his edition of 1793. In 1803 he produced an extensively revised edition of this, known as the First *Variorum.

Regent's Park, London, Open-Air Theatre Founded in 1933 in an enclosure in the park by Sidney Carroll, and run by Robert *Atkins from 1933 to 1943 and 1946 to 1960. Many Shakespeare performances have been given there in the summer months. The theatre archives are held at the *Shakespeare Institute Library.

Rehan, Ada (1860–1916) Irish-born American actress, who played from 1879 to 1899 with Augustin *Daly's company, often in London. Her most famous Shakespearian roles were Kate, in *The *Taming of the Shrew*, and Rosalind, in *As You Like It*.

Reinhardt, Max (1873–1943) Austrian director of spectacular productions of several Shakespeare plays and of a film (1935) of *A *Midsummer Night's Dream*.

religion, Shakespeare's The records of Shakespeare's *baptism, *marriage, and burial, show that he was, as the law required, a conforming member of the Church of England, His works show considerable familiarity with the *Bible, the Book of Common Prayer, and the Homilies.

Richard *Davies, late in the seventeenth century, wrote that Shakespeare 'died a papist'. He cites no evidence. There is some reason to suppose that Shakespeare's father may have had Catholic sympathies (*see* SPIRITUAL TESTAMENT, JOHN SHAKESPEARE'S), and his daughter *Susanna was fined for recusancy, though she later married a staunch Protestant with Puritan leanings.

reported texts *See* BAD QUARTOS.

Reynolds, Frederick (1764–1841) A prolific English dramatist who adapted a number of Shakespeare's comedies in musical versions for *Covent Garden Theatre. They were *A *Midsummer Night's Dream* (1819), *Twelfth Night* (1820), The *Two Gentlemen of Verona* (1821), The *Tempest* (1821), The *Merry Wives of Windsor* (1824), and The *Taming of the Shrew* (1828). The composer Sir Henry *Bishop collaborated with him.

rhyme royal A stanza of seven iambic pentameters, rhyming a b a b b c c, used by Shakespeare in The *Rape of Lucrece*, and in *A *Lover's Complaint*.

Richard II Shakespeare's history play was first published in *quarto in 1597. Richard's abdication (IV. i. 153–323) was omitted, doubtless because of the contemporary political situation, in this and the two subsequent reprints of the quarto (both in 1598). After the succession issue had been resolved, the episode was considered less contentious, and it appeared in the fourth quarto, of 1608, advertised as having 'new additions of the Parliament scene, and the deposing of King Richard; as it hath been lately acted by the King's Majesty's servants, at the Globe.' The First *Folio text (1623) includes a better version of the deposition scene based probably on a prompt-book.

The date of the play is uncertain, but is unlikely to be later than

1595. It is based mainly on *Holinshed, and possibly also on Samuel *Daniel's *First Four Books of the Civil Wars* (1595). It is the first play in Shakespeare's second tetralogy based on English history. Written entirely in verse, it is stylistically very different from the other three. The first recorded performance is one specially commissioned by the Earl of *Essex's supporters on 7 February 1601 as a gesture of support for his rebellion the following day. The players argued that it was 'so old and so long out of use' that they would have 'small or no company at it', but performed it nevertheless. A court case ensued, but the company was exonerated. An improbable performance on a ship captained by William *Keeling is recorded in 1607. It was also given at the *Globe on 12 June 1631.

Nahum *Tate's adaptation, as *The Sicilian Usurper*, appears to have been played twice only, in 1681. Lewis *Theobald's adaptation appeared at *Lincoln's Inn Fields in 1719, with some success. Shakespeare's play was given at *Covent Garden in 1738, with revivals in the two following seasons. It was neglected until Edmund *Kean played in a version by Richard Wroughton at *Drury Lane in 1815, revived from time to time till 1828. W. C. *Macready came closer to Shakespeare in his performances. The most successful nineteenth-century production was Charles *Kean's at the Princess's in 1857, which had eighty-five performances. It was scenically spectacular, archaeologically respectable, and textually short. F. R. *Benson was a distinguished Richard at Stratford-upon-Avon and elsewhere at the turn of the century; C. E. Montague's review of his performance in the *Manchester Guardian* has become a classic of theatre criticism, often anthologized. Beerbohm *Tree's spectacular version at His Majesty's in 1903 included a new version of the pageant of Bolingbroke's entry into London which Charles Kean had introduced, and also a coronation for Henry IV. *Granville-Barker had played Richard in 1899 in a performance in Elizabethan style directed by William *Poel. John *Gielgud, perhaps the greatest exponent of the role in the twentieth century, played it first at the *Old Vic in 1929–30, and also at the Queen's in 1937. Maurice Evans was successful as Richard in both England and America from 1934. Distinguished post-war performances include Michael *Redgrave's at Stratford-upon-Avon (1951), John Neville's at the *Old Vic (1954, etc.), and the *Royal Shakespeare Company production by John *Barton (1973–4) in which Richard *Pasco and Ian *Richardson alternated as Richard and Bolingbroke. Jeremy Irons played a Christ-like Richard in 1986

(Stratford-upon-Avon) and Fiona Shaw played Richard in Deborah *Warner's *Royal National Theatre production (1995, televised 1997).

Richard II is an uneven play, and the scenes of Aumerle's rebellion against Bolingbroke have frequently embarrassed actors and directors, but the role of Richard himself offers unequalled opportunities to actors who can command pathos and speak verse.

Richard III The fourth play in Shakespeare's first historical tetralogy was entered in the *Stationers' Register on 20 October 1597 and printed the same year. It was probably written soon after 3 *Henry VI*, in 1592 or 1593, and is based mainly on *Holinshed's *Chronicles*. There are contemporary allusions to *Burbage's success as Richard, and the play's popularity is also demonstrated by the five reprints of the first edition before it reappeared in the First *Folio (1623). The only specific early performance to be recorded was at Court on 16 November 1633.

In 1700, Colley *Cibber's radical adaptation appeared, with himself as Richard. It is much abbreviated and reshaped, includes material from several of Shakespeare's other history plays, omits Queen Margaret and other important characters, and adds many lines written by Cibber. A theatrically effective melodrama, it held the stage for close on two centuries and provided a leading role in which many actors triumphed. Cibber played Richard till 1733, with a final performance in 1739. James *Quin succeeded him in 1734.

David *Garrick made his sensational London début in the role at Goodman's Fields on 19 October 1741, and continued to play it till 1776. J. P. *Kemble played Richard from 1783, and in 1811 at *Drury Lane restored some of Shakespeare's lines. G. F. *Cooke was famous in the role during the same period, and Edmund *Kean undertook it for his second role at Drury Lane, with enormous success, eloquently recorded in *Hazlitt's reviews. W. C. Macready first played Richard in London in 1819, and in 1821, at *Covent Garden, unsuccessfully attempted more restorations of Shakespeare. Charles *Kean played regularly in Cibber's version, notably in a spectacular production at the Princess's in 1854.

Samuel *Phelps put on a version of Shakespeare's play at *Sadler's Wells in 1845, but reverted to Cibber in 1861. Henry *Irving restored Shakespeare, heavily truncated, at the *Lyceum in 1877, and after this Cibber's influence has gradually faded, though it was felt even in

Laurence *Olivier's film (1955). Geneviève Ward played the restored role of Queen Margaret with great success from 1896 to 1921. F. R. *Benson, Baliol Holloway, and Robert *Atkins all succeeded as Richard.

Laurence Olivier's brilliant performances were given for the *Old Vic in 1944–5 and 1948–9, and for his film version he had John *Gielgud as Clarence and Ralph *Richardson as Buckingham; Margaret was omitted, but Jane Shore was introduced as a non-speaking role. Ian *Holm played Richard in Peter *Hall's Stratford-upon-Avon production, as part of The *Wars of the Roses, in 1963, etc., with Peggy *Ashcroft as Margaret. In 1984, Bill *Alexander directed an intelligent production at Stratford with Antony *Sher as a brilliant Richard. Despite the precedent of Ashcroft's Margaret, Bill Alexander cut the role when the 1984 production toured. Ian *McKellen was a Nazi-style Richard in 1990 at the *Royal National Theatre, a production which became the basis for his film of 1996. The play has been very successful in America, mainly in Cibber's version; Edwin *Booth restored Shakespeare in 1877, but John Barrymore used an adapted text in 1920. Looking for Richard (1996) was an engaging film, directed by Al Pacino, about making a film of Richard III.

In its integration of overall structure and linguistic detail Richard III represents a great advance over Shakespeare's earlier histories, Theatrically it has suffered under the influence of Cibber's adaptation until recent times; directors need to realize its own individual qualities, which are inextricably linked with those of the earlier plays of the tetralogy.

Richardson, Ian (1934–) British actor; he played Hamlet at the Birmingham Repertory Theatre in 1959, and went to Stratford-upon-Avon in 1960. His roles with the *Royal Shakespeare Company included Oberon (1962), Antipholus of Ephesus (1962, etc.), Ford (1964, etc.), Coriolanus and Bertram (1967), Pericles (1969), Angelo and Prospero (1970), Richard II and Bolingbroke (alternately with Richard *Pasco, 1973–4), Berowne (1973), and Iachimo (1974).

Richardson, Sir Ralph (1902–83) English actor who played many Shakespeare roles, most notably Bottom (*Old Vic, 1937) and *Falstaff (Old Vic, 1945).

Riche, Barnabe (c.1540–1617) British soldier and writer; his Riche his Farewell to Military Profession (1581) includes Apollonius and Silla, translated from *Belleforest's version of Bandello, which is the main source of *Twelfth Night.

Rival Poet, The The poet referred to in *Sonnets 78–83, 85, and 86, who at one time and another has been speculatively identified with most poets of Shakespeare's time.

Rivals, The See THE TWO NOBLE KINSMEN.

Riverside edition A one-volume edition of Shakespeare's works published in 1974, edited by G. Blakemore Evans and others, with introductions to the individual works and much ancillary material. A second edition appeared in 1997 including both *Edward III and 'A *Funeral Elegy'.

Roman plays, Shakespeare's *Titus Andronicus, *Julius Caesar, *Antony and Cleopatra, and *Coriolanus. All four of the Roman plays were presented at Stratford-upon-Avon in 1972. *Cymbeline also makes some use of Roman history.

Romances Many of Shakespeare's plays use motifs common in romance literature, such as separation, wanderings, reunion, reconciliation, and forgiveness, but the term is usually confined to his last four tragicomedies, *Pericles, *Cymbeline, The *Winter's Tale, and The *Tempest, sometimes with the addition of The *Two Noble Kinsmen, as in them these elements occur in the greatest concentration. These plays are also known as the *Late Plays or Last Plays.

Romantic Comedies A term sometimes used to distinguish The *Merchant of Venice, *Much Ado About Nothing, *As You Like It, and *Twelfth Night from the *Early Comedies and *'Problem Comedies', though it may also be applied to a wider range of plays.

Romeo and Juliet Shakespeare's early tragedy is based on a long poem by Arthur Brooke, The Tragical History of *Romeus and Juliet (1562), and there are numerous other versions of the story. The play was first printed, in a *bad quarto, in 1597, as 'An excellent conceited tragedy of Romeo and Juliet, as it hath been often (with great applause) played publicly by the Right Honourable the Lord of Hunsdon his servants.' The second quarto, of 1599, declares itself to be 'newly corrected, augmented, and amended', and has about 700 more lines than the first.

Romeo and Juliet has been variously dated from 1591 to 1596. Over the centuries it has been one of Shakespeare's most successful plays. It was acted in 1662, soon after the reopening of the theatres. Thomas Otway borrowed from it for *The History and Fall of Caius Marius* (1679), which ousted Shakespeare's play till 1744, when Theophilus *Cibber revived an adaptation of it, retaining from Otway Juliet's awakening before Romeo's death for a last farewell. David *Garrick's adaptation of 1748 also included his own final duologue for the lovers as well as a dirge for Juliet, with music by Thomas *Arne. His adaptation seems to have been more popular than any other Shakespeare play on the London stage during the second half of the eighteenth century. The reawakening scene was abandoned in major productions during the 1840s. Laurence *Olivier and John *Gielgud changed the roles of Mercutio and Romeo mid-run at the New Theatre in 1934. The production also included Edith *Evans as the Nurse and Peggy *Ashcroft as Juliet. A modern-dress version was directed by Michael *Bogdanov (Stratford-upon-Avon, 1986). The play has continued to be popular and has frequently been filmed, e.g. by Franco *Zeffirelli (1968), and Baz Luhrmann's modern-dress version (1996). It has inspired numerous other works, such as an opera by *Gounod (1867), *Berlioz's dramatic symphony (1839), *Tchaikovsky's fantasy-overture (1869–80), and *Prokofiev's full-length ballet (1938).

Romeus and Juliet, The Tragical History of (1562) A long poem by Arthur *Brooke (d. 1563), on which Shakespeare based *Romeo and Juliet*.

Rosalynde A prose romance by Thomas *Lodge (*c.*1557–1625), printed in 1590; the main source of *As You Like It*.

Rose Theatre *See* ADMIRAL'S MEN.

Rosencrantz and Guildenstern A clever burlesque of *Hamlet* by W. S. *Gilbert first published in 1874 in the magazine *Fun*, with reference to *Irving's performances; acted 1891; revived some years later.

Rossini, Gioacchino (1792–1868) The Italian composer's *Otello* (1816) is the first opera based on Shakespeare's play.

Rowe, Nicholas (1674–1718) English dramatist. He prepared the first edited text of Shakespeare, published in six volumes in 1709. It preserves some of the corruptions of the Fourth *Folio, on which it is based, and includes the non-Shakespearian plays added to the Third *Folio, but Rowe consulted some of the *quartos, too, and restored passages not found in the Folios, such as Hamlet's 'How all occasions . . .' (IV. iv). He provided lists of *Dramatis Personae*, divided the plays into acts and scenes, indicated *locations of scenes, and added *stage directions.

His edition, commissioned by the publisher Jacob Tonson, has forty-five illustrative engravings. It is prefaced by the first formal biography, deriving largely from information provided by Thomas *Betterton, and using much traditional material.

Royal National Theatre After many years of effort, the National Theatre company began to operate at the *Old Vic Theatre under the direction of Laurence *Olivier in 1963, with his production of *Hamlet. Other Shakespeare productions have included *Othello (1964) and The *Merchant of Venice (1970), both with Olivier. Peter *Hall took over the directorship in 1973, and directed John *Gielgud in The *Tempest (1974) and Albert Finney in Hamlet (1975). The theatre's own buildings opened in 1976; Shakespeare productions there have included John Schlesinger's of *Julius Caesar (1977) and Peter Hall's of *Macbeth (1978) with Albert Finney, Othello (1980), with Paul *Scofield, *Coriolanus (1984), with *Ian McKellen, and a season of *late plays in 1988 directed by Peter Hall. It was renamed Royal National Theatre in 1988 when Richard *Eyre took over as Artistic Director, since when notable Shakespeare productions include *Richard III with Ian McKellen (1990), Deborah *Warner's *King Lear (1990), Robert *Lepage's 'mudbath' A *Midsummer Night's Dream (1992), *King Lear with Ian *Holm, and Sam *Mendes's Othello (both 1997). Trevor *Nunn took over as Artistic Director in 1997; his notable Shakespeare productions included *Troilus and Cressida and *Merchant of Venice (both 1999). He was succeeded by Nicholas Hytner in 2003.

Royal Shakespeare Theatre The present building in Stratford-upon-Avon originated in the one opened as the Shakespeare Memorial Theatre in 1879, in which festival performances were given for short periods each year, most notably by F. R. *Benson's company from 1886 to 1919. It was built under the sponsorship of the *Flower family, who have continued to take an active part in its administration.

In 1919 W. *Bridges-Adams took over the artistic direction of the festival. The theatre was incorporated under royal charter as a non-profit making organization in 1925. The next year, the building burned down. The present one was opened in 1932. B. Iden *Payne was director from 1935 to 1942, Milton Rosmer in 1943, Robert

*Atkins from 1944 to 1945, Barry *Jackson from 1946 to 1948, Anthony *Quayle from 1948 to 1952, Anthony Quayle and Glen Byam *Shaw, 1952–6, and Glen Byam Shaw, 1956. Peter *Hall, who became Director in 1960, secured support from the Arts Council, organized the company on a semi-permanent basis, and acquired the Aldwych Theatre as a London home for it.

The theatre became the Royal Shakespeare Theatre in 1961, and Michel Saint-Denis and Peter *Brook became co-directors of the company. Trevor *Nunn was Artistic Director 1968–86, followed by Terry *Hands. The company developed as the major British performers of Shakespeare's plays, with occasional productions of Shakespeare's contemporaries at Stratford-upon-Avon, performances of plays of all periods at the Aldwych, extensive touring operations at home and abroad, and experimental productions in studio theatres. During this time two new theatres were developed, The *Other Place and the *Swan, and in 1982 a London home was set up in the Barbican. Adrian *Noble replaced Terry Hands as Artistic Director in 1991 and was succeeded by Michael Boyd in 2003. The Royal Shakespeare Company's theatre archives are held at the *Shakespeare Birthplace Trust.

Russell, Thomas (1570–1634) A friend of Shakespeare's, who left him £5 and asked him to be an overseer of his will. He seems also to have been a friend of Henry Willoughby, the assumed author of *Willobie his Avisa*. He was the stepfather of Leonard *Digges.

Rutland, Francis Manners, 6th Earl of (1578–1632) On 31 March 1613, his steward recorded a payment 'to Mr Shakespeare in gold about my lord's impresa, 44s.; to Richard Burbage for painting and making it, in gold, 44s.' An 'impresa' was a painted paper or pasteboard shield with emblems or mottoes. Apparently Shakespeare had devised this one. The occasion was the tilt on King *James I's Accession Day, 24 March. Shakespeare portrays such a tilt in *Pericles*, ii. ii.

Rylance, Mark (1960–). Actor and Artistic Director of the *International Shakespeare Globe Centre 1996–2005. His Shakespeare roles include Hamlet (1988), Romeo (1989, both *Royal Shakespeare Company), Touchstone (1994, Theatre at St Clement's Church), Macbeth (1995, Greenwich), Proteus (1996), Henry V (1997), and Cleopatra (1999, all ISGC). Also directed *As You Like It* (1994) and *Macbeth* (1995).

Rylands, George (b. 1902–99) English scholar and critic, for many years Fellow of King's College, Cambridge. He directed many of Shakespeare's plays for the *Marlowe Society, and exercised a strong influence on twentieth-century productions of Shakespeare. He compiled an anthology of passages from Shakespeare, 'The Ages of Man,' which formed the basis of a successful series of recitals by Sir John *Gielgud. He directed the recording of uncut versions of all Shakespeare's plays by the Marlowe Society, along with professional players.

Rymer, Thomas (1641–1713) English historiographer and critic, an adherent of neo-classicism, whose *Short View of Tragedy* (1693) includes a notorious attack on *Othello*: 'the tragical part is plainly none other than a bloody farce, without salt or savour'.

S

Sadler, Hamnet (or Hamlet; d. 1624) Baker of Stratford-upon-Avon. His wife (d. 1614) was called Judith. Shakespeare's twins may have been named after them. Hamnet witnessed Shakespeare's will in 1616, and was left 26s. 8d. to buy a mourning ring.

Sadler's Wells Theatre Performances were given in a 'Musick House' on this site in Islington, London, during the early eighteenth century, and a theatre was built there in 1765. It housed the important Shakespeare productions of Samuel *Phelps from 1844 to 1862. The building deteriorated, and became partly derelict. Lilian *Baylis rebuilt it, and in 1931 it became an additional home for the *Old Vic company. From 1934 it was used primarily as a home for opera and ballet.

Salvini, Tommaso (1829–1916) Italian tragedian, most famous as Othello (which he played in English as well as Italian); also a distinguished Hamlet, Macbeth, Iago, and Lear.

Sauny the Scot *See* TAMING OF THE SHREW, THE.

Saxo Grammaticus (c.1150–1206) The Danish author of *Gesta Danorum*, or *Historia Danica*, first printed in 1514, from which *Belleforest translated the story of Hamlet.

Scheemakers, Peter (1691–1770) Flemish sculptor of the statue of Shakespeare erected in Westminster Abbey by public subscription in 1740, based on the *Chandos portrait. It was frequently copied and imitated, often in porcelain.

Schlegel, August Wilhelm von (1767–1845) German scholar; the translation of Shakespeare's plays begun by him and completed by Ludwig *Tieck has acquired classic status. His 1808 lectures *On Dramatic Art and Literature* propound a Romantic view of Shakespeare related to that of *Coleridge, whom he may have influenced.

Schoenbaum, S. (1927–96) Author of the most comprehensive study of Shakespeare biographies, *Shakespeare's Lives* (1970; revised edition,

1991), which was followed by *William Shakespeare: a Documentary Life* (1975, etc.). The compact edition is the standard biography.

School of Night A phrase in *Love's Labour's Lost* (IV. iii. 250–1) which has been taken to allude to a supposed intellectual circle centring on Sir Walter Ralegh. The group was the subject of Peter Whelan's play, *The School of Night*, produced by the *Royal Shakespeare Company, 1992.

Schubert, Franz (1797–1828) The great Austrian composer wrote music for German translations of three lyrics by Shakespeare: 'Come, thou monarch of the vine' (*Antony and Cleopatra*), 'Hark, hark, the lark' (*Cymbeline*), and 'Who is Sylvia?' (*The *Two Gentlemen of Verona*). The two last are among his most popular songs.

Schücking, Levin Ludwig (1878–1964) German critic, author of *Character Problems in Shakespeare's Plays* (1919), etc., and editor, with Walther Ebisch, of *A Shakespeare Bibliography* (1931, *Supplement*, 1937).

Scofield, Paul (1922–) English actor whose strong presence and careworn looks made him a successful King Lear at the age of only 40 (*RSC). His other Shakespeare roles include Don Armado, Lucio, and Mercutio (Stratford-upon-Avon, 1946–7), the Bastard in *King John*, Hamlet, and the Clown in *The *Winter's Tale* (Stratford-upon-Avon, 1948), Pericles (Rudolf Steiner Hall, 1950), Richard II (Lyric, Hammersmith, 1952–3), Hamlet (Phoenix, etc., 1955), Coriolanus (*Stratford, Ontario, 1961), King Lear (Stratford-upon-Avon, 1962–3), Timon of Athens (Stratford-upon-Avon, 1965), Macbeth (Stratford-upon-Avon, 1967), Prospero (Leeds, etc., 1974–5), and Othello (*National Theatre, 1980). He also played King Lear in Peter *Brook's film (1970). Since 1980 he has been selective about stage roles and only returned to Shakespeare in film versions to play the French King in *Branagh's *Henry V* (1989) and the Ghost in *Zeffirelli's *Hamlet* (1990).

Scoloker, Anthony Known only as the author of *Diaphantus, or the Passions of Love*, 1604, which includes a reference to 'friendly Shakespeare's tragedies, where the comedian rides when the tragedian stands on tip-toe: faith it should please all, like Prince Hamlet.' There is also a description of Hamlet: 'Puts off his clothes, his shirt he only wears, / Much like mad Hamlet; thus as passion tears.'

second-best bed, Shakespeare's *See* HATHAWAY, ANNE.

Second Folio *See* FOLIO, SECOND.

secretary hand The normal handwriting of Shakespeare's time, used in, e.g., his *signatures.

See If You Like It, or 'Tis All a Mistake *See* COMEDY OF ERRORS, THE.

Seneca, Lucius Annaeus (*c*.4 BC–AD 65) Roman philosopher and dramatist. His nine verse tragedies, possibly intended to be declaimed rather than acted, and formally structured, have sensationally bloody themes. They were known in England, were all translated by 1581, and exerted a powerful influence over native playwrights. Shakespeare's most Senecan plays are *Titus Andronicus, *Richard III, and *Julius Caesar; in *Hamlet, Polonius comments that 'Seneca cannot be too heavy, nor Plautus too light' for the players (II. ii. 401–2). Seneca's essays also were influential.

Shadwell, Thomas (*c*.1642–92) English dramatist who in 1674 prepared an operatic version of the *Dryden–*Davenant adaptation of *The *Tempest*. The original music was by a variety of composers. That written for a revival of 1695 has been generally, though not certainly, attributed to Henry *Purcell.

Shadwell also adapted *Timon of Athens as *The History of Timon of Athens, the Man-Hater*, in 1678. Both works were successful, the latter holding the stage till the middle of the eighteenth century.

Shakespeare, Anne Sister of *William, baptized 1571, buried 1579. *See also* HATHAWAY, ANNE.

Shakespeare, Edmund Brother of *William, baptized 1580, probably the 'player' buried in St Saviour's, Southwark, in 1607 'with a forenoon knell of the great bell' which cost twenty shillings.

Shakespeare, Gilbert Brother of *William, baptized 1566; he appears to have worked in London as a haberdasher, and to have been a bachelor; he was buried in Stratford-upon-Avon on 3 February 1612.

Shakespeare, Hamnet Only son of *William, twin of *Judith, baptized 2 February 1585; buried 11 August 1596.

Shakespeare, Joan (*a*) Sister of *William, baptized 15 September 1558; died young. (*b*) Another sister, also Joan, baptized 15 April 1569; married a hatter, William Hart; had four children; lived in the *Birthplace in Henley Street, and by her brother William's will received '£20 and all my wearing apparel . . . and . . . the house with the appurtenances in Stratford wherein she dwelleth for her natural life under the yearly rent of 12*d*.' Her husband was buried one week before William Shakespeare.

Joan continued to live as a widow in Henley Street, and was buried on 4 November 1646. Their daughter, Mary, lived only from 1603 to 1607. Shakespeare left £5 to each of their three sons, William (1600–39), who died unmarried; Thomas (1605, died before 1670), who married, and succeeded his mother in the Birthplace; and Michael (1608–18).

The Birthplace belonged to Susanna *Hall, whose daughter *Elizabeth left it and the adjoining Henley Street house to Thomas's two sons, Thomas (b. 1634) and George (1636–1702). George's descendants occupied the Birthplace till 1806, when it was sold to Thomas Court. Descendants of the Harts are the closest surviving relatives of Shakespeare.

Shakespeare, John (d. 1601) Father of *William, husband of Mary (*Arden), described in Stratford-upon-Avon records as a glover; also dealt in wool. He became a prominent and prosperous townsman, and was elected alderman in 1565 and bailiff in 1568. After about 1576 he seems to have fallen on hard times; he stopped attending council meetings, and was replaced as alderman in 1586. He fell into debt and stopped going to church, perhaps for fear of arrest. He died in September 1601. *See also* SPIRITUAL TESTAMENT, JOHN SHAKESPEARE'S.

Shakespeare, Judith (1585–1662) Daughter of *William, twin of *Hamnet; baptized 2 February 1585; married a vintner, Thomas *Quiney, 10 February 1616. On 26 March, her husband was prosecuted for fornication with Margaret Wheeler, who had died that month along with her baby by Quiney. He confessed, and was sentenced to perform public penance; but this penalty was remitted. This event seems to have caused Shakespeare to alter his *will.

Judith and Thomas had three sons, Shakespeare, who died in infancy, and Richard and Thomas, who both died in 1639, aged 21 and 19. Their father lived till at least 1655. Judith died in 1662, aged 77, and was buried in Stratford-upon-Avon.

Shakespeare, Margaret (1562–3) Sister of *William; baptized 2 December 1562; buried 30 April 1563.

Shakespeare, Richard (1574–1613) Brother of *William; baptized 11 March 1574; buried 4 February 1613.

Shakespeare, Susanna (1583–1649) Daughter of *William; baptized 26 May 1583. Her name occurs in a recusant list of 1606 for failing to receive communion on Easter Sunday, which implies that she was suspected of having Catholic sympathies. She married John *Hall on 5 June 1607. Their daughter, *Elizabeth, was baptized on 21 February 1608. On 15 July 1615 she sued John Lane for slanderously saying that she 'had the running of the reins and had been naught with Ralph Smith at [?and] John Palmer.' For thus accusing her of having venereal disease and of committing adultery, Lane was excommunicated. These events are dramatized in Peter Whelan's play *The Herbal Bed*, first performed in The *Other Place in 1996. She and her husband were the executors of Shakespeare's *will, and she inherited *New Place and most of his other lands and property. Hall died in 1635. Susanna continued to live at New Place with her daughter and son-in-law, Elizabeth and Thomas *Nash. She died on 11 July 1649 and was buried next to her husband in the chancel of *Holy Trinity Church. Her gravestone is inscribed:

> Witty above her sex, but that's not all;
> Wise to salvation was good Mistress Hall.
> Something of Shakespeare was in that, but this
> Wholly of him with whom she's now in bliss.
> Then, passenger, hast ne'er a tear
>   To weep with her that wept with all?
> That wept, yet set herself to cheer
>   Them up with comforts cordial.
> Her love shall live, her mercy spread,
> When thou hast ne'er a tear to shed.

Shakespeare, William (1564–1616) The principal entries relating directly to his life and career are: APOCRYPHAL WORKS; ARMS, SHAKESPEARE'S; AUTHORSHIP; BAPTISM, SHAKESPEARE'S; BIRTHDAY, SHAKESPEARE'S; BIRTHPLACE, SHAKESPEARE'S; BLACKFRIARS GATEHOUSE; CHRONOLOGY; CRABTREE, SHAKESPEARE'S; DARK LADY OF THE SONNETS; DEDICATIONS; EPITAPH, SHAKESPEARE'S; FOLIO, THE FIRST; GRAMMAR SCHOOL, STRATFORD-UPON-AVON; HATHAWAY, ANNE; LOST YEARS, SHAKESPEARE'S; MARRIAGE, SHAKESPEARE'S; MONUMENT, SHAKESPEARE'S; NEW PLACE; PORTRAITS OF SHAKESPEARE; RELIGION, SHAKESPEARE'S;

SIGNATURES, SHAKESPEARE'S; TITHES; WELCOMBE ENCLOSURES; WILL, SHAKESPEARE'S. There is a separate entry for each of his works.

Shakespeare, William, as actor Shakespeare's name heads the list of 'the principal actors in all these plays' in the First *Folio and of the 'principal comedians' in the 1616 Folio reprint of Ben *Jonson's *Every Man in his Humour*, acted in 1598. He is also listed among the 'principal tragedians' in Jonson's *Sejanus*, acted in 1603. We cannot certainly name any parts as his. John *Davies, in enigmatic lines, wrote 'Hadst thou not played some kingly parts in sport . . .' *Rowe's enquiries yielded only the report 'that the top of his performance was the Ghost in his own *Hamlet*'. George *Steevens, in 1778, published a legend that he played Adam in *As You Like It*. Phrases in *Sonnets 110 and 111 suggest distaste for a life which makes him 'a motley to the view' and for 'public means which public manners breeds'.

Shakespeare Apocrypha, The *See* APOCRYPHAL WORKS.

Shakespeare Association Founded in 1916 by Sir Israel Gollancz, the Association held regular meetings, and published papers, monographs, facsimiles of rare texts, and a series of *facsimiles of Shakespeare quartos. The Association is no longer active.

Shakespeare Association of America A scholarly society founded in 1923. Its first organ was the *Shakespeare Association Bulletin*, founded in 1924, developed in 1950 into *Shakespeare Quarterly*. Since 1973, an annual meeting has been held which includes a series of lectures, seminars, and workshops.

Shakespeare Bibliothek, Munich A library and research centre for postgraduate study of Shakespeare and the English Renaissance of the University of Munich, founded by W. H. *Clemen in 1964. It is open to visiting scholars, and is especially rich in materials concerning Shakespeare in Germany.

Shakespeare Birthplace Trust Founded shortly after the *Birthplace was bought for the nation in 1847, the Trust owns and administers the five historic Shakespeare houses in or near Stratford-upon-Avon, and also arranges cultural and educational activities, including courses for students at all levels. Its headquarters, the Shakespeare Centre in Henley Street, houses extensive library and records collections, including the production archives of the *Royal Shakespeare Company. The Centre is also the headquarters of the *International

Shakespeare Association. The Trust was directed by Levi Fox from 1945 to 1989, when he was succeeded by Roger Pringle.

Shakespeare Centre *See* SHAKESPEARE BIRTHPLACE TRUST.

Shakespeare Conference *See* SHAKESPEARE INSTITUTE.

Shakespeare Gallery *See* BOYDELL'S SHAKESPEARE GALLERY.

Shakespeare Gesellschaft The German Shakespeare Society founded at Weimar in 1865. It publishes the *Shakespeare Jahrbuch*. In 1964 it divided into East and West, but the two groups combined again after the reunification of Germany in 1989.

Shakespeare Institute Allardyce *Nicoll founded the Shakespeare Institute in 1951 as a graduate centre of the University of Birmingham specializing in the study of Shakespeare and his contemporaries. It was originally housed in Mason Croft, Stratford-upon-Avon, an eighteenth-century house formerly the home of the novelist Marie Corelli. Later Directors were T. J. B. Spencer (from 1961), Philip Brockbank (from 1979), Stanley Wells (from 1988), Peter Holland (from 1997), Russell Jackson (from 2002) and Kate McCluskie (from 2005). During Spencer's directorship and for some years thereafter the Institute operated mainly in Birmingham, but its work has centred on Stratford again since 1989. It holds extensive collections of books, microfilms, and other research materials. The home of the biennial International Shakespeare Conference, whose membership is by invitation, it has a close connection with *Shakespeare Survey*, also founded by Nicoll and later edited by Wells. Successive Directors have been General Editors of the *New Penguin, *New Cambridge, and *Oxford editions.

Shakespeare Memorial Library, Birmingham Founded in 1864, destroyed by fire in 1879, but soon restored, it is part of the Birmingham Central Reference Library, and has an important collection of printed and other materials.

Shakespeare Memorial Theatre *See* ROYAL SHAKESPEARE THEATRE.

Shakespeare Newsletter An occasional publication founded in 1951, edited by Louis Marder 1951–91, and by Thomas A. Pendleton and John W. Mahon 1991– . It includes news items, reviews, digests of books and articles, bibliographies, etc.

Shakespeare Quarterly Official publication of the *Shakespeare Association of America, first published in 1950, succeeding the

Shakespeare Association Bulletin; it includes articles and notes, reviews of books and performances, and an annual bibliography, now published on CD-ROM, which is currently the most extensive reference tool for Shakespeare studies.

Shakespeare Society A scholarly organization founded in London in 1840 by J. P. *Collier and others which published much original material. Collier's forgeries resulted in its disbandment in 1853.

Shakespeare Studies An annual American volume of scholarly and critical articles and reviews, founded in 1965 and edited by J. Leeds Barroll and others.

Shakespeare Survey A British annual publication, founded in 1948 by Allardyce *Nicoll; he was succeeded as editor by Kenneth *Muir (from 1966), Stanley Wells (from 1981) and Peter Holland (from 2000). Each volume has a specific theme, and includes critical and scholarly articles along with surveys of current Shakespeare studies. Alternate volumes have included a selection of papers given at the previous year's *Shakespeare Conference.

Shakespeare's birthday *See* BIRTHDAY, SHAKESPEARE'S.

'Shall I die?' A lyric in nine stanzas of ten lines each, ascribed to William Shakespeare in a Bodleian Library manuscript collection of poems which dates probably from the late 1630s. Another, unascribed version is in the Beinecke Library, Yale University. The poem was first included in a Shakespeare edition in the *Oxford Complete Works (1986). Its authorship has been disputed.

Sharpham, Edward (1576–1608) Dramatist. His *The Fleir* (*c*.1605) has Shakespearian echoes and includes a probable reference to stage business in early performances of *A *Midsummer Night's Dream*: 'Faith, like Thisbe in the play, 'a has almost killed himself with the scabbard.'

Shaw, George Bernard (1856–1950) The great dramatist's many writings concerned with Shakespeare include many brilliant reviews contributed to the *Saturday Review* between 1895 and 1898; a short play, *The Dark Lady of the Sonnets* (1910), which is a piece of propaganda for a *National Theatre; a substitute Act V for *Cymbeline* (*Cymbeline Refinished*, 1945); and a puppet play, *Shakes versus Shav* (1949). They are collected by Edwin Wilson as *Shaw on Shakespeare* (1961, etc.).

GEORGE BERNARD SHAW: *review of* Cymbeline *at the Lyceum Theatre; from* The Saturday Review, *26 September 1896*

With the single exception of Homer, there is no eminent writer, not even Sir Walter Scott, whom I can despise so entirely as I despise Shakespear when I measure my mind against his. The intensity of my impatience with him occasionally reaches such a pitch, that it would positively be a relief to me to dig him up and throw stones at him, knowing as I do how incapable he and his worshippers are of understanding any less obvious form of indignity. To read Cymbeline and to think of Goethe, of Wagner, of Ibsen, is, for me, to imperil the habit of studied moderation of statement which years of public responsibility as a journalist have made almost second nature in me.

But I am bound to add that I pity the man who cannot enjoy Shakespear. He has outlasted thousands of abler thinkers, and will outlast a thousand more. His gift of telling a story (provided some one else told it to him first); his enormous power over language, as conspicuous in his senseless and silly abuse of it as in his miracles of expression; his humor; his sense of idiosyncratic character; and his prodigious fund of that vital energy which is, it seems, the true differentiating property behind the faculties, good, bad, or indifferent, of the man of genius, enable him to entertain us so effectively that the imaginary scenes and people he has created become more real to us than our actual life—at least, until our knowledge and grip of actual life begins to deepen and glow beyond the common.

Shaw, Glen Byam (1904–86) Actor and director, co-director with Anthony *Quayle of the *Shakespeare Memorial Theatre, Stratford-upon-Avon, 1952–6; Director, 1956–9.

Sheep-Shearing, The *See* MORGAN, MCNAMARA.

Sher, Antony (1951–) South African-born actor, artist, and author. His Shakespeare roles include Lear's Fool (1982), Richard III (1984), Shylock, Malvolio (1987), Leontes (1998), Macbeth (1999), all *Royal Shakespeare Company, Titus Andronicus (Market Theatre, 1995, also televised). *The Year of the King* (1985) charts his preparation for the role of Richard III in 1984, and *Woza Shakespeare!* (1996) covers the 1995 *Titus Andronicus*.

Shostakovitch, Dmitri (1906–75) The Russian composer wrote the musical scores for Grigori *Kozintsev's films of *Hamlet (1964) and *King Lear (1971). His opera *Katerina Ismailova* (1934), also known as *Lady Macbeth of Mtensk*, is not based on Shakespeare.

Shottery *See* HATHAWAY, ANNE.

Sibelius, Jean (1865–1957) The Finnish composer wrote incidental music for The *Tempest in 1926. He also has an impressive setting of 'Come away, death' (*Twelfth Night*).

Sicilian Usurper, The *See* TATE, NAHUM.

Siddons, Mrs Sarah (1755–1831) The great tragic actress was the sister of John Philip and Charles *Kemble. Her most famous part was Lady Macbeth; she was also remarkable as Desdemona, Ophelia, Volumnia, Constance, Queen Katherine, Rosalind, and Hermione.

Sidney, Sir Philip (1554–86) *See* ARCADIA.

signatures, Shakespeare's The six undisputed signatures are on a deposition in the Belott–*Mountjoy suit (11 May 1612), on a conveyance of the *Blackfriars Gatehouse (10 March 1613), on the mortgage of the Blackfriars Gatehouse (11 March 1613), and on the three sheets of the *will (25 March 1616). There are many forgeries, and a few other signatures that may be genuine, including one in a copy of *Florio's translation of *Montaigne in the British Library, and one in William Lambarde's *Archaionomia* (1568) in the *Folger Library.

Signet Shakespeare An American paperback edition of Shakespeare's works, one play per volume, under the General Editorship of Sylvan Barnet, with introductions, notes on the page, and selected criticism. It was published from 1963 to 1968, and in collected form in 1972.

One of the three signatures on Shakespeare's will (1616)

Sinden, Sir Donald (1923–) English actor whose Shakespeare roles have included Romeo (1947, His Majesty's), Duke of York (1963), Malvolio, Henry VIII (both 1969), Benedick, King Lear (1976), Othello (1979, all *Royal Shakespeare Company).

Sir Thomas More A play written for the *Admiral's Men, surviving in an incomplete scribal transcript submitted to Sir Edmund Tilney, *Master of the Revels, perhaps about 1593, perhaps about 1601, who required revisions, which were supplied in five different hands. One of these, known as Hand D, is believed by many to be Shakespeare's. If so, it is his only surviving literary manuscript. It is a scene of three pages depicting More, as Sheriff of London, pacifying apprentices in a May-day rebellion against foreigners. Studies of handwriting, spelling, style, and thought have supported the attribution to Shakespeare. The revisions did not satisfy the censor. The play's first known professional performance was given in London in 1954; in 1964, Ian *McKellen played More in a Nottingham Playhouse production directed by Frank Dunlop, and in 1990 Ken Bones played the title role at the Shaw Theatre. The RSC produced it in the Swan in 2005.

Sisson, C. J. (1885–1966) Scholar and critic, especially expert in the handwriting of Shakespeare's time. His edition of Shakespeare was published in 1954, and is supplemented by *New Readings in Shakespeare* (2 vols., 1956), discussions of individual textual problems.

Smetana, Bedrich (1824–84) The Czech composer wrote a symphonic poem, *Richard III* (1858).

Smith, John Christopher (1712–95) An English composer of German origin who wrote the music for musical versions of A *Midsummer Night's Dream (The Fairies*, 1755) and The *Tempest (1756), both at *Drury Lane.

Smock Alley Theatre A theatre in Dublin established during the Restoration. A copy of the Third *Folio used by the company as a prompt-book shows that at least fourteen of Shakespeare's plays were performed there during the late seventeenth century. During the eighteenth century, many leading English actors performed there.

Soest portrait of Shakespeare A painting by the Dutch artist Gerard Soest, who settled in London in 1656 and died in 1681. The figure

The Soest portrait

is dressed in a late seventeenth-century conception of early seventeenth-century costume. David Piper (*see* PORTRAITS OF SHAKESPEARE) says that it 'may well reflect a tradition in living memory, early in the second half of the seventeenth century, of the poet's appearance'. It, or a copy probably by the artist, now hangs in the *Shakespeare Centre, Stratford-upon-Avon.

soliloquy Shakespeare often uses the convention by which characters address themselves or the audience, sometimes while alone, sometimes as an aside while other characters are present.

Sonnets One hundred and fifty-four sonnets were published in 1609 as *Shakespeare's Sonnets never before imprinted* in a volume bearing a dedication by the publisher, Thomas *Thorpe, to 'Mr W. H.' Two of the sonnets, Nos. 138 and 144, had already been printed, in inferior texts, in 1599, in The *Passionate Pilgrim*. Most of the sonnets were reprinted in 1640 by John Benson.

Their date of composition is unknown. Francis *Meres referred in

1598 to Shakespeare's 'sugared sonnets among his private friends'. Sonnet cycles had an extraordinary vogue during the 1590s. Otherwise, conjectures are based on stylistic evidence, including parallels with the plays; on possible topical allusions (especially in No. 107, known as the 'dating sonnet', though the event referred to has been variously identified); and on theories about the persons and events which form the subject-matter of the sonnets. Most scholars assign them to 1592–8, though for different reasons.

All the sonnets but three are in the 'Shakespearian' form, having three quatrains of ten-syllabled lines followed by a couplet, and rhyming abab cdcd efef gg. The exceptions are No. 99, which has an additional, introductory line; No. 126, which has only twelve lines and is entirely in couplets; and No. 145, which is in octosyllabics.

The first one hundred and twenty-six sonnets are addressed partly to a young man. The first seventeen implore him to marry and beget children. In Nos. 40 to 42, the friend steals the poet's mistress. In Nos. 78 to 86, a *rival poet wins the affection of the friend, who appears also to be the writer's patron. Nos. 127 to 152 are addressed mainly to the writer's mistress, a dark woman. Nos. 153 and 154 are versions of a Greek epigram, and are sometimes believed not to be by Shakespeare.

There are differing opinions about whether the sonnets are autobiographical. 'With this key,' wrote Wordsworth, 'Shakespeare unlocked his heart.' 'If so,' retorted Browning, 'the less Shakespeare he.' Though they portray or allude to related situations, they do not tell a coherent story. The order in which they are printed is not necessarily the order of their composition. Many attempts have been made to rearrange them into a more logical sequence, but none has achieved general acceptance.

Many identifications have been offered of the poet's friend and his mistress. The poem *Willobie his Avisa* has been thought to have some connection with the story behind the sonnets. The friend has often, though not always, been supposed to be the dedicatee, 'Mr W. H.', described by Thorpe as 'the only begetter of these ensuing sonnets'. The two favourite candidates have been Henry *Wriothesley, 3rd Earl of Southampton (though he was not 'Mr', and the initials are reversed), and William *Herbert, 3rd Earl of Pembroke (whose rank is also a problem). Nominations for the 'rival poet' and the black woman (often known as the *'dark lady') have come, gone, and come again: none has had more than temporary acceptance. Public readings are occasionally given and Derek Jarman's *The Angelic Conversation* (1985) is a film including sonnets read by Judi *Dench.

To read all the sonnets consecutively is difficult. Shakespeare's varied handling of the form requires the reader to make constant adjustments of response. Some of the poems are intellectually contorted, introspective, and enigmatic. Others are among the most confident and lyrical love poems in English.

sources of Shakespeare's works Most of Shakespeare's plays, like those of his contemporaries, are based on history, or on other stories that had already been told. Bernard *Shaw referred mischievously to Shakespeare's 'gift of telling a story (provided someone else told it to him first)'. But Shakespeare almost always transformed his inherited material.

The entries on individual works name their major sources. Geoffrey Bullough's *Narrative and Dramatic Sources of Shakespeare* (8 vols., 1957–75) reprints the major sources with valuable critical essays on Shakespeare's use of them in each work.

Southampton, Earl of *See* WRIOTHESLEY, HENRY.

Spevack, Marvin Compiler of *A Complete and Systematic Concordance to the Works of Shakespeare* (6 vols., 1968–70). It is keyed to the *Riverside edition. Vols. I–III list all uses of all words in the text, without context, and also give separate character concordances to each play. Vols. IV–VI list the words alphabetically for the works as a whole, and give context. Supplementary volumes appeared in 1975: Vol. VII is a concordance to stage directions and speech-prefixes, and Vol. VIII to the *'bad' quartos, etc. *The Harvard Concordance to Shakespeare* (1973) is a single-volume work based on Vols. IV–VI.

'Spiritual Testament', John Shakespeare's A booklet containing a handwritten Catholic protestation of faith by John *Shakespeare in fourteen articles discovered in the rafters of his house in Henley Street, Stratford-upon-Avon, in 1757. John *Jordan submitted a transcript of all of it except the first leaf (which by then was missing) for publication in *The Gentleman's Magazine* in 1784, but it was rejected. *Malone studied the original and printed it in his 'Historical Account of the English Stage' in his 1790 edition of Shakespeare's works, along with a transcript of the missing first page which Jordan was somehow able to supply. By this time, Malone was beginning to lose faith in the document's authenticity.

The original booklet is now lost, and we depend for our knowledge of it on Malone's printed transcript. For a long time Jordan was suspected of having forged the entire document, but about 1923 a Spanish version of the same basic statement, a 'Last Will of the Soul, made in health for the Christian to secure himself from the temptations of the Devil at the hour of death' and drawn up by Carlo Borromeo, who died in 1585, was discovered in the British Museum. It is known that British Jesuit missionaries, including Edmund Campion, visited Borromeo in 1580 and disseminated thousands of copies of the document on their return to England.

In 1966 an early printed English translation was acquired by the *Folger Library, which proves that the document as printed by Malone was genuine, except for the first page, as to which Malone's suspicions of Jordan are justified.

The loss of the original document leaves several questions unanswered, but it does seem that at some point in his life Shakespeare's father subscribed to the Catholic faith.

Sprague, Arthur Colby (1895–91) American scholar who was highly influential in the study of the stage history of Shakespeare, and the critical application of its results. His main books are *Shakespeare and the Actors* (1944), *Shakespearian Players and Performances* (1953), and *Shakespeare's Histories: Plays for the Stage* (1964).

Spurgeon, Caroline (1869–1941) *See* IMAGERY.

stage directions The stage directions in the early editions of Shakespeare's plays are a mixture of those that he wrote himself and, in editions printed from manuscripts which had passed through the theatre (*see* PROMPT-BOOK), of modifications of these by theatre personnel concerned with the practical needs of performance. Sometimes these can be distinguished on the basis of hypotheses about the manuscript from which the play was printed. Directions tend to be sparse, as the scripts were for performance, not for reading, and Shakespeare must usually have been at hand to amplify them orally when necessary.

Most modern editors vary the directions and add to them, in differing degrees according to the aims of the edition.

Stanford, Sir Charles Villiers (1852–1924) Irish composer of an opera based on *Much Ado About Nothing*, with that title, performed at *Covent Garden in 1901.

Stationers' Register In Shakespeare's time, printing and publication were the monopoly of the Stationers' Company. Members who wished to publish a book were required to enter its title in a register, and to pay a fee, which gave them a copyright in it. Not all bothered to do so, but the register is a valuable source of information, especially about the date of works not printed immediately on registration. For example, the earliest record of *Troilus and Cressida* is an entry of 7 February 1603, though it was not printed till 1609.

Steevens, George (1736–1800) English scholar who published an edition of twenty of Shakespeare's plays in 1766, a complete edition, based on Dr *Johnson's but with additional notes by himself, in 1773 (revised 1778, revised again by Isaac *Reed, 1785), and his final edition, as an answer to *Malone's, in 1793. He realized the value to an editor of the *quartos, and had an exceptional knowledge of Elizabethan literature.

He enjoyed both the friendship and the enmity of many literary figures of his time, including David *Garrick, who lent him quartos of Shakespeare's plays from his library, and Dr Johnson. In his 1793 edition, he provided obscene notes to bawdy passages, attributing them to two worthy clergymen with whom he had quarrelled.

Stein, Peter (1937–) German director who, in 1970, formed Berlin's Schaubuhne am Halleschen. He first approached Shakespeare in 1976 with *Shakespeare's Memory*, a dramatized investigation into Renaissance thought. This production inspired an *As You Like It the following year. Other productions include *Titus Andronicus (1992, Rome), *Julius Caesar (1992, Salzburg), *Antony and Cleopatra (1994, Salzburg).

Stephens, Sir Robert (1931–95) English actor who joined the *National Theatre in 1963 and played Horatio in their inaugural production of *Hamlet. Played *Falstaff in 1 and 2 *Henry IV, in 1991 (Stratford-upon-Avon), and King Lear (Stratford, 1993) in his last stage role.

Stevenson, Juliet (1956–) British actress whose strong, intelligent portrayal of Shakespeare heroines for the *Royal Shakespeare Company have made her one of Britain's foremost classical actresses. Roles include Hippolyta/Titania (1981, doubled), Isabella (1983), Rosalind, Cressida (both 1985, all RSC).

Stewart, Patrick (1940–) English actor with the *Royal Shakespeare Company 1966–82. His many Shakespeare roles include King John (1970), Oberon (1977), Shylock, Enobarbus (1978), Leontes, Titus Andronicus (1981), and Henry IV in Parts 1 and 2 (1982), all Royal Shakespeare Company, Prospero (Delacorte Theatre, New York, 1995), and Othello (Washington, DC, 1997).

Stoll, Elmer Edgar (1874–1959) American critic who reacted against A. C. *Bradley and insisted that study of Shakespeare's plays should be based on the dramatic conventions of the time at which they were written. His best-known book is *Art and Artifice in Shakespeare* (1933).

Strachey, Lytton (1880–1932) English man of letters whose essay on 'Shakespeare's Final Period' (1904) attacks the sentimental view of Shakespeare's *late plays.

Stratford, Ontario The festival here began in 1953, with two plays directed by Tyrone *Guthrie on an open stage incorporating Elizabethan features and designed by Tanya *Moiseiwitsch which has influenced the design of many subsequent theatres. At first it was covered by a tent; the permanent building was opened in 1957. It has continued to present Shakespeare's plays, with modifications to the stage and the use of additional auditoria, often with great success. A useful reference book is Alan Somerset's *The Stratford Festival Story: a catalogue-index to the Stratford Ontario Festival 1953–1990* (1991).

Strauss, Richard (1864–1949) The German composer wrote a tone poem, *Macbeth* (1888), and also set three of Ophelia's songs.

Strehler, Giorgio (1921–97) Italian director who founded Piccolo Teatro, Milan, in 1947, and the Théâtre de l'Europe, Paris, in 1983. An unbending perfectionist, who found that Shakespeare's plays accommodated his ability to combine elements of realism and fantasy. Productions include *Richard II, The *Tempest, *Romeo and Juliet (1948), *Richard III (1950), *Henry IV (1951), *Macbeth, *Coriolanus (both 1952), *Julius Caesar (1953), *Henry VI trilogy (1955), *King Lear (1972), The *Tempest (1978).

Students, The *See* LOVE'S LABOUR'S LOST.

Sullivan, Sir Arthur (1842–1900) W. S. Gilbert's great collaborator made his first success with incidental music for The *Tempest (1861); he composed settings for several Shakespeare songs, of which 'Orpheus with his Lute' is the best known, and, later, incidental music for *The *Merchant of Venice* (1871), **Henry VIII* (1877), and **Macbeth* (1888).

Supposes A play published in 1573, translated by George *Gascoigne from Ariosto's *I Suppositi*, the first extant English play written entirely in prose, used by Shakespeare for the Bianca plot of *The *Taming of the Shrew*.

Suzman, Janet (1939–) South African-born actress whose work with the *Royal Shakespeare Company 1963–72 included Rosaline, Portia, Ophelia (all 1965), Katharina, Celia (both 1967), Beatrice, Rosalind (both 1968), Cleopatra, Lavinia (both 1972). In 1988 she returned to Shakespeare to direct a deliberately politicized *Othello* at the Market Theatre, Johannesburg.

Swan Theatre Built on the Bankside, London, about 1595; drawn by *de Witt; the *Lord Chamberlain's Men probably played in it in 1596; it had 'fallen to decay' by 1632.

Swan Theatre, Stratford-upon-Avon Built in 1986 in the shell of the former *Shakespeare Memorial Theatre. The design is loosely based on theatres of Shakespeare's time, such as the *Swan. The initial purpose was to present infrequently produced plays by Renaissance and Restoration dramatists, but in recent years the programme has broadened to include more recent classics and new writing. See *This Golden Round* (1989), edited by Ronnie Mulryne and Margaret Shewring.

Taming of a Shrew, The An anonymous play, registered and published in 1594, generally believed to be a *bad quarto of The *Taming of the Shrew or of an earlier play from which both derive.

Taming of the Shrew, The Shakespeare's comedy, written probably in the early 1590s, was first printed in the First *Folio (1623). A play printed as The *Taming of a Shrew in 1594, once believed to be Shakespeare's source, is now generally regarded as a *bad quarto. It includes a continuation and conclusion of the Christopher Sly episodes omitted from the Folio which may derive from a Shakespearian original, and are sometimes performed and included in editions. Shakespeare's plot of Bianca and her suitors derives from *Supposes, translated by George *Gascoigne from Ariosto's I Suppositi.

For long after the Restoration, performances were normally in adaptation, such as John Lacy's Sauny the Scot (1667), Christopher Bullock's The Cobbler of Preston (1716), Charles Johnson's of the same title and date, and, above all, David *Garrick's *Catherine and Petruchio, of 1754, which held the stage until late in the nineteenth century. The first revival of Shakespeare's play was in 1844, under the auspices of Benjamin Webster and J. R. *Planché, in a production which, uniquely for its time, attempted to revive Elizabethan staging methods. Samuel *Phelps played both the original play and Garrick's adaptation. Augustin *Daly's production of 1887 shortened and rearranged Shakespeare's text and had Ada *Rehan as a splendid Kate; it was given in both America and England.

Many later productions, and Franco *Zeffirelli's film (1966), have treated the play as an uproarious farce, or as male brutality as in Charles *Marowitz's adaptation (1973) and Michael *Bogdanov's radical 1978 production (Stratford-upon-Avon). Among those which have shown that it can be both amusing and touching when played in its own terms was John *Barton and Peter *Hall's at Stratford-upon-Avon in 1960, with Peter O'Toole and Peggy *Ashcroft as Petruchio and Kate, replaced in a revival with almost equal success by Derek Godfrey and Vanessa *Redgrave.

Tarlton, Richard (d. 1588) Comic actor, a favourite of Queen *Elizabeth; sometimes sentimentally identified with Yorick in *Hamlet.

Tate, Nahum (1652–1715) Irish poet and playwright, librettist of *Purcell's opera *Dido and Aeneas*, author of 'While shepherds watched their flocks by night'; Poet Laureate, 1692. He adapted *Richard II in 1680; this was rapidly suppressed on political grounds; Tate revised it again as *The Sicilian Usurper*, without success. In 1681 he adapted *Coriolanus, as *The Ingratitude of a Commonwealth*, also unsuccessfully. But his version of *King Lear, 1681, which omits the Fool, introduces a love affair between Edgar and Cordelia, and finally commits Lear, Gloucester, and Kent to peaceful retirement, succeeded in supplanting Shakespeare's play from the stage, and went on being played, with modifications and restorations, until W. C. *Macready returned to Shakespeare's text in 1838.

Tchaikovsky, Peter Ilyich (1840–93) The great Russian composer wrote a symphonic fantasy on The *Tempest (1873), a fantasy overture on *Hamlet (1888), incidental music to the same play (1891), and a fantasy overture on *Romeo and Juliet (1869, revised 1870, final version, 1880).

Tempest, The Shakespeare's tragicomedy was first printed in the First *Folio (1623), where it is well printed, with divisions into acts and scenes. It was played at Court on 1 November 1611, and was probably written not long before. No source for the plot is known, though Shakespeare appears to have used accounts of the wreck of a ship called the *Sea-Venture* which sailed for Virginia in June 1609 and was wrecked on the coast of Bermuda. The storm in Shakespeare's play seems to be based on a letter of William Strachey describing the wreck which was written on 15 July 1610 and circulated in manuscript, though it was not published till 1625. Other books, such as *Florio's translation of *Montaigne and *Golding's of *Ovid, influenced individual passages of the play, sometimes quite closely.

The Tempest was performed as part of the festivities for the marriage of *James I's daughter, Princess Elizabeth, to the Elector Palatine during the winter of 1612/13. An adaptation by William *Davenant and John *Dryden was played at the Duke's Theatre, *Lincoln's Inn Fields, in 1667. Miranda is matched by a young man, Hippolito, who has never seen a woman, and she is given a younger sister, Dorinda.

Caliban has a sister, Sycorax, and Ariel has an attendant, Milcha. Thomas *Shadwell's operatic version of this play was given at the *Dorset Garden Theatre in 1674, in a spectacular production; music for a revival of 1695 is attributed to Henry *Purcell.

David *Garrick presented an operatic version of the Dryden–Davenant text, with music by J. C. *Smith, at *Drury Lane in 1756, but restored Shakespeare's play in the following year. J. P. *Kemble gave a modified version of the adaptation at Drury Lane from 1789, and did more to purify the text in his *Covent Garden version of 1806, in which he played Prospero. A musical version by Frederick *Reynolds, the music arranged by Henry *Bishop, appeared at Covent Garden in 1821, with W. C. *Macready (to his regret) as Prospero. Macready played Shakespeare's text at the same theatre in 1838, as did Samuel *Phelps at *Sadler's Wells in 1847, etc. Charles *Kean's spectacular revival at the Princess's in 1857 was severely shortened. Beerbohm *Tree's revival at the *Haymarket in 1904 also emphasized spectacle, and centred on Caliban, Tree's own role. John *Gielgud played Prospero at the *Old Vic in 1930 and 1940, at Stratford-upon-Avon in Peter *Brook's production of 1957, at the *National Theatre in 1974, and on film in Peter Greenaway's *Prospero's Books* (1991). The play was included in Peter *Hall's season of *late plays (*National Theatre, 1988), and Sam *Mendes directed a deliberately theatrical production with Simon Russell Beale as an unusually austere Ariel (Stratford-upon-Avon, 1993). There have been film versions directed by Derek Jarman (1980) and Peter Greenaway (1991), and the science fiction classic, *The Forbidden Planet* (1956), was loosely based on the play. Thomas Adès's opera was performed at Covent Garden in 2003.

The Tempest uses plot-elements which relate it to the other *Late Plays', or *romances, but it focuses on the end of the story and concentrates romance material into a neo-classical framework which relates it to one of Shakespeare's earliest plays, *The *Comedy of Errors*. The play has sometimes been regarded as his farewell to his art, but both Prospero and the whole play are multi-faceted in ways that make it infinitely suggestive. It has inspired other works of art, including an opera by Frank *Martin (1956), a fantasia by *Berlioz, a symphonic fantasy by *Tchaikovsky, a sequence of poems, *The Sea and the Mirror*, by W. H. Auden, and many paintings.

Temple Garden Scene 1 *Henry VI*, II. iv, invented by Shakespeare, in which Richard Plantagenet invites his supporters to pluck white roses, while the supporters of his opponent, the Earl of Somerset, pluck red roses. The Earl of Warwick prophesies that

> this brawl today,
> Grown to this faction in the Temple Garden,
> Shall send between the Red Rose and the White
> A thousand souls to death and deadly night! (ll. 124–7)

Terence (Publius Terentius Afer, *c*.185–159 BC) Roman dramatist who, like *Plautus, imitated Greek comedies, and whose plays were known and studied in Elizabethan England, providing models for contemporary dramaturgy. He probably exerted a direct influence on Shakespeare.

Terry, Dame Ellen (1848–1928) English actress, best known for her performances with Henry *Irving; mother of Gordon *Craig. Her principal Shakespeare roles were Beatrice, Ophelia, Portia, Desdemona, Juliet, Viola, Lady Macbeth, Imogen, Queen Katherine, and Volumnia.

Her correspondence with Bernard *Shaw (published in 1931) and her delightful autobiography, *The Story of My Life* (1908), are full of insights into the theatre of her time. There is an Ellen Terry Museum in her former house in Smallhythe, Kent.

Theatre, The Built by James *Burbage in 1576 in Shoreditch, London; the first English theatre; pulled down from 28 December 1598 by Burbage's sons and others after disagreements with the landlord, Giles Allen. The timber was ferried across the river to Bankside and used to build the *Globe.

Theobald, Lewis (1688–1744) Writer, translator, and dramatist. In 1726 he published *Shakespeare Restored*, an attack on Alexander *Pope's edition of 1725. Pope responded by making him the hero of the original *Dunciad* (1728):

> There hapless Shakespeare, yet of Theobald sore,
> Wished he had blotted for himself before.

But *Shakespeare Restored* includes the most famous of all Shakespeare emendations—in the description of *Falstaff's death, 'a babbled of green fields' for 'a Table of greene fields' (*Henry V*, II. iii. 19–20).

In 1733 he published his complete edition which includes many emendations that have since been regularly accepted; he is regarded now as the first of Shakespeare's major editors. In 1719 he presented an adaptation of *Richard II* which had some success; and in 1727 he prepared for the stage *The Double Falsehood* (*see* CARDENIO).

theophany Appearance of a god, as of Jupiter in *Cymbeline*, v. iv.

Third Folio *See* FOLIO, THIRD.

Thomas, Ambroise (1811–96) The French composer wrote an opera (1868) based on *Hamlet*.

Thomas, Lord Cromwell An anonymous play registered in the *Stationers' Register in 1602, published in that year as 'by W. S.', and included in the second issue of the Third *Folio, but no longer ascribed to Shakespeare.

Thomas of Woodstock *See* WOODSTOCK.

Thomson, James *See* CORIOLANUS.

Thorndike, Dame Sybil (1882–1976) English actress. She played many Shakespeare roles with Ben *Greet's company in America from 1904 to 1907 and at the *Old Vic from 1914 to 1918. Later Shakespeare roles included Lady Macbeth (Paris, 1921, Prince's, 1926, etc.), Queen Katherine (Empire, 1925), Volumnia (with Laurence *Olivier, Old Vic, 1938), and Constance (Old Vic, 1941). She was married to Sir Lewis *Casson.

Thorpe, Thomas Publisher of Shakespeare's *Sonnets in 1609, and author of the dedication to Mr W. H.

Throne of Blood A Japanese film (*Kumonoso-jo*) based on *Macbeth, directed by Akira *Kurosawa, and made in 1957.

Tieck, Johann Ludwig (1773–1853) German writer and Shakespeare critic who completed *Schlegel's translation of the works.

Tillyard, E. M. W. (1889–1962) English scholar who wrote *The Elizabethan World Picture* (1943), a useful exposition of some aspects of Renaissance thought, *Shakespeare's History Plays* (1994), an influential study, and other books on Shakespeare's plays.

Timon of Athens The tragedy, on which Shakespeare probably collaborated with Thomas *Middleton, was first printed in the First *Folio (1623), probably from an uncompleted manuscript. Its date is uncertain, but in style and content it seems related to *King Lear* and the later plays, and it is usually dated about 1607–8. Editors have to make decisions on textual discrepancies and inconsistencies, and a still greater degree of tinkering is necessary to prepare the text for performance.

Thomas *Shadwell's adaptation, as *The History of Timon of Athens, the Man-Hater*, was successfully acted in 1678; Henry *Purcell wrote music for it in 1694. It was frequently revived till the middle of the eighteenth century. Richard Cumberland's adaptation was played at *Drury Lane in 1771–2, and in Dublin, with J. P. *Kemble, in 1783. Another, unpublished version, apparently by Thomas Hull, who acted Flavius, was given at *Covent Garden in 1786.

George Lamb presented Shakespeare's play with omissions and with some material from Cumberland in the last scene at Drury Lane in 1816. Edmund *Kean's performance as Timon is the subject of a fine review by Leigh Hunt. Samuel *Phelps successfully produced a carefully prepared version of Shakespeare's text (omitting the Fool) at *Sadler's Wells in 1851 and 1856, playing Timon himself. More recent Timons have included F. R. *Benson (Stratford-upon-Avon, 1892), Robert *Atkins (*Old Vic, 1922), and Wilfred Walter (Stratford-upon-Avon, 1928). Barry *Jackson presented a *modern-dress version in Birmingham in 1947, Tyrone *Guthrie directed the play at the Old Vic in 1952, and Michael *Benthall directed Ralph *Richardson in an abbreviated text at the same theatre in 1956. John Schlesinger produced an authentic text, with some rearrangements, at Stratford-upon-Avon, in 1965, with Paul *Scofield as a memorable Timon. It is rarely seen on the large stage but small-scale productions have included The *Other Place (1980), Young Vic (1991), and Red Shift's 1989 touring production which cast a woman as Timon. Gregory Doran directed Michael *Pennington in the title-role for the Royal Shakespeare Theatre in 1999, using Duke Ellington's jazz suite. There have been few performances in America, but it was played in a successful modern-dress production at *Stratford, Ontario in 1963.

Unless anyone accepts the challenge of making a satisfactory acting version, *Timon of Athens* will not be a popular play, but the nature of the text gives it great fascination for the student of Shakespeare's working methods, and some of its episodes are fine in their own right.

tithes In 1605, Shakespeare paid £440 for a half-interest in the lease of certain tithes in the Stratford-upon-Avon area. His interest brought him £60 a year, above his yearly rents of £5 and £17. Shakespeare's friend Anthony *Nash collected the tithes for him. In 1611

Shakespeare joined two other leaseholders in a chancery court suit to protect their rights.

Titus Andronicus Shakespeare's early tragedy was first printed in 1594 in a *quarto of which the only known copy was discovered in Sweden in 1904. It was reprinted in 1600 and 1611. The 1611 quarto was reprinted in the First *Folio, with the addition of the whole of III. ii, which presumably came from a manuscript, and a few other lines.

The date of the play's composition is problematical; it may be as early as 1589. Francis *Meres included it in his list of Shakespeare's plays in 1598, but scholars have often been reluctant to believe that Shakespeare wrote all of it, a doubt first fostered in 1687 by Edward *Ravenscroft. Sources of the play have been suggested in *Ovid's *Metamorphoses*, *Seneca's *Thyestes* and *Trodes*, and a chapbook which survives only in an eighteenth-century version, discovered in 1936.

*Henslowe recorded performances of a 'Tittus and Vespaccia' in 1592 and a 'Titus & Ondronicus' in 1594. Either of these may or may not have been Shakespeare's play. It appears to have been popular in Shakespeare's time. An early drawing related to it is in the *Longleat manuscript.

A version by Edward Ravenscroft was played in 1687, and was revived several times till 1725. No further performances are known until 1839, when an adaptation by one N. H. Bannister was given in Philadelphia. It reappeared in London in 1852, when a black actor, Ira *Aldridge, played Aaron, apparently in Ravenscroft's adaptation.

Shakespeare's play was given at the *Old Vic in 1923, when the last act aroused laughter. Peter *Brook's historic production was given at Stratford-upon-Avon in 1955, with Laurence *Olivier as an immensely moving Titus. Later productions have included Trevor *Nunn's, also at Stratford-upon-Avon, in 1972, and the success of Deborah *Warner's full-text 1987 Stratford-upon-Avon production did much to improve the theatrical reputation of the play. Julie Taymor directed a film version, *Titus* (1999), with Anthony Hopkins in the title-role.

If Shakespeare was ever 'of an age', it was in *Titus Andronicus*, but, given tactful handling, the play's scenes of suffering can still be powerful.

Tokyo Globe, Japan A thrust-stage theatre opened in 1988 specializing in Shakespeare productions. Visiting touring companies have included *Royal Shakespeare Company, *Cheek by Jowl, and the *English Shakespeare Company.

Tolstoy, Count Leo (1828–1910) The great Russian novelist's essay *Shakespeare and the Drama* (1906) is an uncomprehending attack on *King Lear*.

Tom O'Bedlam A term used for an inmate of the lunatic asylum, Bedlam Hospital, London, the role adopted by Edgar in *King Lear*.

topical allusions There are a few clear topical allusions in Shakespeare's plays (*see*, e.g., ESSEX, EARL OF; MARLOWE, CHRISTOPHER; BOY ACTORS). Unexplained passages in some plays, especially *Love's Labour's Lost*, probably held topical significance for their first audiences, and many attempts have been made to show that Shakespeare bodied forth contemporary events, personalities, and issues under the guise of history or fiction (*see* e.g. LOPEZ, RODERIGO; JAMES I).

Tragedies The First *Folio distinguishes eleven plays as tragedies: in order of printing *Coriolanus*, *Titus Andronicus*, *Romeo and Juliet*, *Timon of Athens*, *Julius Caesar*, *Macbeth*, *Hamlet*, *King Lear*, *Othello*, *Antony and Cleopatra*, and *Cymbeline*. The last is now classed as a *comedy, or *romance.

   Troilus and Cressida, now classed as a comedy or *problem play, was to have been grouped among the tragedies, but was withdrawn and placed between the *histories and tragedies.

   Four of Shakespeare's histories, 3 *Henry VI*, *King John*, *Richard II*, and *Richard III*, have strongly tragic characteristics, including the death of the protagonist.

Tree, Sir Herbert Beerbohm (1853–1917) English actor and theatre manager who controlled the *Haymarket Theatre from 1887 to 1897, when he moved to Her Majesty's (later His Majesty's). He produced and acted in many lavish and spectacular versions of Shakespeare's plays in the tradition of Charles *Kean and Henry *Irving.

Troilus and Cressida Shakespeare's play was entered in the *Stationers' Register on 7 February 1603 'as it is acted by my Lord Chamberlain's Men'. This appears to be a *blocking entry, and the first *quarto did not appear till 1609. Its original title-page described it as having been 'acted by the King's Majesty's Servants at the Globe'. During the printing this title was replaced by a *'cancel', which omits the reference to performance. This issue also adds an epistle according to which this is 'a new play, never staled with the stage, never clapper-clawed with the palms of the vulgar, and yet passing full of the palm comical'. There is no satisfactory explanation of this discrepancy.

The text printed in the *Folio (1623) includes the Prologue and about forty-five lines not printed in the quarto. On both title-pages of the quarto, the play is called a history (a word which then had no more specific meaning than 'story'). The Epistle clearly classes it as a comedy. There is evidence that it was to have been included among the tragedies in the Folio, but that its printing there had to be delayed for copyright reasons, with the result that it was finally placed between the histories and the tragedies. The printing difficulties are reflected in the fact that it is not listed in the 'Catalogue' of plays at the beginning of the volume.

The classification of the play is still disputed; it can be regarded as a comedy, a history, a tragedy, or a satire. It is often classed among the *problem plays. It is usually assumed to have been written not very long before its entry in the Stationers' Register. Its difficult style has given rise to the theory that it was intended for a specialized audience, perhaps at one of the *Inns of Court. The most important source is Homer's *Iliad*, mainly in George *Chapman's translation, along with William Caxton's *Recuyell of the Histories of Troy* (1475) and John Lydgate's *Troybook* (c.1412–20). Shakespeare also probably knew other treatments of the Troy story, including Chaucer's *Troilus and Criseyde*.

The play seems to have been performed in Dublin during the Restoration period, and *Dryden's radical adaptation, *Troilus and Cressida, or Truth Found Too Late*, first performed at *Dorset Garden in 1679, held the stage until 1734. It includes a powerful quarrel scene between Troilus and Hector. J. P. *Kemble made an unperformed adaptation, but the first recorded performance in modern times was at Munich in 1898. In England, an unsuccessful costume-reading in 1907 was followed by William *Poel's production of an abbreviated text with the Elizabethan Stage Society in 1912, with a remarkable cast including Edith *Evans as Cressida, Esmé Percy as Troilus, and Hermione Gingold as Cassandra. The production was repeated at Stratford-upon-Avon in 1913.

Since then the play has grown in popularity, especially in University productions. It was first performed at the *Old Vic in 1923. B. Iden *Payne directed it at Stratford-upon-Avon in 1936, with Donald *Wolfit as Ulysses, and in 1938 came a *modern-dress version, directed by Michael MacOwan, at the Westminster. The play gained in significance because of the political climate. Tyrone *Guthrie directed another modern-dress production at the Old Vic in 1956. Peter *Hall and John *Barton directed it at Stratford-upon-Avon in 1960, with Dorothy *Tutin as Cressida and Max Adrian as Pandarus, and John Barton also directed it there in 1968 and 1976. Juliet *Stevenson was a fine Cressida in 1985, and Sam *Mendes directed a strong ensemble cast in 1990 with Simon Russell Beale as a caustic Thersites, both at Stratford-upon-Avon. Trevor Nunn's lavish production for the National in 1999 adjusted the text to begin and end with Cressida.

Troilus and Cressida is perhaps Shakespeare's most pessimistic play, a profound examination of human values, especially in relation to love and war, in the light of eternity. It does not seek popular appeal, but has found receptive audiences for the first time in the twentieth century.

Troublesome Reign of John, King of England, The An anonymous play published in two parts in 1591, strongly anti-Catholic in tone, used by Shakespeare as a source for *King John*.

True Tragedy of Richard Duke of York, The *See* 'CONTENTION' PLAYS.

Tutin, Dame Dorothy (1930–2001) English actress whose Shakespeare roles included Juliet (1958, 1961), Viola (1958, 1960), Ophelia (1958), Portia (1960), Cressida (1960, etc.), Desdemona (1961), and Rosalind (1967–8), at Stratford upon-Avon as well as Lady Macbeth (Guildford, etc., 1976), Cleopatra (*Prospect Players, 1977), and Queen Katherine in *Henry VIII* (Chichester, 1991).

Twelfth Night Shakespeare's comedy was first printed in the First *Folio (1623). It is based mainly on the tale of Apollonius and Silla in Barnabe *Riche's *Farewell to Military Profession* (1581).

Francis *Meres does not mention it, and internal references suggest that it was written about 1601. John *Manningham saw a performance at the *Middle Temple on 2 February 1602. Court performances are recorded in 1618 and 1623, and Leonard *Digges alluded to the play's popularity in lines printed in 1640. *Pepys saw Thomas *Betterton play Sir Toby Belch in 1661 at *Lincoln's Inn Fields. He did not admire the play. A distant adaptation by Charles Burnaby, *Love Betrayed*, was published in 1703. Shakespeare's play was revived at *Drury Lane in 1741, with Charles *Macklin as Malvolio, and continued to be played regularly both there and at *Covent Garden. Frederick *Reynolds's musical version, with music by Henry

*Bishop, appeared at Covent Garden in 1820, and was successful for some years.

Shakespeare's play was revived at the *Haymarket in 1846 for Charlotte *Cushman (as Viola) and her sister Susan (as Olivia). Samuel *Phelps produced it at *Sadler's Wells in 1848, playing Malvolio, and again in 1857. Kate Terry played both Viola and Sebastian at the Olympic in 1865. Henry *Irving was Malvolio in his *Lyceum production of 1884, with Ellen *Terry as Viola. Ada *Rehan was admired as Viola in an adaptation produced by Augustin *Daly in 1893 (New York) and 1894 (London). William *Poel's several productions with the Elizabethan Stage Society included one at the Middle Temple in 1897. His methods contrasted with those of Beerbohm *Tree at His Majesty's in 1901.

Harley *Granville-Barker's revolutionary production was given at the Savoy in 1912. There have been many productions at the *Old Vic and Stratford-upon-Avon. At the Old Vic, Edith *Evans was Viola in 1932; Laurence *Olivier played Toby Belch in 1937, for a Tyrone *Guthrie production in which Viola and Sebastian were again, regrettably, doubled; and Peggy *Ashcroft played Viola for Hugh Hunt in 1950. At Stratford-upon-Avon, Vivien Leigh played Viola, and Laurence Olivier Malvolio, in John *Gielgud's production of 1955; Peter *Hall (1958 and 1960) had Dorothy *Tutin as Viola; John *Barton (1969, etc.) directed a beautifully balanced production with Judi *Dench as Viola and Donald *Sinden as Malvolio. *Cheek by Jowl offered an inventive and economical staging with a strong ensemble cast in 1986, and Kenneth *Branagh directed the play for the Renaissance Theatre Company in 1988 (televised 1989). A bitter-sweet film version of 1996, directed by Trevor *Nunn, maintained a skilful balance between the various plots.

Twelfth Night, unquestionably one of the greatest of Shakespeare's comedies, has delighted critics and audiences alike. It contains many excellent acting roles, and different directors have varied the emphases, stressing sometimes the merry, sometimes the melancholy aspects, but the play has rarely failed to please audiences all over the world.

Twine, Laurence (fl. 1576) Writer and translator whose *The Pattern of Painful Adventures*, registered in 1576, provided Shakespeare with a source for *Pericles*. An edition of 1607 may have drawn Shakespeare's attention to the subject. The book also had a direct influence on George *Wilkins's *The Painful Adventures of Pericles Prince of Tyre* (1608).

Twins, The *See* COMEDY OF ERRORS, THE.

Two Gentlemen of Verona, The Shakespeare's early comedy was first printed in the First *Folio (1623), probably from a transcript of a *prompt-book. It is the first of his plays mentioned by Francis *Meres in 1598, and may be judged on stylistic grounds to be one of his earliest plays. It is based on part of Montemayor's *Diana*, perhaps indirectly.

The first recorded performance was at *Drury Lane in 1762, in an adaptation by Benjamin Victor. Shakespeare's play was given at *Covent Garden in 1784. J. P. *Kemble played a revised version, based partly on Victor, at Covent Garden in 1808, which proved unpopular. A spectacular musical version by Frederick *Reynolds was given at Covent Garden in 1821. Later nineteenth-century productions by W. C. *Macready, Samuel *Phelps, Charles *Kean, and Augustin *Daly had little success.

Harley *Granville-Barker directed it at the Court Theatre in 1904, and there have been a number of other twentieth-century productions, including ones by *Bridges-Adams (Stratford-upon-Avon, 1925), B. Iden *Payne (Stratford-upon-Avon, 1938), Denis Carey (Bristol Old Vic, 1951), Michael *Langham (*Old Vic, 1956), Peter *Hall (Stratford-upon-Avon, 1960), and Robin *Phillips (Stratford-upon-Avon, 1970; *Stratford, Ontario, 1975). The inclusion of popular pre-war ballads throughout David Thacker's 1991 production (Stratford-upon-Avon) helped to produce a rare commercial success, and the play was chosen for the inaugural Shakespeare production for the *International Shakespeare Globe Centre Company in 1996.

The play has never had great success, but it contains lyrical verse of great beauty, and Lance is the first in the line of Shakespeare's great clowns. His dog, Crab, is perhaps the most effective non-speaking role in the canon. The song 'Who is Silvia' has had independent popularity, especially in *Schubert's setting.

Two Noble Kinsmen, The This romance was first printed in 1634 as 'by the memorable worthies of their time, Mr John Fletcher, and Mr William Shakespeare, Gent.'. This attribution is now accepted by most scholars, and the scenes generally ascribed to Shakespeare are I. i–iii, III. i, and all of Act V except Scene ii. The play includes a dance identical with one in *Beaumont's *Masque of the Inner Temple and Gray's Inn*, performed in 1613, and is usually believed to have been written in the same year. The major source is Chaucer's *Knight's Tale*.

William *Davenant's adaptation, *The Rivals*, was successfully played from 1664–7. The original play was first revived at the *Old Vic in 1928, and has been occasionally played since then, notably as the inaugural production at the *Swan Theatre, Stratford-upon-Avon in 1986, where Imogen Stubbs was particularly effective as the Jailer's Daughter. It offers opportunities for spectacle, and has some impressive verse in Shakespeare's late style along with some touching and amusing episodes.

U

University Wits A term applied to the main university-educated playwrights of the 1580s, Robert *Greene, Christopher *Marlowe, and Thomas *Nashe, all of Cambridge, and John *Lyly, George *Peele, and Thomas *Lodge, of Oxford.

upper level *See* LORDS' ROOM.

Upstart Crow *See* GREENE, ROBERT.

Ur-Hamlet Title given to a lost play on the basis of allusions by Thomas *Nashe, Thomas *Lodge, Philip *Henslowe, and others. It has sometimes been supposed to be by Thomas *Kyd, but the evidence is questionable. Its relationship to Shakespeare's play is unknown.

V

Variorum editions Properly editions 'cum notis variorum', i.e. with notes by various people. The First Variorum is the fifth reprint of George *Steevens's edition, edited by *Isaac Reed in 1803, which reprints much material by *Johnson, *Malone, and others. The Second Variorum (1813) is a reprint of this. The Third Variorum is known as the Boswell–Malone Variorum (1821; *see* MALONE), and includes Prefaces from most of the eighteenth-century editions. It is the first to include the *Poems. The New Variorum edition (*see* FURNESS, H. H.) is often loosely referred to as 'the Variorum'.

Vaughan Williams, Ralph (1872–1958) The great English composer wrote music for F. R. *Benson's Stratford-upon-Avon productions of *Richard II*, 2 *Henry IV*, and *Richard III* in 1913. His opera *Sir John in Love* (1929) is based on The *Merry Wives of Windsor*; the cantata *In Windsor Forest* (1929) is based on the opera. The *Serenade to Music* (1938) sets lines from the last act of The *Merchant of Venice*. It was originally written for sixteen specified solo singers and orchestra for the jubilee of the conductor, Sir Henry Wood, but is also heard in a purely orchestral version. Vaughan Williams also wrote settings of Shakespeare as solo songs and part-songs.

Venus and Adonis Shakespeare's narrative poem was first published in 1593, probably from his own manuscript, perhaps under his supervision, by Richard *Field, who also came from Stratford-upon-Avon. It has a dedication to Henry *Wriothesley, 3rd Earl of Southampton, which refers to it as 'the first heir of my invention'. This presumably means that it was Shakespeare's first published work, or his first poem. It is written in a six-line stanza, rhyming a b a b c c, and has 1,194 lines.

Venus and Adonis is an early example of the Ovidian narrative poem popular in the 1590s. Its highly wrought style, resembling that of *Love's Labour's Lost*, creates difficulties for the modern reader; but it is a brilliant example of its kind, displaying a wit and elegance that link it with Shakespeare's *early comedies.

Verdi, Giuseppe (1813–1901) The great Italian composer wrote three

The dedication to Venus and Adonis, *from the only surviving copy of the first edition, in the Bodleian Library, Oxford*

operas based on Shakespeare's plays: *Macbeth* (1847, revised 1865), and his two final masterpieces, *Otello* (1887) and *Falstaff* (1893), based mainly on The **Merry Wives of Windsor*.

Vertue, George *See* NEW PLACE.

Vestris, (Madame) Elizabeth (1797–1856) English singer, actress, and theatre manager, whose main importance in relation to Shakespeare is the revival of **Love's Labour's Lost* for the first time since the Restoration, at **Covent Garden in 1839, under the joint management of herself and her husband, Charles Mathews, and the production of the first unadapted (though abbreviated) version of A **Midsummer Night's Dream*, also at Covent Garden, in 1840. Her artistic adviser in these enterprises was J. R. **Planché.

villages, the Shakespeare John **Jordan (1746–1809) related a story based on that of Shakespeare's **crabtree adding that Shakespeare refused to return to Bidford to renew the drinking contest, saying he had drunk with

> Piping Pebworth, dancing Marston,
> Haunted Hillborough, hungry Grafton,
> Dadging Exhall, papist Wixford,
> Beggarly Broom, and drunken Bidford.

These are all villages close to Stratford-upon-Avon.

> VOLTAIRE *(1694–1778) on the barbarities of* Hamlet; *adapted from the translation in H. H. Furness's New Variorum edition, 2 vols. (Philadelphia, PA, 1877), ii. 381.*
>
> ---
>
> *Hamlet* is a vulgar and barbarous drama, which would not be tolerated by the vilest populace of France or Italy. Hamlet becomes crazy in the second act, and his mistress becomes crazy in the third. The Prince slays his mistress's father under the pretence of killing a rat, and the heroine throws herself into a river. A grave is dug on the stage, and the gravediggers speak characteristically in riddles while holding skulls in their hands. Hamlet responds to their nasty vulgarities in sillinesses no less disgusting. In the meantime another of the actors conquers Poland. Hamlet, his mother and his father-in-law carouse on the stage; songs are sung at table, there is quarrelling, fighting, killing—one would imagine this piece to be the work of a drunken savage. But amidst all those nasty vulgarities, which to this day make the English drama so absurd and barbarous, there are to be found in *Hamlet*, by a bizarrerie still greater, some sublime passages worthy of the greatest genius. It seems as though nature had mingled in Shakespeare's brain the greatest conceivable strength and grandeur with whatsoever witless vulgarity can devise that is lowest and most detestable.

vocabulary, Shakespeare's *Spevack's *Concordance* lists 29,066 different words in Shakespeare's works, and 884,647 words altogether. *See* the Appendix: Some Facts and Figures.

Voltaire (François-Marie Arouet; 1694–1778) The French philosopher helped to spread knowledge of Shakespeare's plays in Europe, but often experienced difficulty in reconciling his admiration for Shakespeare with his own neo-classical literary principles.

Vortigern *See* IRELAND, WILLIAM HENRY.

W

W. H., Mr *See* SONNETS.

Wagner, Richard (1813–83) The great German composer's early opera, *Das Liebesverbot* (1836), is based on Shakespeare's *Measure for Measure*.

Walton, Sir William (1902–83) The English composer wrote distinguished incidental music for Laurence *Oliver's films of *Henry V* (1944), *Hamlet* (1948), and *Richard III* (1955). He also wrote the music for a film of *As You Like It* (1936), and for John *Gielgud's stage production of *Macbeth* (1942).

Wanamaker, Sam (1919–93) American stage and film actor who became well known for the extraordinary energy he channelled into establishing a replica of the Globe Theatre on its original Southwark site. In 1970 he became the Executive Director of the Globe Playhouse Trust and began two decades of vigorous planning and fund-raising. He died before the theatre was officially opened in 1997.

Warburton, William (1698–1779) Clergyman and scholar who edited Shakespeare's works in eight volumes in 1747, basing his text on *Pope's, whose literary executor and editor he was. Some of his own emendations have been influential.

Ward, John (1629–81) Vicar of Stratford-upon-Avon, 1662–81. His notebooks include a few facts about Shakespeare and some legends, including 'Shakespeare, Drayton, and Ben Jonson had a merry meeting, and it seems drank too hard, for Shakespeare died of a fever there contracted'.

Warlock, Peter (Philip Heseltine; 1894–1930) The English composer wrote popular settings of several lyrics by Shakespeare.

Warner, Deborah (1959–) British director renowned for directing small-scale, emotionally charged productions for Kick Theatre, 1980–6, and for successful full-text versions of the relatively unpopular *Titus Andronicus* and *King John* for the *Royal Shakespeare

Company 1987–8. Other Shakespeare productions include *King Lear* (1990), *Richard II* with Fiona Shaw in the title role (1995, both *Royal National Theatre), and *Coriolanus* (1993, Salzburg Festival).

Wars of the Roses, The John *Barton's adaptation of *1, 2* and *3 *Henry VI* and *Richard III*, acted at Stratford-upon-Avon in 1963 in three parts, as *Henry VI*, *Edward IV*, and *Richard III*. It was also televised. The plays were directed by Barton and Peter *Hall. Also the name given to the *English Shakespeare Company's sequence of history plays (1986, filmed 1989), which included both the first and second tetralogies.

Webster, John (1580?–1634?) English dramatist; the Epistle to his play *The White Devil* (1612) includes a reference to 'the right happy and copious industry of Master Shakespeare, Master Dekker, and Master Heywood'.

Weever, John (1576–1632) English poet, author of a sonnet in praise of Shakespeare published in 1599, and of lines referring to *Julius Caesar* published in 1601.

Weird Sisters The normal form of reference in *Macbeth* to the characters usually known now as the three witches.

Welcombe enclosures In 1614 proceedings were instigated to enclose land at Welcombe, within the parish of Stratford-upon-Avon, in which Shakespeare had an interest in the *tithes. He and his cousin, Thomas Greene, were to be compensated for any loss. The Stratford-upon-Avon Corporation opposed the scheme. The conflict dragged on for several years. A number of Greene's notes about it have survived. Shakespeare's attitude is uncertain. He may have favoured the scheme, as is suggested in Edward *Bond's play *Bingo* (1973).

Welles, Orson (1915–85) American actor and director; his Shakespeare roles include Mercutio (1933), Hamlet (1934), Brutus (1938, in his own modern-dress production), and *Falstaff (in adaptation, 1939). His first London appearance was as Othello in his own production (1951). He played King Lear in his own production in New York (1956), and Falstaff in his adaptation, *Chimes at Midnight*, in Dublin (1960); this was filmed in 1966. He also filmed *Macbeth* (1949), *Othello* (1951), and began work on The *Merchant of Venice* but it was never completed.

Whateley, Ann *See* MARRIAGE, SHAKESPEARE'S.

Wheeler, Margaret *See* SHAKESPEARE, JUDITH.

Whetstone, George (1554?–1587?) English author whose two-part play *Promos and Cassandra* (1578) is a principal source for **Measure for Measure*. Whetsone retold the story in prose in his *Heptameron of Civil Discourses* (1582), which Shakespeare may also have known.

Whiter, the Revd Walter (1758–1832) English philologist whose *Specimen of a Commentary on Shakespeare* (1794) anticipates *imagery studies of the twentieth century. It was almost entirely neglected for a century and a half, but was reprinted, with Whiter's own revisions, edited by Alan Over and Mary Bell, in 1967.

Wilkins, George (fl. 1603–8) A writer of whom little is known. His work includes *The Painful Adventures of Pericles Prince of Tyre* (1608), a prose tale based partly on Shakespeare's **Pericles*, and also on Laurence *Twine's *The Pattern of Painful Adventures*. Wilkins is sometimes supposed to have had a hand in *Pericles*, too.

will, Shakespeare's Shakespeare's will was drawn up for him by Francis *Collins in January 1616, and was revised on 25 March. The principal bequest was of *New Place, the Henley Street property, the property in Old Stratford, the *Blackfriars Gatehouse, and all his other property to his daughter *Susanna. References to his other daughter, *Judith, suggest lack of confidence in her husband, Thomas Quiney, whom she married on 2 February. She receives £150, the interest on a further £150 if she is still alive and married three years later, and a silver-gilt bowl. Shakespeare's granddaughter, Elizabeth *Hall, received the rest of his plate. To his sister, Joan *Hart, Shakespeare left the house in Henley Street at an annual rent of 12*d*., and his clothes. Other bequests are £5 to her three sons, £5 to Thomas *Russell, £13 6*s*. 8*d*. to Francis Collins, 26*s*. 8*d*. each to Hamnet *Sadler, Anthony *Nash, and John *Nash, neighbours of Shakespeare, to buy mourning rings; the same to John *Heminges, Richard *Burbage, and Henry *Condell for the same purpose; his sword to Thomas *Russell; £1 to his godson, William Walker; £10 to the poor of Stratford-upon-Avon; and his second-best bed to his wife (*see* Hathaway, Anne). The will bears three of Shakespeare's six authenticated *signatures.

Willobie his Avisa A poem by Henry Willobie (born about 1575), printed in 1594. Commendatory verses include the first literary reference to Shakespeare by name:

> Yet Tarquin plucked his glistering grape,
> And Shakespeare paints poor Lucrece' rape.

The poem tells how Avisa, an inn-keeper's wife, rejected many suitors, including 'Henrico Willobego', who confided his love to 'his familiar friend, W.S.', recently recovered from a similar passion. W. S. 'in viewing afar off the course of this loving comedy . . . determined to see whether it would sort to a happier end for this new actor than it did for the old player.' Willobie was related by marriage to Shakespeare's friend, Thomas *Russell. It is possible that Shakespeare is the Mr W.S. of the deliberately enigmatic poem.

Willow Song A song with traditional words and music sung by Desdemona (*Othello*, iv. iii).

Wilmcote A village two-and-a-half miles north-west of Stratford-upon-Avon; Shakespeare's grandfather, Robert Arden, bequeathed two estates there, Asbyes, to Shakespeare's mother, Mary *Arden. *See* MARY ARDEN'S HOUSE.

Wilson, John (1595–1674) Musician who became Professor of Music at Oxford in 1656 and a Gentleman of the Chapel Royal in 1662. His *Cheerful Airs or Ballads* (1660) includes settings of 'Take, O take those lips away' (*Measure for Measure*) and 'Lawn as white as driven snow' (*Winter's Tale*). He may be the 'Jack Wilson' referred to in a stage direction (ii. i) in the *Folio text of *Much Ado About Nothing*, apparently a performer of the singing role of Balthazar.

Wilson, John Dover (1881–1969) English scholar and critic. His writings include *The Essential Shakespeare*, described as a 'biographical adventure' (1932), *The Manuscript of Shakespeare's 'Hamlet' and the Problems of its Transmission* (1934), *What Happens in 'Hamlet'* (1935), *The Fortunes of Falstaff* (1953), *Shakespeare's Happy Comedies* (1962), and an autobiography, *Milestones on the Dover Road* (1969).

He was the General Editor, along with (initially) Sir A. T. Quiller-Couch, of the *New Cambridge edition of Shakespeare, which began with *The *Tempest* in 1921 and was completed with the *Sonnets in 1966.

Winter's Tale, The Shakespeare's tragicomedy was first printed in the First *Folio (1623). Simon *Forman saw it at the *Globe on 15 May 1611, and a Court performance on 5 November of that year is recorded. The dance of satyrs in iv. iv seems to derive from *Jonson's

masque *Oberon*, performed on 1 January 1611, and the composition of
the play is usually ascribed to that year. It is based mainly on Robert
*Greene's prose tale *Pandosto*, printed in 1588.

The play seems to have been popular in its own time; seven
Court performances are recorded before 1640. It was not played
again until 1741, when it was given at both Goodman's Fields
and *Covent Garden. Later eighteenth-century performances were
usually in severely abbreviated versions, of which David *Garrick's, as
Florizel and Perdita (1756), was the most successful. It concentrates on
the last two acts, reflecting disapproval of the wide time-span of the
original play.

John Philip *Kemble used a much fuller text at *Drury Lane in
1802, when he played Leontes, with Sarah *Siddons as Hermione.
W. C. *Macready played Leontes frequently from 1815 to 1843; at
Covent Garden in 1837 he had Helena *Faucit as his Hermione.
Samuel *Phelps presented the play successfully at *Sadler's Wells in
1845, and Charles *Kean put on a spectacular version at the Princess's
in 1856, with great success. Mary Anderson doubled Hermione and
Perdita in 1887, also in an abbreviation.

Beerbohm *Tree directed Ellen *Terry as Hermione at His Majesty's
in 1906. Harley *Granville-Barker's historic Savoy production of 1912,
using an almost complete text, was not a popular success. There have
been numerous *Old Vic and Stratford-upon-Avon productions. Peter
*Brook directed it at the Phoenix in 1951, with John *Gielgud as
Leontes, Diana Wynyard as Hermione, and Flora Robson as Paulina.
In Trevor *Nunn's Stratford-upon-Avon production of 1969, Judi
*Dench doubled Hermione and Perdita. Peter *Hall included the play
in a season of *Late Plays in 1988 (*National Theatre), and Adrian
*Noble directed a large-scale production in 1992 (*Royal Shakespeare
Company) which toured internationally. Theatre de Complicite
staged an inventive touring production in the same year, with a
virtuoso performance from Kathryn Hunter playing Mamillius,
Time, Antigonus, and Autolycus.

Formerly criticized for improbability and structural irregularity,
The Winter's Tale has risen in critical esteem during the twentieth
century, and is now recognized as one of Shakespeare's richest poetic
dramas, wide-ranging, powerful in psychological suggestiveness,
varied in comic effect, tempering romance with astringency, poeti-
cally resonant, having some of the qualities of myth, yet also profoundly human.

Wolfit, Sir Donald (1902–68) English actor–manager. He played many Shakespeare roles, including Hamlet at Stratford-upon-Avon in 1936. In 1937 he formed his own Shakespearian company with which he played Hamlet, Macbeth, Shylock, and Malvolio. The company toured widely in the provinces and overseas, and gave occasional London seasons.

Wolfit's other Shakespeare roles included Petruchio, Othello, Iago, Benedick, *Falstaff, Richard III, Bottom, Iachimo, and King Lear, the role in which he was most admired. He gave his last Shakespeare performances in 1953, except for recital programmes.

Woodstock An anonymous play of uncertain date, surviving only in manuscript, dealing with the early part of the reign of Richard II and the murder of his uncle, Thomas of Woodstock, Duke of Gloucester. Shakespeare may have known the play, and it has even been suggested that he designed *Richard II* as a sequel to it.

World Shakespeare Congress A meeting with this title, at which scholarly papers were delivered, was held in Vancouver in 1971,

---

VIRGINIA WOOLF *(1882–1941): an extract from her diary for 13 April 1930*

I read Shakespeare *directly* I have finished writing, when my mind is agape & red & hot. Then it is astonishing. I never yet knew how amazing his stretch & speed & word coining power is, until I felt it utterly outpace & outrace my own, seeming to start equal & then I see him draw ahead & do things I could not in my wildest tumult & utmost press of mind imagine. Even the less known & worser plays are written at a speed that is quicker than anybody else's quickest; & the words drop so fast one can't pick them up. Look at this, Upon a gather'd lily almost wither'd (that is a pure accident: I happen to light on it.) Evidently the pliancy of his mind was so complete that he could furbish out any train of thought; &, relaxing lets fall a shower of such unregarded flowers. Why then should anyone else attempt to write. This is not 'writing' at all. Indeed, I could say that Shre surpasses literature altogether, if I knew what I meant.

under the auspices of Simon Fraser University. From it developed the *International Shakespeare Association, with responsibility for organizing future Congresses.

Wotton, Sir Henry (1568–1639) Poet, diplomat, translator; in a letter of 2 July 1613, to his nephew, Sir Edmund Bacon, he gave an account of the burning down of the *Globe Theatre on 29 June during a performance (which he did not attend) of *Henry VIII* (**All is True*).

Wriothesley, Henry, 3rd Earl of Southampton (1573–1624) Shakespeare's patron, recipient of his only two dedications, those to *Venus and Adonis* (1593), and The **Rape of Lucrece* (1594). He encouraged other writers, such as *Florio and *Nashe. *Rowe records a legend that he gave Shakespeare £1,000. He has often been identified with the Mr W. H. to whom Thomas *Thorpe dedicated Shakespeare's *Sonnets. A performance of *Love's Labour's Lost* was arranged for Queen Anne at his London home in January 1605.

Y

Yorkshire Tragedy, A A domestic tragedy published in 1608 and ascribed to Shakespeare both in the *Stationers' Register and on the
title-page. It was reprinted in 1619. It was not included in the First
*Folio (1623), but appears in the second issue of the Third *Folio
(1664). It is based on a contemporary murder case. It is now generally
ascribed to Thomas *Middleton.

Z

Zadek, Peter (1926–) German director, head of Bochum Theatre 1972–5, and Deutsches Schauspielhaus, Hamburg 1985–9, known for experimental, iconoclastic Shakespeare revivals. Productions include *Measure for Measure* (1967, Bremen), *King Lear* (1974), *Othello* (1976), *Hamlet* (1977), The *Merchant of Venice*, *Measure for Measure* (both 1990), *Antony and Cleopatra* (1994, Vienna).

Zeffirelli, Franco (1923–) Italian stage and film director famous for large-scale, spectacular productions: he directed *Romeo and Juliet* at the *Old Vic in 1960, and a film of the same play in 1968; his production of *Othello* at Stratford-upon-Avon in 1961, with John *Gielgud as Othello, was visually splendid but less successful dramatically. He also filmed The *Taming of the Shrew* (1966) with Richard *Burton and Elizabeth Taylor, and *Hamlet* (1990) with Mel Gibson.

The Characters of Shakespeare's Plays

A Selective Finding List

Aaron, a Moor, loved by Tamora, *Titus Andronicus*
Abbess (Emilia), *Comedy of Errors*
Abergavenny, George Neville, Lord, *All is True*
Abhorson, an executioner, *Measure for Measure*
Abraham, Montague's servant, *Romeo and Juliet*
Achilles, Greek warrior, *Troilus and Cressida*
Adam, an old servant, *As You Like It*
Adrian, a Volscian, *Coriolanus*
Adrian, attendant on Alonso, *Tempest*
Adriana, wife of Antipholus of Ephesus, *Comedy of Errors*
Aemilia, *see* Emilia, an Abbess
Aemilius, a Roman nobleman, *Titus Andronicus*
Aeneas, Trojan commander, *Troilus and Cressida*
Aeschines, lord of Tyre, *Pericles*
Agamemnon, Greek commander, *Troilus and Cressida*
Agrippa, friend of Octavius, *Antony and Cleopatra*
Aguecheek, Sir Andrew, suitor of Olivia, *Twelfth Night*
Ajax, Greek commander, *Troilus and Cressida*
Alarbus, Tamora's eldest son, *Titus Andronicus*
Albany, Duke of, Goneril's husband, *King Lear*
Alcibiades, Athenian captain, *Timon of Athens*
Alençon, Duke of, *1 Henry VI*
Alexander, Cressida's servant, *Troilus and Cressida*
Alexas, a eunuch, *Antony and Cleopatra*
Alice, a waiting-woman, *Henry V*
Aliena, name taken by Celia, *As You Like It*
Alonso, King of Naples, *Tempest*
Amiens, a lord, *As You Like It*
Andromache, Hector's wife, *Troilus and Cressida*
Andronicus, Marcus, Titus' brother, *Titus Andronicus*
Angelo, a goldsmith, *Comedy of Errors*
Angelo, the Duke's deputy, *Measure for Measure*
Angus, a nobleman, *Macbeth*

Anne, Lady (Neville), wife of Richard III, *Richard III*
Antenor, Trojan warrior, *Troilus and Cressida*
Antigonus, Paulina's husband, *Winter's Tale*
Antiochus, King of Antioch, *Pericles*
Antipholus of Ephesus, and of Syracuse, twins, *Comedy of Errors*
Antonio, a merchant, *Merchant of Venice*
Antonio, Leonato's brother, *Much Ado About Nothing*
Antonio, Prospero's brother, *Tempest*
Antonio, a sea-captain, *Twelfth Night*
Antonio, Proteus's father, *Two Gentlemen of Verona*
Antony, Mark, *Julius Caesar, Antony and Cleopatra*
Apemantus, a cynic, *Timon of Athens*
Apothecary, *Romeo and Juliet*
Aragon, Prince of, *Merchant of Venice*
Archidamus, Bohemian lord, *Winter's Tale*
Arcite, *Two Noble Kinsmen*
Ariel, a spirit, *Tempest*
Armado, Don Adriano de, a Spaniard, *Love's Labour's Lost*
Artemidorus, *Julius Caesar*
Artesius, an Athenian soldier, *Two Noble Kinsmen*
Arthur, Duke of Brittaine (Prince), *King John*
Arviragus, Cymbeline's son, known as Cadwal, *Cymbeline*
Audrey, wooed by Touchstone, *As You Like It*
Aufidius, Tullus, Volscian leader, *Coriolanus*
Aumerle, Duke of, later **Duke of York**, *Richard II, Henry V*
Autolycus, a rogue, *Winter's Tale*
Auvergne, Countess of, *1 Henry VI*

Bagot, favourite of Richard, *Richard II*
Balthasar, a merchant, *Comedy of Errors*
Balthasar, Portia's servant, *Merchant of Venice*
Balthasar, Don Pedro's attendant, *Much Ado About Nothing*
Balthasar, Romeo's servant, *Romeo and Juliet*
Banquo, Scottish nobleman, *Macbeth*
Baptista Minola, father of Katherine and Bianca, *Taming of the Shrew*
Bardolph, Lieutenant (or **Corporal)**, *Merry Wives of Windsor*, 1 and 2
  Henry IV, Henry V
Bardolph, Lord, *2 Henry IV*
Barnardine, a prisoner, *Measure for Measure*
Barnardo, a sentry, *Hamlet*
Bartholomew, a page, *Taming of the Shrew*

Bassanio, Portia's suitor, *Merchant of Venice*
Basset, a Lancastrian, *1 Henry VI*
Bassianus, Saturninus' brother, *Titus Andronicus*
Bates, John, a soldier, *Henry V*
Beatrice, Leonato's niece, *Much Ado About Nothing*
Bedford, Duke of, *see* John (of Lancaster)
Belarius, known as Morgan, *Cymbeline*
Belch, Sir Toby, *Twelfth Night*
Benedick, a lord of Padua, *Much Ado About Nothing*
Benvolio, friend of Romeo, *Romeo and Juliet*
Berkeley, Earl, *Richard II*
Berowne, *see* Biron
Bertram, Count of Roussillon, *All's Well that Ends Well*
Bianca, a courtesan, *Othello*
Bianca Minola, Katherine's sister, *Taming of the Shrew*
Bigot, Lord, *King John*
Biondello, Lucentio's servant, *Taming of the Shrew*
Biron, in love with Rosaline, *Love's Labour's Lost*
Blanche of Spain, Lady, *King John*
Blunt, Sir James, *Richard III*
Blunt, Sir John, *2 Henry IV*
Blunt, Sir Walter, *1 Henry IV*
Boleyn, Anne, *All is True*
Bolingbroke, Harry, Duke of Hereford, later **Henry IV**, *Richard II*, *1
  and 2 Henry IV*
Bolingbroke, Roger, a sorcerer, *2 Henry VI*
Bona, Lady, the French Queen's sister, *3 Henry VI*
Borachio, follower of Don John, *Much Ado About Nothing*
Bottom, Nick, a weaver, *Midsummer Night's Dream*
Boult, servant in a brothel, *Pericles*
Bourbon, John, Duke of, *Henry V*
Bourbon, Lord, *3 Henry VI*
Bourchier, Cardinal, *Richard III*
Boyet, a lord, *Love's Labour's Lost*
Brabanzio, Desdemona's father, *Othello*
Brakenbury, Sir Robert, Lieutenant of the Tower, *Richard III*
Brandon, Charles, *see* Suffolk, Duke of
Brandon, Sir William, an officer, *All is True*
Brooke, false name of Ford, *Merry Wives of Windsor*
Brutus, Junius, a tribune, *Coriolanus*

Brutus, Marcus Junius, *Julius Caesar*
Buckingham, Edward Stafford, Duke of, *All is True*
Buckingham, Henry Stafford, Duke of, *Richard III*
Buckingham, Humphrey Stafford, Duke of, *2 Henry VI*
Bullcalf, Peter, *2 Henry IV*
Burgundy, Duke of, Cordelia's suitor, *King Lear*
Burgundy, Duke of (Philip the Good), *Henry V*, *1 Henry VI*
Bushy, favourite of Richard, *Richard II*
Butts, Doctor, the King's physician, *All is True*

Cade, Jack, a rebel, *2 Henry VI*
Cadwal, name taken by Arviragus, *Cymbeline*
Caesar, Octavius, *Julius Caesar*, *Antony and Cleopatra*
Caithness, Scottish nobleman, *Macbeth*
Caius, name taken by Kent, *King Lear*
Caius, Doctor, a Frenchman, *Merry Wives of Windsor*
Caius Cassius, *see* Cassius
Caius Ligarius, *see* Ligarius
Caius Lucius, *see* Lucius
Caius Martius, *see* Coriolanus
Calchas, Trojan priest, *Troilus and Cressida*
Caliban, 'a savage and deformed slave', *Tempest*
Calpurnia, Caesar's wife, *Julius Caesar*
Cambio, name taken by Lucentio, *Taming of the Shrew*
Cambridge, Richard (Plantagenet), Earl of, *Henry V*
Camidius, Antony's lieutenant-general, *Antony and Cleopatra*
Camillo, Sicilian lord, *Winter's Tale*
Campeius, Cardinal, papal legate, *All is True*
Canterbury, Archbishop of, *see* Bourchier *and* Cranmer
Canterbury, Archbishop of (Henry Chicheley), *Henry V*
Canterbury, Archbishop of (William Warham), *All is True*
Caphis, a servant, *Timon of Athens*
Capulet, Cousin, *Romeo and Juliet*
Capulet, Lady, Juliet's mother, *Romeo and Juliet*
Capulet, 'Old', Juliet's father, *Romeo and Juliet*
Caputius, a Spanish ambassador, *All is True*
Carlisle, Bishop of, *Richard II*
Casca, a conspirator, *Julius Caesar*
Cassandra, Priam's daughter, a prophetess, *Troilus and Cressida*
Cassio, Michael, a Florentine, *Othello*

Cassius, Caius, *Julius Caesar*
Catesby, Sir William, *Richard III*
Catherine of France, Princess, later **Queen of Henry V**, *Henry V*
Cato, Young, Marcus Cato's son, *Julius Caesar*
Celia, Duke Frederick's daughter, *As You Like It*
Ceres (impersonated by Ariel), *Tempest*
Cerimon, a physician, *Pericles*
Cesario, name taken by Viola, *Twelfth Night*
Charles VI, King of France, *Henry V*
Charles the Dauphin, later Charles VII of France, *1 Henry VI*
Charles the Wrestler, *As You Like It*
Charmian, Cleopatra's attendant, *Antony and Cleopatra*
Châtillon, a French lord, *King John*
Chiron, son of Tamora, *Titus Andronicus*
Cicero, *Julius Caesar*
Cimber, Metellus, a conspirator, *Julius Caesar*
Cinna, a conspirator, *Julius Caesar*
Cinna, a poet, *Julius Caesar*
Clarence, George, Duke of, *3 Henry VI*, *Richard III*
Clarence, Thomas, Duke of, *2 Henry IV*, *Henry V* (non-speaking)
Claudio, Brutus' servant, *Julius Caesar*
Claudio, betrothed to Juliet, *Measure for Measure*
Claudio, betrothed to Hero, *Much Ado About Nothing*
Claudius, King of Denmark, *Hamlet*
Cleomenes, Sicilian lord, *Winter's Tale*
Cleon, Governor of Tarsus, *Pericles*
Clifford, John (Young Clifford), *2 and 3 Henry VI*
Clifford, Thomas, Lord (Old Clifford), *2 Henry VI*
Clitus, Brutus' servant, *Julius Caesar*
Cloten, Cymbeline's stepson, *Cymbeline*
Cobweb, a fairy, *Midsummer Night's Dream*
Coleville, Sir John, *2 Henry IV*
Cominius, Roman commander, *Coriolanus*
Conrad, follower of Don John, *Much Ado About Nothing*
Constable of France (Charles Delabreth), *Henry V*
Constance, Lady, Arthur's mother, *King John*
Cordelia, Lear's youngest daughter, *King Lear*
Corin, an old shepherd, *As You Like It*
Coriolanus, *see* Martius, Caius
Cornelius, a physician, *Cymbeline*

Cornelius, a courtier, *Hamlet*
Cornwall, Duke of, Regan's husband, *King Lear*
Costard, a clown, *Love's Labour's Lost*
Court, Alexander, a soldier, *Henry V*
Courtesan, *Comedy of Errors*
Crab, a dog, *Two Gentlemen of Verona*
Cranmer, Thomas, Archbishop of Canterbury, *All is True*
Cromwell, Thomas, *All is True*
Curan, a courtier, *King Lear*
Curio, Orsino's attendant, *Twelfth Night*
Curtis, a servant, *Taming of the Shrew*

Dardanius, Brutus' servant, *Julius Caesar*
Dauphin, *see* Charles *and* Louis
Davy, Shallow's servant, *2 Henry IV*
Decius Brutus, a conspirator, *Julius Caesar*
Decretas, friend of Antony, *Antony and Cleopatra*
Deiphobus, son of Priam, *Troilus and Cressida*
Delabreth, *see* Constable of France
Demetrius, Roman soldier, *Antony and Cleopatra*
Demetrius, in love with Hermia, *Midsummer Night's Dream*
Demetrius, son of Tamora, *Titus Andronicus*
Denis, Oliver's servant, *As You Like It*
Denny, Sir Anthony, *All is True*
Derby, Thomas Lord Stanley, Earl of, *Richard III*
Desdemona, Othello's wife, *Othello*
Diana, the goddess, *Pericles*
Diana Capilet, a widow's daughter, *All's Well that Ends Well*
Dick, the Butcher of Ashford, *2 Henry VI*
Diomed, Cleopatra's attendant, *Antony and Cleopatra*
Diomedes, Greek general, *Troilus and Cressida*
Dion, Sicilian lord, *Winter's Tale*
Dioniza, Cleon's wife, *Pericles*
Dogberry, a constable, *Much Ado About Nothing*
Dolabella, friend of Octavius, *Antony and Cleopatra*
Doll Tearsheet, *see* Tearsheet, Doll
Donalbain, son of Duncan, *Macbeth*
Dorcas, a shepherdess, *Winter's Tale*
Doricles, name taken by Florizel, *Winter's Tale*
Dorset, Thomas Gray, Marquis of, *Richard III*

Douglas, Archibald, Earl of, *1 Henry IV*
Dromio of Ephesus, and of Syracuse, twins, *Comedy of Errors*
Duke (Senior), The, *As You Like It*
Dull, Anthony, a constable, *Love's Labour's Lost*
Dumaine, Captain (two), *All's Well that Ends Well*
Dumaine, in love with Katharine, *Love's Labour's Lost*
Duncan, King of Scotland, *Macbeth*

Edgar, Gloucester's legitimate son, *King Lear*
Edmond, Gloucester's bastard son, *King Lear*
Edward, Earl of March, later **Edward IV**, *2* and *3 Henry VI*, *Richard III*
Edward, Earl of Warwick, Clarence's son, *Richard III*
Edward, Prince of Wales, son of **Henry VI**, *3 Henry VI*, (ghost of) *Richard III*
Edward, Prince of Wales, later **Edward V**, *3 Henry VI*, *Richard III*
Egeon, merchant of Syracuse, *Comedy of Errors*
Egeus, Hermia's father, *Midsummer Night's Dream*
Eglamour, Sir, a knight, *Two Gentlemen of Verona*
Elbow, 'a simple constable', *Measure for Measure*
Eleanor, Queen, John's mother, *King John*
Elizabeth, Princess (afterwards **Elizabeth I**; non-speaking), *All is True*
Ely, Bishop of (John Fordham), *Henry V*
Ely, Bishop of (John Morton), *Richard III*
Emilia, an Abbess, *Comedy of Errors*
Emilia, Iago's wife, *Othello*
Emilia, attendant on Hermione, *Winter's Tale*
Emilia, Hippolyta's sister, *Two Noble Kinsmen*
Emmanuel, Clerk of Chatham, *2 Henry VI*
Enobarbus, Domitius, Roman soldier, *Antony and Cleopatra*
Ephesus, Duke of, *See* Solinus
Eros, Antony's servant, *Antony and Cleopatra*
Erpingham, Sir Thomas, *Henry V*
Escalus, a lord, *Measure for Measure*
Escalus, Prince of Verona, *Romeo and Juliet*
Escanes, *see* Aeschines
Essex, Earl of, *King John*
Evans, Sir Hugh, a Welsh parson, *Merry Wives of Windsor*
Exeter, Thomas Beaufort, Duke of, *Henry V*, *1 Henry VI*
Exeter, Henry Holland, Duke of, *3 Henry VI*
Exton, *see* Piers of Exton

Fabian, Olivia's servant, *Twelfth Night*

Falconbridge, Lady, *King John*
Falconbridge, Philip, the Bastard, *King John*
Falconbridge, Robert, *King John*
Falstaff, Sir John, *Merry Wives of Windsor*, 1 and 2 *Henry IV*
Fang, a sheriff's officer, 2 *Henry IV*
Fastolf, Sir John, a cowardly knight, 1 *Henry VI*
Father that has killed his son, *see* Soldier
Feeble, Francis, a woman's tailor, 2 *Henry IV*
Fenton, Anne Page's suitor, *Merry Wives of Windsor*
Ferdinand, Alonso's son, *Tempest*
Ferdinand, King of Navarre, *Love's Labour's Lost*
Feste, Olivia's fool, *Twelfth Night*
Fidele, name taken by Innogen, *Cymbeline*
Filario, *see* Philario
Fitzwater, Lord, *Richard II*
Flaminius, Timon's servant, *Timon of Athens*
Flavius, a tribune, *Julius Caesar*
Flavius, a soldier (non-speaking), *Julius Caesar*
Flavius, Timon's steward, *Timon of Athens*
Fleance, Banquo's son, *Macbeth*
Florence, Duke of, *All's Well that Ends Well*
Florizel, Prince, in love with Perdita, *Winter's Tale*
Fluellen, Welsh officer, *Henry V*
Flute, Francis, a bellows-mender, *Midsummer Night's Dream*
Ford, Frank, sometimes disguised as Brooke, *Merry Wives of Windsor*
Ford, Mistress Alice, Frank's wife, *Merry Wives of Windsor*
Fortinbras, Prince of Norway, *Hamlet*
France, King of, Cordelia's successful suitor, *King Lear*
France, King of, *All's Well that Ends Well*
France, King of, *see also* Charles VI, Charles the Dauphin, Louis XI, Philip
France, Princess of, *Love's Labour's Lost*
Francesca, a nun, *Measure for Measure*
Francis, a drawer, 1 and 2 *Henry IV*
Francis, Friar, *Much Ado About Nothing*
Francisco, a sentry, *Hamlet*
Francisco, a lord, *Tempest*
Frederick, Duke, Celia's father, *As You Like It*
Froth, 'a foolish gentleman', *Measure for Measure*

Gadshill, a robber, *1 Henry IV*

Gallus, a soldier (non-speaking), *Antony and Cleopatra*

Ganymede, name taken by Rosalind, *As You Like It*

Gardiner, Stephen, Bishop of Winchester, *All is True*

Gargrave, Sir Thomas, *1 Henry VI*

Gaunt, John of, Duke of Lancaster, *Richard II*

Gerald, a schoolmaster, *Two Noble Kinsmen*

Gertrude, Queen of Denmark, *Hamlet*

Giacomo, *Cymbeline*

Glasdale, Sir William, *1 Henry VI*

Glendower, Owen, *see* Glyndŵr

Gloucester, Earl of, *King Lear*

Gloucester, Eleanor de Bohum, Duchess of, *Richard II*

Gloucester, Eleanor Cobham, Duchess of, *2 Henry VI*

Gloucester, Richard, Duke of, later **Richard III**, *1*, *2*, and *3 Henry VI*, *Richard III*

Gloucester, Prince Humphrey, later **Duke of**, *2 Henry IV*, *Henry V*, *1* and *2 Henry VI*

Glyndŵr, Owain, *1 Henry IV*

Gobbo, Lancelot, Shylock's servant, *Merchant of Venice*

Gobbo, 'Old', Lancelot's father, *Merchant of Venice*

Goneril, Duchess of Albany, Lear's eldest daughter, *King Lear*

Gonzalo, 'an honest old counsellor', *Tempest*

Goodfellow, Robin, *see* Puck

Gough, Matthew, *2 Henry VI*

Gower, a messenger, *2 Henry IV*

Gower, Captain, *Henry V*

Gower (John), the presenter, *Pericles*

Grandpré, a French lord, *Henry V*

Gray, Lord, *Richard III*

Graziano, Bassanio's friend, *Merchant of Venice*

Graziano, Brabantio's brother, *Othello*

Green, favourite of Richard, *Richard II*

Gregory, Capulet's servant, *Romeo and Juliet*

Gremio, suitor to Bianca, *Taming of the Shrew*

Grey, Sir Thomas, a traitor, *Henry V*

Griffith, Queen Katherine's gentleman-usher, *All is True*

Groom of the Stable, *Richard II*

Grumio, Petruccio's servant, *Taming of the Shrew*

Guiderius, Cymbeline's son, known as Polydore, *Cymbeline*

Guildenstern, a courtier, *Hamlet*
Guildford, Sir Henry, *All is True*
Gurney, James, Lady Faulconbridge's servant, *King John*

Hal, Prince, *see* Henry (Harry), Prince of Wales
Harcourt, an officer, *2 Henry IV*
Harfleur, Governor of, *Henry V*
Harry Bolingbroke, Duke of Hereford, later **Henry IV**, *Richard II, 1 Henry IV, 2 Henry IV*
Hastings, Lord, *2 Henry IV*
Hastings, Lord, *3 Henry VI, Richard III*
Hastings, a pursuivant, *Richard III*
Hecate, goddess of the moon, *Macbeth*
Hector, son of Priam, *Troilus and Cressida*
Helen, a physician's daughter, *All's Well that Ends Well*
Helen, an attendant, *Cymbeline*
Helen of Troy, *Troilus and Cressida*
Helena, in love with Demetrius, *Midsummer Night's Dream*
Helenus, a priest, son of Priam, *Troilus and Cressida*
Helicanus, lord of Tyre, *Pericles*
Henry, Prince, later **Henry III**, *King John*
Henry (Harry), Prince of Wales, later **Henry V**, *1* and *2 Henry IV, Henry V*
Henry VI, *1, 2*, and *3 Henry VI*, (corpse and ghost) *Richard III*
Henry Tudor, Earl of Richmond, later **Henry VII**, *3 Henry VI, Richard III*
Herbert, Sir Walter, a soldier, *Richard III*
Hermia, loved by Lysander, *Midsummer Night's Dream*
Hermione, Leontes's queen, *Winter's Tale*
Hero, Leonato's daughter, *Much Ado About Nothing*
Hippolyta, Queen of the Amazons, *Midsummer Night's Dream*, *Two Noble Kinsmen*
Holofernes, a schoolmaster, *Love's Labour's Lost*
Horatio, Hamlet's friend, *Hamlet*
Hortensio, suitor of Bianca, *Taming of the Shrew*
Hortensius, a servant, *Timon of Athens*
Host, *Two Gentlemen of Verona*
Host of the Garter Inn, *Merry Wives of Windsor*
Hostess, *see* Quickly, Mistress
Hostilius, *Timon of Athens*
Hotspur (Henry Percy), *Richard II, 1 Henry IV*

Hubert (de Burgh), *King John*
Hume, John, a priest, *2 Henry VI*
Humphrey, Prince, Duke of Gloucester, *see* Gloucester
Hymen, god of marriage, *As You Like It*, *Two Noble Kinsmen*

Iachimo, *see* Giacomo
Iago, Othello's ensign, *Othello*
Iden, Alexander (later **Sir)**, *2 Henry VI*
Innogen, Cymbeline's daughter, *Cymbeline*
Iras, attendant of Cleopatra, *Antony and Cleopatra*
Iris, a spirit, *Tempest*
Isabel of France, Richard's Queen, *Richard II*
Isabel, Queen of France, *Henry V*
Isabella, Claudio's sister, *Measure for Measure*

Jailer, *Two Noble Kinsmen*
Jailer's Daughter, *Two Noble Kinsmen*
Jamy, Captain, a Scottish officer, *Henry V*
Jaquenetta, a wench, *Love's Labour's Lost*
Jaques, a lord, *As You Like It*
Jaques de Bois, Orlando's brother, *As You Like It*
Jessica, Shylock's daughter, *Merchant of Venice*
Joan of Arc (Joan la Pucelle), *1 Henry VI*
John, Don, the Bastard, *Much Ado About Nothing*
John, Friar, *Romeo and Juliet*
John of Gaunt, *see* Gaunt
John of Lancaster, Prince, later **Duke of Bedford**, *1* and *2 Henry IV*,
	Henry V, 1 Henry VI
Jordan, Margery (or **Margaret)**, a witch, *2 Henry VI*
Joseph, a servant, *Taming of the Shrew*
Julia, lover of Proteus, *Two Gentlemen of Verona*
Juliet, Claudio's betrothed, *Measure for Measure*
Junius Brutus, a tribune, *Coriolanus*
Juno, a spirit, *Tempest*
Jupiter, King of the gods, *Cymbeline*

Katherine, loved by Dumaine, *Love's Labour's Lost*
Katherine, Queen of Henry VIII, *All is True*
Katherine Minola, the shrew, *The Taming of the Shrew*
Kent, Earl of, *King Lear*

Laertes, Polonius's son, *Hamlet*
Lafeu, an old lord, *All's Well that Ends Well*

Lance, Proteus's servant, *Two Gentlemen of Verona*
Lartius, Titus, Roman general, *Coriolanus*
Laurence, Friar, *Romeo and Juliet*
Lavatch, the Countess's fool, *All's Well that Ends Well*
Lavinia, Titus' daughter, *Titus Andronicus*
Le Beau, a courtier, *As You Like It*
Le Fer, Monsieur, a French soldier, *Henry V*
Lennox, a thane, *Macbeth*
Leonardo, Bassanio's servant, *Merchant of Venice*
Leonato, governor of Messina, Hero's father, *Much Ado About Nothing*
Leonine, a murderer, *Pericles*
Leontes, King of Sicilia, *Winter's Tale*
Lepidus, Marcus Aemilius, *Julius Caesar*, *Antony and Cleopatra*
Lichorida, Marina's nurse, *Pericles*
Limoges, Duke of Austria, *King John*
Ligarius, Caius, a conspirator, *Julius Caesar*
Lincoln, Bishop of, *All is True*
Lion, played by Snug, *Midsummer Night's Dream*
Lodovico, kinsman of Brabanzio, *Othello*
Lodowick, Friar, role assumed by Vincentio, *Measure for Measure*
Longueville, in love with Maria, *Love's Labour's Lost*
Lorenzo, in love with Jessica, *Merchant of Venice*
Louis XI of France, *3 Henry VI*
Louis the Dauphin, later **Louis VIII**, *King John*
Louis the Dauphin, son of Charles VI, *Henry V*
Lovell, Sir Thomas, Chancellor of the Exchequer, *All is True*
Luce, *see* Nell
Lucentio, Bianca's suitor, *Taming of the Shrew*
Lucetta, Julia's waiting-woman, *Two Gentlemen of Verona*
Luciana, Adriana's sister, *Comedy of Errors*
Lucilius, servant of Timon, *Timon of Athens*
Lucillius, friend of Brutus, *Julius Caesar*
Lucio, 'a fantastic', *Measure for Measure*
Lucius, young servant of Brutus, *Julius Caesar*
Lucius, a lord, and his servant, *Timon of Athens*
Lucius, Titus' eldest son, *Titus Andronicus*
Lucius, Caius, Roman ambassador, *Cymbeline*
Lucius, Young, Lucius' son, *Titus Andronicus*
Lucullus, a lord, *Timon of Athens*
Lucy, Sir William, *1 Henry VI*

Lysander, in love with Hermia, *Midsummer Night's Dream*
Lysimachus, governor of Mytilene, *Pericles*

Macduff, thane of Fife, and his Lady and Son, *Macbeth*
MacMorris, an Irish officer, *Henry V*
Maecenas, friend of Octavius, *Antony and Cleopatra*
Malcolm, later King of Scotland, *Macbeth*
Malvolio, Olivia' steward, *Twelfth Night*
Mamillius, Leontes' son, *Winter's Tale*
Marcellus, a soldier, *Hamlet*
Marcus Antonius, *see* Mark Antony
Mardian, a eunuch, *Antony and Cleopatra*
Margaret, attendant on Hero, *Much Ado About Nothing*
Margaret, Queen, *1*, *2*, and *3 Henry VI*, *Richard III*
Margareton, bastard son of Priam, *Troilus and Cressida*
Maria, loved by Longueville, *Love's Labour's Lost*
Maria, attendant on Olivia, *Twelfth Night*
Mariana, friend of Diana's mother, *All's Well that Ends Well*
Mariana, of the 'moated grange', *Measure for Measure*
Marina, Pericles' daughter, *Pericles*
Mark Antony, *Julius Caesar*, *Antony and Cleopatra*
Martext, Sir Oliver, a country clergyman, *As You Like It*
Martius, Caius (Coriolanus), *Coriolanus*
Martius, Young, Coriolanus' son, *Coriolanus*
Martius, son of Titus, *Titus Andronicus*
Marullus, *see* Murellus
Melun, a French lord, *King John*
Menas, a pirate, *Antony and Cleopatra*
Menecrates, friend of Pompey, *Antony and Cleopatra*
Menelaus, Helen's husband, *Troilus and Cressida*
Menenius Agrippa, friend of Coriolanus, *Coriolanus*
Menteith, Scottish nobleman, *Macbeth*
Mercadé, a messenger, *Love's Labour's Lost*
Mercutio, friend of Romeo, *Romeo and Juliet*
Messala, friend of Brutus, *Julius Caesar*
Metellus Cimber, *see* Cimber
Michael, Sir, associate of the Archbishop of Canterbury, *1 Henry IV*
Milan, Duke of, Silvia's father, *Two Gentlemen of Verona*
Miranda, Prospero's daughter, *Tempest*
Montague, 'Old' and **Lady**, Romeo's parents, *Romeo and Juliet*

Montague, John Neville, Marquis of, *3 Henry VI*
Montano, Governor of Cyprus, *Othello*
Montgomery, Sir John, *3 Henry VI*
Montjoy, French herald, *Henry V*
Moonshine, played by Starveling, *Midsummer Night's Dream*
Mopsa, a shepherdess, *Winter's Tale*
Morgan, name taken by Belarius, *Cymbeline*
Morocco, Prince of, suitor to Portia, *Merchant of Venice*
Mortimer, Edmund, Earl of March, *1 Henry IV, 1 Henry VI*
Mortimer, Lady, Edmund's Welsh wife, *1 Henry IV*
Mortimer, Sir Hugh, *3 Henry VI*
Mortimer, Sir John, *3 Henry VI*
Morton, *2 Henry IV*
Mote, Armado's page, *Love's Labour's Lost*
Mote, a fairy, *Midsummer Night's Dream*
Mouldy, Ralph, *2 Henry IV*
Mowbray, John, Duke of Norfolk, *3 Henry VI*
Mowbray, Thomas, Duke of Norfolk, *Richard II*
Mowbray, Thomas, Lord, *2 Henry IV*
Mugs, a carrier, *1 Henry IV*
Murellus, a tribune, *Julius Caesar*
Mustardseed, a fairy, *Midsummer Night's Dream*
Mutius, Titus' youngest son, *Titus Andronicus*

Nathaniel, a servant, *Taming of the Shrew*
Nathaniel, Sir, a curate, *Love's Labour's Lost*
Nell, a country wench, *Two Noble Kinsmen*
Nell, a kitchen-maid, *Comedy of Errors*
Nerissa, Portia's waiting-gentlewoman, *Merchant of Venice*
Nestor, aged Greek commander, *Troilus and Cressida*
Nicanor, a Roman spy, *Coriolanus*
Nicholas, a servant, *Taming of the Shrew*
Nim, Corporal, *Merry Wives of Windsor*, *Henry V*
Norfolk, Duchess of, *All is True*
Norfolk, John Mowbray, Duke of, *3 Henry VI*
Norfolk, John Howard, Duke of, *Richard III*
Norfolk, Thomas Howard, 2nd Duke of, *see* Surrey, Earl of
Norfolk, Thomas Mowbray, Duke of, *Richard II*
Northumberland, Henry Percy, 1st Earl of, *Richard II, 1 and 2 Henry IV*
Northumberland, Henry Percy, 3rd Earl of, *3 Henry VI*

Northumberland, Lady, *2 Henry IV*
Nurse (Angelica), Juliet's, *Romeo and Juliet*

Oatcake, Hugh, a watchman, *Much Ado About Nothing*
Oberon, King of the Fairies, *Midsummer Night's Dream*
Octavia, Octavius' sister, *Antony and Cleopatra*
Octavius Caesar, *Julius Caesar*, *Antony and Cleopatra*
Oliver de Bois, Orlando's eldest brother, *As You Like It*
Olivia, a countess, loved by Orsino, *Twelfth Night*
Ophelia, Polonius's daughter, *Hamlet*
Orlando de Bois, in love with Rosalind, *As You Like It*
Orléans, Bastard of (Dunois), *1 Henry VI*
Orléans, Duke of, *Henry V*
Orléans, Master-Gunner of, and his son, *1 Henry VI*
Orsino, Duke (or Count) of Illyria, *Twelfth Night*
Osric, a foppish courtier, *Hamlet*
Oswald, Goneril's steward, *King Lear*
Overdone, Mistress, a bawd, *Measure for Measure*
Oxford, John de Vere, Earl of, *3 Henry VI*, *Richard III*

Pacorus, a soldier, *Antony and Cleopatra*
Page, Anne, loved by Fenton, *Merry Wives of Windsor*
Page, Master George (or Thomas), Anne's father, *Merry Wives of Windsor*
Page, Mistress Meg, Anne's mother, *Merry Wives of Windsor*
Page, William, Anne's schoolboy brother, *Merry Wives of Windsor*
Painter, a, *Timon of Athens*
Palamon, *Two Noble Kinsmen*
Pandarus, Cressida's uncle, *Troilus and Cressida*
Pandolf, Cardinal, *King John*
Panthino, Antonio's servant, *Two Gentlemen of Verona*
Paris, betrothed to Juliet, *Romeo and Juliet*
Paris, Priam's second son, *Troilus and Cressida*
Paris, Governor of, *1 Henry VI*
Paroles, cowardly follower of Bertram, *All's Well that Ends Well*
Patch-breech, a fisherman, *Pericles*
Patience, Katherine's waiting-woman, *All is True*
Patroclus, companion of Achilles, *Troilus and Cressida*
Paulina, Antigonus's wife, *Winter's Tale*
Peaseblossom, a fairy, *Midsummer Night's Dream*
Pedant, *Taming of the Shrew*

Pedro, Don, Prince of Aragon, *Much Ado About Nothing*
Pembroke, William Herbert, Earl of, *3 Henry VI*
Pembroke, William Marshal, Earl of, *King John*
Percy, Henry, *see* Northumberland
Percy, Lady ('Kate'), Hotspur's wife, *1* and *2 Henry IV*
Percy, Thomas, Earl of Worcester, *1 Henry IV*
Perdita, Leontes' daughter, *Winter's Tale*
Peter, Nurse's servant, *Romeo and Juliet*
Peter, a servant, *Taming of the Shrew*
Peter, Friar, *Measure for Measure*
Peter of Pomfret, a prophet, *King John*
Peto, companion of Falstaff, *2 Henry IV*
Petruccio, follower of the Capulets, *Romeo and Juliet*
Petruccio, Katherine's suitor, *Taming of the Shrew*
Philario, friend of Posthumus, *Cymbeline*
Philemon, Cerimon's servant, *Pericles*
Philharmonus, a soothsayer, *Cymbeline*
Philip, a servant, *Taming of the Shrew*
Philip, King of France, *King John*
Philo, friend of Antony, *Antony and Cleopatra*
Philostrate, Theseus' Master of the Revels, *Midsummer Night's Dream*
Philotus, a servant, *Timon of Athens*
Phoebe, loved by Silvius, *As You Like It*
Phrynia, a prostitute, *Timon of Athens*
Piers of Exton, Sir, *Richard II*
Pilch, a fisherman, *Pericles*
Pinch, Doctor, a schoolmaster and exorcist, *Comedy of Errors*
Pindarus, a bondman, *Julius Caesar*
Pirithous, friend of Theseus, *Two Noble Kinsmen*
Pisanio, Posthumus' servant, *Cymbeline*
Pistol, Ensign (Lieutenant), *2 Henry IV*, *Henry V*, *Merry Wives of Windsor*
Poet, a, *Timon of Athens, Julius Caesar*
Poins, Edward (Ned), *1* and *2 Henry IV*
Polixenes, King of Bohemia, *Winter's Tale*
Polonius, a lord, *Hamlet*
Polydore, name taken by Guiderius, *Cymbeline*
Pompeius, Sextus (Pompey), son of Pompey the Great, *Antony and Cleopatra*
Pompey Bum, a bawd, *Measure for Measure*
Popillius Laena, a senator, *Julius Caesar*

Portia, Brutus' wife, *Julius Caesar*
Portia, loved by Bassanio, *Merchant of Venice*
Posthumus Leonatus, Innogen's husband, *Cymbeline*
Potpan, a servant, *Romeo and Juliet*
Priam, King of Troy, *Troilus and Cressida*
Proculeius, *Antony and Cleopatra*
Prospero, formerly Duke of Milan, *Tempest*
Proteus, a gentleman, loved by Julia, *Two Gentlemen of Verona*
Publius, a senator, *Julius Caesar*
Publius, Marcus' son, *Titus Andronicus*
Puck (or Robin Goodfellow), *Midsummer Night's Dream*
Pyramus, played by Bottom, *Midsummer Night's Dream*

Quickly, Mistress, 1 and 2 *Henry IV*, *Henry V*, *Merry Wives of Windsor*
Quince, Peter, a carpenter, *Midsummer Night's Dream*
Quintus, son of Titus, *Titus Andronicus*

Ralph, a servant, *Taming of the Shrew*
Rambures, a French lord, *Henry V*
Ratcliff, Sir Richard, follower of Richard, *Richard III*
Rebeck, Hugh, a musician, *Romeo and Juliet*
Regan, Duchess of Cornwall, Lear's second daughter, *King Lear*
René, Duke of Anjou, King of Naples, 1 *Henry VI*
Reynaldo, the Countess's steward, *All's Well that Ends Well*
Reynaldo, Polonius's servant, *Hamlet*
Richmond, Henry, Earl of, *see* Henry Tudor
Rivers, Lord (Anthony Woodville, Lord Scales), 3 *Henry VI*, *Richard III*
Robert, a servant, *Merry Wives of Windsor*
Robin, an apprentice, 2 *Henry VI*
Robin, Falstaff's page, *Merry Wives of Windsor*
Rochester, Bishop of, *All is True*
Roderigo, in love with Desdemona, *Othello*
Rogero, *see* Ruggiero
Rosalind, loved by Orlando, *As You Like It*
Rosaline, loved by Biron, *Love's Labour's Lost*
Rosencrantz, a courtier, *Hamlet*
Ross, Lord, *Richard II*
Ross, Thane of, *Macbeth*
Roussillon, Countess of, *All's Well that Ends Well*
Rugby, John, Dr Caius' servant, *Merry Wives of Windsor*
Ruggiero, a gentleman, *Winter's Tale*

Rumour, the presenter, *2 Henry IV*
Rutland, Edmund, Earl of, *3 Henry VI*

Salarino, friend of Antonio, *Merchant of Venice*
Salerio (perhaps a mistake for Solanio or Salarino), *Merchant of Venice*
Salisbury, William Longsword, Earl of, *King John*
Salisbury, John Montacute, Earl of, *Richard II*
Salisbury, Richard Neville, Earl of, *2 Henry VI*
Salisbury, Thomas Montacute, Earl of, *Henry V, 1 Henry VI*
Samson, a servant, *Romeo and Juliet*
Sands, Lord (Sir William Sands), *All is True*
Saturninus, Emperor of Rome, *Titus Andronicus*
Saye, Lord, *2 Henry VI*
Scales, Lord, *2 Henry VI*
Scarus, friend of Antony, *Antony and Cleopatra*
Scrope, Henry, Lord, of Masham, *Henry V*
Scrope, Richard, Archbishop of York, *1 and 2 Henry IV*
Scrope, Sir Stephen, *Richard II*
Seacoal, Francis, a scribe, *Much Ado About Nothing*
Seacoal, George, a literate watchman, *Much Ado About Nothing*
Sebastian, name taken by Julia, *Two Gentlemen of Verona*
Sebastian, Viola's twin brother, *Twelfth Night*
Sebastian, Alonso's brother, *Tempest*
Seleucus, Cleopatra's treasurer, *Antony and Cleopatra*
Sempronius, a lord, *Timon of Athens*
Sempronius, kinsman of the Andronici, *Titus Andronicus*
Servilius, servant of Timon, *Timon of Athens*
Seyton, Macbeth's armourer, *Macbeth*
Shadow, Simon, *2 Henry IV*
Shallow, Robert, 'a country justice', *2 Henry IV, Merry Wives of Windsor*
Shylock, a usurer, *Merchant of Venice*
Sicilius Leonatus, Posthumus's father (and his dead wife and sons), *Cymbeline*
Sicinius Velutus, a tribune, *Coriolanus*
Silence, a country justice, *2 Henry IV*
Silius, an officer, *Antony and Cleopatra*
Silvia, the Duke of Milan's daughter, *Two Gentlemen of Verona*
Silvius, a shepherd, *As You Like It*
Simonides, Thaisa's father, King of Pentapolis, *Pericles*

Simpcox, Simon, and **Mrs Simpcox**, *2 Henry VI*
Simple, Peter, Slender's servant, *Merry Wives of Windsor*
Siward, Earl of Northumberland, *Macbeth*
Siward, Young, *Macbeth*
Slender, Abraham, Shallow's cousin, *Merry Wives of Windsor*
Sly, Christopher, 'a drunken tinker', *Taming of the Shrew*
Smith, the Weaver, *2 Henry VI*
Snare, an officer, *2 Henry IV*
Snout, Tom, a tinker, *Midsummer Night's Dream*
Snug, a joiner, *Midsummer Night's Dream*
Solanio, friend of Antonio, *Merchant of Venice*
Soldier that has killed his father, *3 Henry VI*
Soldier that has killed his son, *3 Henry VI*
Solinus, Duke of Ephesus, *Comedy of Errors*
Somerset, Edmund Beaufort, 2nd Duke of, *2 Henry VI*
Somerset, Henry Beaufort, 3rd Duke of, and **Edmund, 4th Duke of**,
    confused, *3 Henry VI*
Somerset, John Beaufort, Earl of, later **1st Duke of**, confused with
    Edmund, 2nd Duke of, *1 Henry VI*
Somerville, Sir John, a Lancastrian, *3 Henry VI*
Soundpost, James, a musician, *Romeo and Juliet*
Southwell, John, a priest, *2 Henry VI*
Speed, Valentine's servant, *Two Gentlemen of Verona*
Stafford, Sir Humphrey, *2 Henry VI*
Stafford, Lord, a Yorkist, *3 Henry VI*
Stafford, William, *2 Henry VI*
Stanley, Sir John, *2 Henry VI*
Stanley, Thomas, Lord, Earl of Derby, *Richard III*
Stanley, Sir William, *3 Henry VI*
Starveling, Robin, a tailor, *Midsummer Night's Dream*
Stefano, servant of Portia, *Merchant of Venice*
Stefano, a 'drunken butler', *Tempest*
Strato, Brutus' servant, *Julius Caesar*
Suffolk, Charles Brandon, Duke of, *All is True*
Suffolk, William de la Pole, Earl of, later **Duke of**, *1* and *2 Henry VI*
Sugarsop, a servant, *Taming of the Shrew*
Surrey, Thomas Fitzalan, Earl of (non-speaking), *2 Henry IV*
Surrey, Thomas Holland, Duke of, *Richard II*
Surrey, Thomas Howard, Earl of, later **Duke of Norfolk**, *All is*
    True

Talbot, John, Lord, later **Earl of Shrewsbury**, *1 Henry VI*
Talbot, John ('Young'), *1 Henry VI*
Tamora, Queen of the Goths, *Titus Andronicus*
Taurus, Octavius' lieutenant-general, *Antony and Cleopatra*
Tearsheet, Doll, a whore, *2 Henry IV*
Thaisa, Pericles' wife, *Pericles*
Thaliart, lord of Antioch, *Pericles*
Thersites, Achilles' fool, *Troilus and Cressida*
Theseus, Duke of Athens, *Midsummer Night's Dream*, *Two Noble Kinsmen*
Thidias, *Antony and Cleopatra*
Thisbe, played by Flute, *Midsummer Night's Dream*
Thomas, Friar, *Measure for Measure*
Thump, Peter, Horner's servant, *2 Henry VI*
Thurio, suitor of Silvia, *Two Gentlemen of Verona*
Thyreus, *see* Thidias
Timandra, a prostitute, *Timon of Athens*
Time (as Chorus), *Winter's Tale*
Timothy, a taborer, *Two Noble Kinsmen*
Tirrel, Sir James, *Richard III*
Titania, Queen of the Fairies, *Midsummer Night's Dream*
Titinius, friend of Brutus, *Julius Caesar*
Titus, a servant, *Timon of Athens*
Tom, Poor, name taken by Edgar, *King Lear*
Topas, Sir, impersonated by Feste, *Twelfth Night*
Touchstone, Duke Frederick's jester, *As You Like It*
Tranio, Lucentio's servant, *Taming of the Shrew*
Travers, a servant, *2 Henry IV*
Trebonius, a conspirator, *Julius Caesar*
Tressel, a gentleman, *Richard III*
Trinculo, a jester, *Tempest*
Tubal, friend of Shylock, *Merchant of Venice*
Tybalt, Juliet's cousin, *Romeo and Juliet*

Ulysses, Greek commander, *Troilus and Cressida*
Ursula, attendant on Hero, *Much Ado About Nothing*
Urswick, Sir Christopher, a priest, *Richard III*

Valentine, a gentleman, *Two Gentlemen of Verona*
Valentine, kinsman of the Andronici, *Titus Andronicus*
Valentine, attendant on Orsino, *Twelfth Night*
Valeria, friend of Virgilia, *Coriolanus*

Valerius, a Theban, *Two Noble Kinsmen*
Valtemand, a courtier, *Hamlet*
Varrius, friend of Pompey, *Antony and Cleopatra*
Varrius, friend of the Duke (non-speaking), *Measure for Measure*
Varro, *Timon of Athens*
Varrus, Brutus' man, *Julius Caesar*
Vaughan, Sir Thomas, *Richard III*
Vaux, Sir Nicholas, *All is True*
Vaux, Sir William, *2 Henry VI*
Venice, Duke of, *Merchant of Venice, Othello*
Ventidius, one of Antony's generals, *Antony and Cleopatra*
Ventidius, a debtor, *Timon of Athens*
Verges, a headborough, *Much Ado About Nothing*
Vernon, a Yorkist, *1 Henry VI*
Vernon, Sir Richard, follower of Hotspur, *1 Henry IV*
Vincentio, Duke of Vienna, *Measure for Measure*
Vincentio, Lucentio's father, *Taming of the Shrew*
Viola, twin sister of Sebastian, *Twelfth Night*
Violenta (non-speaking), *All's Well that Ends Well*
Virgilia, Coriolanus' wife, *Coriolanus*
Voltemand, *see* Valtemand
Volumnia, Coriolanus' mother, *Coriolanus*
Volumnius, friend of Brutus, *Julius Caesar*

Wall, played by Snout, *Midsummer Night's Dream*
Walter, a servant, *Taming of the Shrew*
Wart, Thomas, a recruit, *2 Henry IV*
Warwick, Earl of, a Yorkist, *2 and 3 Henry VI*
Warwick, Earl of, *2 Henry IV, Henry V, 1 Henry VI*
Weird Sisters, *Macbeth*
Westminster, Abbot of, *Richard II*
Westmorland, Ralph Neville, 1st Earl of, *1 and 2 Henry IV, Henry V*
Westmorland, Ralph Neville, 2nd Earl of, *3 Henry VI*
Whitmore, Walter, *2 Henry VI*
William, a countryman, *As You Like It*
Williams, Michael, a soldier, *Henry V*
Willoughby, Lord, *Richard II*
Winchester, Bishop of (later **Cardinal)**, *1 and 2 Henry VI*
Wolsey, Cardinal, *All is True*

A Conjectural Chronology of Shakespeare's Works

It is particularly difficult to establish the dates of composition and the relative chronology of the early works, up to those named by Francis Meres in his *Palladis Tamia* of 1598. The following table is based on the 'Canon and Chronology' section in *William Shakespeare: A Textual Companion*, by Stanley Wells and Gary Taylor, with John Jowett and William Montgomery (1987), where more detailed information and discussion may be found.

The Two Gentlemen of Verona	1590–1
The Taming of the Shrew	1590–1
The First Part of the Contention (Henry VI, Part Two)	1591
Richard Duke of York (Henry VI, Part Three)	1591
Henry VI, Part One	1592
Titus Andronicus	1592
Richard III	1592–3
Venus and Adonis	1592–3
The Rape of Lucrece	1593–4
The Comedy of Errors	1594
Love's Labour's Lost	1594–5
Richard II	1595
Romeo and Juliet	1595
A Midsummer Night's Dream	1595
King John	1596
The Merchant of Venice	1596–7
Henry IV, Part One	1596–7
The Merry Wives of Windsor	1597–8
Henry IV, Part Two	1597–8
Much Ado About Nothing	1598
Henry V	1598–9
Julius Caesar	1599
As You Like It	1599–1600
Hamlet	1600–1
Twelfth Night	1600–1
Troilus and Cressida	1602
The Sonnets	1593–1603
A Lover's Complaint	1603–4

Sir Thomas More	1603–4
Measure for Measure	1603
Othello	1603–4
All's Well that Ends Well	1604–5
Timon of Athens	1605
King Lear	1605–6
Macbeth	1606
Antony and Cleopatra	1606
Pericles	1607
Coriolanus	1608
The Winter's Tale	1609
Cymbeline	1610
The Tempest	1611
Henry VIII (All is True)	1613
The Two Noble Kinsmen	1613–14

Some Facts and Figures

The following figures are based on *A Complete and Systematic Concordance to the Works of Shakespeare* by Marvin Spevack (Hildesheim, 1968–80), based on the first edition of *The Riverside Shakespeare* (1974) which, unlike the Oxford Shakespeare, prints conflated texts of, for example, *Hamlet*, *King Lear*, and *Othello*.

Plays by Length

PLAYS	LINES	PLAYS	WORDS
Hamlet	4,042	*Hamlet*	29,551
Coriolanus	3,752	*Richard III*	28,309
Cymbeline	3,707	*Cymbeline*	26,778
Richard III	3,667	*Coriolanus*	26,579
Othello	3,551	*Othello*	25,887
Troilus and Cressida	3,531	*2 Henry IV*	25,706
Antony and Cleopatra	3,522	*Henry V*	25,577
King Lear	3,487	*Troilus and Cressida*	25,516
The Winter's Tale	3,348	*King Lear*	25,221
2 Henry IV	3,326	*The Winter's Tale*	24,543
Henry V	3,297	*2 Henry VI*	24,450
The Two Noble Kinsmen	3,261	*1 Henry IV*	23,955
All is True	3,221	*Romeo and Juliet*	23,913
2 Henry VI	3,130	*Antony and Cleopatra*	23,742
Romeo and Juliet	3,099	*The Two Noble Kinsmen*	23,403
1 Henry IV	3,081	*All is True*	23,325
All's Well that Ends Well	3,013	*3 Henry VI*	23,295
3 Henry VI	2,915	*All's Well that Ends Well*	22,550
Measure for Measure	2,891	*Richard II*	21,809
The Merry Wives of Windsor	2,891	*As You Like It*	21,305
Love's Labour's Lost	2,829	*Measure for Measure*	21,269
As You Like It	2,810	*The Merry Wives of Windsor*	21,119
Richard II	2,796	*Love's Labour's Lost*	21,033
Much Ado About Nothing	2,787	*The Merchant of Venice*	20,921
The Merchant of Venice	2,701	*Much Ado About Nothing*	20,768
1 Henry VI	2,695	*1 Henry VI*	20,515
The Taming of the Shrew	2,676	*The Taming of the Shrew*	20,411
King John	2,638		

PLAYS	LINES	PLAYS	WORDS
Julius Caesar	2,591	King John	20,386
Twelfth Night	2,591	Titus Andronicus	19,790
Titus Andronicus	2,538	Twelfth Night	19,401
Timon of Athens	2,488	Julius Caesar	19,110
Pericles	2,459	Timon of Athens	17,748
Macbeth	2,349	Pericles	17,723
The Two Gentlemen of Verona	2,288	The Two Gentlemen of Verona	16,883
The Tempest	2,283		
A Midsummer Night's Dream	2,192	Macbeth	16,436
The Comedy of Errors	1,787	A Midsummer Night's Dream	16,087
		The Tempest	16,036
		The Comedy of Errors	14,369

Plays by Percentage of Verse and Prose

PLAYS arranged according to the chronology in *William Shakespeare: A Textual Companion* by Stanley Wells and Gary Taylor (Oxford, 1987).

PLAY	VERSE	PROSE
The Two Gentlemen of Verona	73.5	26.5
The Taming of the Shrew	80.5	19.5
2 Henry VI	84.3	15.7
3 Henry VI	99.9	0.1
1 Henry VI	99.7	0.3
Titus Andronicus	98.6	1.4
Richard III	98.1	1.9
The Comedy of Errors	87.1	12.9
Love's Labour's Lost	65.4	34.6
Richard II	100	0.0
Romeo and Juliet	86.5	13.5
A Midsummer Night's Dream	80.2	19.8
King John	100	0.0
The Merchant of Venice	78	22
1 Henry IV	56.2	43.8
The Merry Wives of Windsor	12.2	87.8
2 Henry IV	48.7	51.3
Much Ado About Nothing	27.5	72.5
Henry V	60	40
Julius Caesar	92.6	7.4

PLAY	VERSE	PROSE
As You Like It	43.6	56.4
Hamlet	73	27
Twelfth Night	38.8	61.2
Troilus and Cressida	70.1	29.9
Measure for Measure	62.4	37.6
Othello	82	18
All's Well that Ends Well	54.3	45.7
Timon of Athens	77.1	22.9
King Lear	75.9	24.1
Macbeth	93.8	6.2
Antony and Cleopatra	92.3	7.7
Pericles	83.4	16.6
Coriolanus	79.6	20.4
The Winter's Tale	75.6	24.4
Cymbeline	87	13
The Tempest	80.4	19.6
All is True	97.8	2.2
The Two Noble Kinsmen	95.3	4.7

Longest Scenes

PLAY	SCENE	NO. OF LINES
Love's Labour's Lost	v. ii	914
The Winter's Tale	iv. ii	843
Hamlet	ii. ii	607
King John	ii. i	599
1 Henry IV	ii. v	553
Measure for Measure	iii. i	538
Measure for Measure	v. i	538
Timon of Athens	iv. iii	537
The Tempest	i. ii	506
Titus Andronicus	i. i	491
Cymbeline	v. vi	486

Longest Roles: Male

PLAY	CHARACTER	NO. OF LINES
Hamlet	Hamlet	1,507
Richard III	Richard III	1,145
Othello	Iago	1,094

PLAY	CHARACTER	NO. OF LINES
Henry V	Henry V	1,036
Coriolanus	Coriolanus	886
Othello	Othello	879
Measure for Measure	Duke Vincentio	858
Timon of Athens	Timon	849
Antony and Cleopatra	Antony	824
Richard II	Richard II	755

Longest Roles: Female

PLAY	CHARACTER	NO. OF LINES
As You Like It	Rosalind	721
Antony and Cleopatra	Cleopatra	670
Cymbeline	Innogen	591
The Merchant of Venice	Portia	578
Romeo and Juliet	Juliet	541
All's Well that Ends Well	Helen	477
Measure for Measure	Isabella	424
Othello	Desdemona	391
The Two Noble Kinsmen	Emilia	368
All is True	Queen Katherine	374

The Longest Word in Shakespeare

The longest word is 'honorificabilitudinitatibus' (*Love's Labour's Lost*, v. i. 41).

Further Reading

Complete Works

The Complete Works. General editors, Stanley Wells and Gary Taylor. Oxford, 2nd edn. 2005

The Norton Shakespeare. General editor, Stephen Greenblatt. New York, 1997

The Riverside Shakespeare. General editor, G. Blakemore Evans. 2nd edn. Boston, 1997

Annotated Editions of Single Plays

Arden Shakespeare Third Series. General editors, Richard Proudfoot, Ann Thompson, and David Kastan. 1995–

Arden Shakespeare. General editors, Una M. Ellis-Fermor, H. F. Brooks, Harold Jenkins, and Brian Morris. 1951–82

New Cambridge Shakespeare. General editors, Philip Brockbank, Brian Gibbons, *et al.* 1984–

New Penguin Shakespeare. General editors, T. J. B. Spencer and Stanley Wells. 1967–

Oxford Shakespeare. General editor, Stanley Wells. 1982–

General Works of Reference

McDonald, Russ, *The Bedford Companion to Shakespeare: An Introduction with Documents.* Boston, 1996

Wells, Stanley (ed.), *The Cambridge Companion to Shakespeare Studies.* Cambridge, 1986

Wells, Stanley, and Lena Orlin (ed.), *Shakespeare: An Oxford Guide*, Oxford, 2003

Dobson, Michael, and Stanley Wells (ed.), *The Oxford Companion to Shakespeare*, Oxford, 2001

Bibliography

Wells, Stanley (ed.), *Shakespeare: A Bibliographical Guide.* New edn. Oxford, 1990. Articles reviewing and listing literature on selected play groups and subjects.

Periodicals

Shakespeare Survey, 1948– . An annual publication. Includes 'Year's contribution to Shakespearian study', and checklist of productions. Indexes published every ten years.

Shakespeare Quarterly, 1950– . Includes articles, performance reviews, and an annual bibliography for Shakespeare-related criticism and performances.

Shakespeare Bulletin, 1982– . Originally the publication of the New York Shakespeare Society, now a journal of performance criticism and scholarship on Shakespeare and Renaissance drama. From 1992 incorporates Shakespeare on Film Newsletter.

Biography and Overall Studies of Life and Career

Greenblatt, Stephen, *Will in the World*, London, 2004

Greer, Germaine, *Shakespeare*. Oxford, 1986

Honan, Park, *Shakespeare: A Life*. Oxford, 1998

Schoenbaum, S., *William Shakespeare: A Compact Documentary Life*. Oxford, 1977; reprinted 1987

—— *Shakespeare's Lives*. Oxford, 1970; revised 1990

Wells, Stanley, *Shakespeare: A Dramatic Life*. London, 1994; paperback with additional chapter, published as *Shakespeare: the Poet and his Plays*, 1997

The Text: Facsimiles

Hinman, C., *The First Folio of Shakespeare: The Norton Facsimile*, 2nd edn. New York, 1996

Muir, K., and M. Allen (eds.), *Shakespeare's Plays in Quarto: A Facsimile Edition*. Berkeley, 1981

The Text

Blayney, Peter W. M., *The First Folio of Shakespeare*. Washington, DC, 1991

Ioppolo, Grace, *Revising Shakespeare*. Cambridge, Mass., 1991

Taylor, Gary, and Michael Warren (eds.), *The Division of the Kingdoms: Shakespeare's Two Versions of 'King Lear'*. Oxford, 1983

Wells, Stanley, *Re-Editing Shakespeare for the Modern Reader*. Oxford, 1984

Wells, Stanley and Gary Taylor, with John Jowett and William
   Montgomery, *William Shakespeare: A Textual Companion*. Oxford, 1987.
   The General Introduction provides a valuable overview of the textual
   situation

Concordance

Spevack, Marvin (comp.), *Harvard Shakespeare Concordance*. Cambridge,
   Mass., 1973

Language

Abbott, E. A., *A Shakespearian Grammar: An Attempt to Illustrate Some of the
   Differences Between Elizabethan and Modern English*, London, 1883, etc.

Blake, N. F., *The Language of Shakespeare*. Basingstoke, 1988

Crystal, David and Ben, *Shakespeare's Words*, London, 2002

Onions, C. T., *A Shakespeare Glossary*. Revised by R. D. Eagleson. Oxford,
   1986

Partridge, Eric, *Shakespeare's Bawdy: A Literary and Psychological essay and
   a Comprehensive Glossary*. London, 1947, etc.

Williams, Gordon, *A Glossary of Shakespeare's Sexual Language*. Atlantic
   Highlands, NJ, 1997

Sources

Bate, Jonathan, *Shakespeare and Ovid*. Oxford, 1993

Bullough, G., *Narrative and Dramatic Sources of Shakespeare*. 8 vols.,
   London, 1957–75

Shakespeare Criticism and Reputation

Bate, Jonathan, *The Genius of Shakespeare*. London, 1997

—— (ed.), *The Romantics on Shakespeare*. Harmondsworth, 1992

Eastman, A. M., *A Short History of Shakespearean Criticism*. New York, 1968

Grady, Hugh, *The Modernist Shakespeare: Critical Texts in a Material World*.
   Oxford, 1991

Johnson, Samuel, *Samuel Johnson on Shakespeare*, ed. H. R. Woudhuysen.
   London, 1989

Lenz, C. R. S., and others (eds.), *The Woman's Part: Feminist Criticism of
   Shakespeare*. Urbana, Ill., 1980

Vickers, Brian, *Appropriating Shakespeare: Contemporary Critical Quarrels*. London, 1993

—— (ed.), *Shakespeare: The Critical Heritage*, 6 vols. London, 1974–81

Wells, Stanley, *Shakespeare: For All Time*, London, 2002

Shakespeare in Performance

Barton, John, *Playing Shakespeare*. London, 1984

Bate, Jonathan, and Russell Jackson (eds.), *Shakespeare: An Illustrated Stage History*. Oxford, 1996

Bentley, G. E., *The Profession of Dramatist in Shakespeare's Time, 1590–1642*. Princeton, 1971

—— *The Profession of Player in Shakespeare's Time, 1590–1642*. Princeton, 1984

Berry, Cicely, *The Actor and his Text*. London, 1987

Berry, Ralph, *On Directing Shakespeare*. London, 1977; revised 1989

Brockbank, Philip (ed.), *Players of Shakespeare*. Cambridge, 1985

Brook, Peter, *The Empty Space*. London, 1968

Brown, John Russell, *Shakespeare's Plays in Performance*. London, 1966

David, Richard, *Shakespeare in the Theatre*. Cambridge, 1978

Gurr, Andrew, *The Shakespearian Playing Companies*. Oxford, 1996

—— *The Shakespearean Stage 1574–1642*. 3rd edn. Cambridge, 1992

—— *Playgoing in Shakespeare's London*. Cambridge, 1987

Halio, Jay L., *Understanding Shakespeare's Plays in Performance*. Manchester, 1988

Hapgood, Robert, *Shakespeare the Theatre Poet*. Oxford, 1988

Holland, Peter, *English Shakespeares: Shakespeare on the English Stage in the 1990s*. New York, 1997

Jackson, Russell, and Robert Smallwood (eds.), *Players of Shakespeare 2*. Cambridge, 1988

—— (eds.), *Players of Shakespeare 3*. Cambridge, 1993

Kennedy, Dennis, *Looking at Shakespeare: A Visual History of Twentieth-Century Performance*. Cambridge, 1993

Mulryne, J. R., and J. C. Bulman, Shakespeare in performance series. Manchester, 1982– . Each volume is devoted to a single play and includes detailed discussion of selected productions.

Odell, G. C. D., *Shakespeare from Betterton to Irving*. 2 vols., New York, 1920

Parsons, Keith, and Pamela Mason (eds.), *Shakespeare in Performance*. London, 1995

Styan, J. L., *The Shakespeare Revolution: Criticism and Performance in the Twentieth Century*. Cambridge, 1977

Wells, Stanley (ed.), *Shakespeare in the Theatre: An Anthology of Criticism*. Oxford, 1997

Wells, Stanley, and Sarah Stanton (ed.), *The Cambridge Companion to Shakespeare on Stage*, Cambridge, 2002

Shakespeare on Film

Burt, Richard, and Lynda Boose (eds.), *Shakespeare, the Movie: Popularizing the Plays on Film, TV, and Video*. London, 1997

Davies, E. A., *Filming Shakespeare's Plays*. Cambridge, 1988

——and Stanley Wells (ed.), *Shakespeare and the Moving Image*. Cambridge 1994

Jackson, Russell (ed.), *The Cambridge Companion to Shakespeare on Film*, Cambridge, 2000

Rothwell, Kenneth S., and A. Henkin Melzer, *Shakespeare on Screen: An International Filmography and Videography*. London, 1990. Covers productions 1899–1989. Includes indexes of actors, directors, critics, etc.

——*A History of Shakespeare on Screen: a Century of Film and Television*. Cambridge, 1999